Dark Shadows Episode Guide
Volume 2

Dark Shadows Episode Guide
Volume 2
by
Hanley Jennings Peterson

Table of Contents

Enter Cousin Barnabas — The Dapper Doppelgänger

Episode #211 — Kinescope. The next morning, Liz and Jason are arguing in the drawing room about Willie; is he gone, or not? McGuire says he doesn't know where his friend is, but Liz doesn't believe him. Seems Willie's belongings are still upstairs. Mrs. Johnson comes in, asking about Mr. Loomis. Liz walks out. Mrs. Johnson tells McGuire she saw Willie around the tool shed last night and knew he wasn't leaving. Blah, blah, Willie, and Jason is perplexed. Mrs. Johnson admits she's going to miss Willie as they talked quite a bit (at least somebody didn't full-on hate him, but this is real Willie, not faux fiver perv Willie). Anyway, Jason asks what they talked about and she says the Collins family and its history, mostly, and some rather long, bullshit rehash ensues. Walking into the foyer, Mrs. J says Willie was interested in Barnabas Collins and was sorry to hear he died in England. She goes on to reveal that Willie seemed especially interested in the jewelry in the portrait and the legend of Naomi Collins being buried with gifted pirate gems. More rehash and Mrs. J tells Jason about Eagle Hill Cemetery. Mrs. J goes off to do some work and Jason leaves the house.

At Eagle Hill, Crazy Pants Old Man Coot Caretaker shows up and finds the gate/door of the Collins mausoleum is open, then starts gibbering about *eeevillll* (shoot this annoyance already). McGuire shows up and gets the 'evil — go away!' warning. McGuire asks if anyone was around lately and Crazy Old Coot mentions Willie, blah, blah, then points out the broken lock to the crypt gate — *"EVIL!"* (if only Jason would smother this guy). McGuire's all 'fuck you, I'm going into the crypt.' More blah, blah (God, this episode truly sucks). As Jason and the caretaker are leaving, McGuire notices a cigarette butt on one of the sarcophagi, which he pockets. Unfortunately, he goes without performing a mercy killing on behalf of the viewing audience.

Jason's back at Collinwood and Liz wants to know if Willie's gone, but McGuire doesn't know (didn't they already have this conversation?). Mrs. Johnson comes along and asks if Willie is going to be there for dinner. Nobody knows. Jason goes upstairs. Mrs. J confides to Liz that she thinks something has happened to Mr. Loomis, what with him just up and disappearing like he did (huh, somebody actually gives a damn). Liz goes upstairs and Mrs. Johnson bitches about nobody hanging anything up (Jason left his coat on the foyer table). A knock sounds on the door and she opens it. There's a male visitor, whom we only see from the back. In a very cultured voice, he asks if he's at Collinwood and may he please see Mrs. Elizabeth Collins Stoddard? He's a cousin, from England. Mrs. Johnson, looking a bit stunned, invites him in and starts to go upstairs. The man walks toward the portrait of Barnabas and when he turns around, we see that he looks *exactly* like Barnabas Collins. He calls after Mrs. Johnson, telling her to inform Liz that it's her cousin, *Barnabas* Collins who's come to call. (Just like in *Varney the Vampire.* New neighbor, Sir Francis Varney, is a dead ringer to Bannerworth family ancestor Runnagate Bannerworth, whose life-size portrait hangs in the Bannerworth mansion)

Episode #212 — Barnabas is patiently waiting in the foyer as Liz comes downstairs, amazed and pleasantly surprised at her visitor. She points out the resemblance to the Barnabas in the portrait. As the two discuss the painting, Barnabas gestures and he's wearing the exact same ring as the man in the picture. Barnabas is very courtly, gentlemanlike and refined of manner. He tells Liz that his ancestor namesake married after moving to England. They go into the drawing room and Barnabas says he's the last of the line in England. Liz asks if he's in Collinsport for business or pleasure. He says a visit, initially, but he hopes to settle there. Liz wants to talk the English side of the family and invites him to dinner, but Barnabas says no, thanks, he just wanted to stop in and say hello. He goes on to announce that Collinwood is just like he remembered — from the stories he heard as a child, he feels like he's lived there. He also says a few things about the Old House and Liz is impressed with his knowledge of family history.

In the foyer, David and Vicki have come downstairs, talking Willie. David rightfully opines that Vicki didn't like him much, but he does and hopes he comes back (me, too! Unless it's skeezy Willie, he could be dead for all I care). David then goes out to play. Meanwhile, Liz is in the drawing room, telling Barnabas to stop by anytime. Vicki comes along and Liz makes the introductions. Barnabas charms by saying Victoria is such a beautiful name, he couldn't *possibly* call her Vicki (oh, brother). After bidding farewell with a courtly bow,

Barnabas leaves. Liz and Vicki, blah, blah Barnabas. Vicki asks if Jason found Willie yet.

At the Old House, David's playing on the stairs just inside the front door when Barnabas comes in. David thinks he's the ghost of the portrait Barnabas, but is told, nope, I'm your cousin, that's why we can talk. David reveals that he talks to ghosts, even at the Old House. He shows him Josette's portrait and tells how her picture glows, jasmine fills the room and she's very helpful, especially to Collinses. David offers to show Barnabas around, but he says no, thanks, he knows all about the Old House and its secret places. David then invites his cousin to watch a sunrise with him sometime, then asks him why he suddenly seems so sad. He doesn't really get an answer and Barnabas says something about being home.

David's back at Collinwood and asks if Willie's back. Vicki tells him no, and to stop asking (but, Vicki, inquiring minds want to know!). Liz joins them and David mentions running into Barnabas at the Old House. Blah, blah. He says Barnabas talks funny, like people in books (I guess he means old fashioned). Liz wanders off to the kitchen, I think. David walks over to the portrait (watch out for that giant boom mic shadow!) and says the man in the painting seems angry, but cousin Barnabas seems sad.

Still in the Old House parlor, Barnabas looks at the portrait of Josette and asks why she didn't protect *him* when he was turned into something his own father loathed. He claims the house for himself and tells her to tell his old man, if his spirit is hanging around, that he's broken the chains he'd been bound in (is it necessary for me to state the obvious re: the chained coffin Willie found?).

Episode #213 — The next day, Jason goes to the drawing room and asks Liz if Willie was there last night. Negatory. He goes on to say that someone must have broken in during the night, because all of Willie's belongings are gone. Liz says a break-in is impossible (are you sure? You people *never* seem to lock the front door). She then reminds Brogue Blarney that he owes her five hundred dollars, but Jason says he's saving the cash for Willie. Liz hopes 'ole Willie never comes back and Jason assures her he never told his friend about the dead hubby in the basement. Carolyn comes downstairs and hears them arguing, so she walks in and asks what the quarrel is about. Liz claims it's nothing. Carolyn doesn't believe her and, upset, leaves the house.

Burke and Joe are hanging out at the Blue Whale (remember when Joe hated him? Good times). Carolyn comes in. Joe says hi, but when Burke walks over and says hello, she glares at him, says nothing, and walks away. Suddenly self-aware, Burke tells Joe that he deserved it (Joe agrees), but says he can't do any-thing about it. Joe suggests apologizing for acting a cad and points out that he and Carolyn got over their differences and are now friends (but you're a great guy, Joe, Burke is a selfish jerk). Eventually, Burke decides to give it a shot and walks over to Carolyn's table, offers to buy her a drink and have a talk. She's not interested and asks him to go away, she wants to be left alone. Burke returns to the bar and Joe goes over and Carolyn explains she's upset and wor-ried about her mother and Jason. Joe says he's there to help, all she has to do is ask. Carolyn mentions that he and Burke seem chummy and Joe says they no longer have a beef. Good guy Joe declares her to be acting like a brat by avoid-ing Burke. She admits she's afraid to talk to him because she still has feelings for the lunk (she's still carrying a torch for him, it seems. Dummy). Joe encour-ages her to talk to Devlin, then leaves to meet Maggie (this conversation was very quiet and adult; no shrieking, high theatrics or melodrama; a nice change). Burke and Carolyn glance at each other from across the room.

Carolyn approaches Burke and agrees to have a drink. They head back to the table where Burke apologizes to her in a vague sort of way. She fills in what he's not saying — he used her. He says he wants to be friends and that she's an attractive, desirable woman and Carolyn quickly cuts him off, telling him to shove that old cliché. She apologizes for blowing up, he apologizes again and blah, blah. Upset again, Carolyn decides to leave and refuses his offer of a ride home, as she wants to be alone. Burke bullshits about wishing things could be different and Carolyn finally leaves.

In the drawing room, Liz and McGuire are bitching about the money for Willie and Liz wants to know if he's gone. She then asks Jason how much for *him* to leave for good? Carolyn comes home and, through the closed door, hears them squabbling about eighteen years ago, Jason's help and Liz saying she wished she'd never met the not-so-lucky charm. Carolyn walks in and McGuire bitches at her for barging in (screw you, Darby O'Gill, it's not your house). She asks what the hell is going on and sort of tells Brogue Blarney to shove the attitude. Liz says they were arguing about her and the night Willie tried to — "bother" her (is that what we're calling the near rape by faux fiver Willie?). Liz then suddenly announces she has a headache and sweeps upstairs. Carolyn asks McGuire what they were really fighting about. Jason bullshits and Carolyn calls him on it, saying she knows Liz is afraid of him and she'll find out why. He then issues a warning that doing so will get Liz into serious trouble. Ass.

Episode #214 — Night and Vicki goes to the Old House looking for David. The front doors mysteriously close and she can't open them. Barnabas comes downstairs (so he just keeps wandering around the property, then? Isn't that a little weird?) and easily opens the door, knowing it can be a bit tricky some- times (convenient, as no one had a problem with it before, like Matthew; re- member him?). Gosh, it's like he's spent a lot of time here, Vicki observes. Barnabas explains that his knowledge is culled from letters, journals and stories handed down through the generations (right). He then says the house will last forever and blah, blah what the Old House represents. He then begins waxing rhapsodic on the construction and some bullshit about workmen dying or suf- fering severe injuries (oh, like the men rumored to be accidentally encased in cement at the Merchandise Mart?), then basically says the house was one of misery and how a father and son fought (does this seem like set-up? It does to me).

Back at Collinwood, Roger comes home from a business trip to Boston. He's greeted by Kitten and tells her that he's brought back a recipe for Mrs. Johnson, but doubts it will do any good. Carolyn recalls how, when she was little, he al- ways used to bring back a gift for her from his trips and was like a father to her. Retiring to the drawing room, Roger pours a drink and asks after Liz and is told she's fine, physically, but Jason is still causing problems. She updates him about Willie being gone and Roger gets off a wonderfully snarky line about not keeping the jet-set down (hilarious). Carolyn also mentions the newest visitor to the Collins homestead; cousin Barnabas, whom Roger has never heard of. Vicki and Barnabas walk in; introductions are made and Barnabas makes an odd comment about the "aliveness" of Collinwood.

Vicki and Carolyn are in the foyer, discussing Barnabas. Vicki says that he has quite an imagination and seems a bit strange and tells about the meeting in the Old House. Carolyn chalks it up to Barnabas being a keen family historian, but Vicki insists it's more than that; it's like he *lived* at the Old House.

Barnabas and Roger have gone to the study. Roger offers a drink, blah, blah a discussion of amontillado ensues. Barnabas proposes a bizarre toast to eternal health. Roger notices that Barnabas is wearing the ring so prominently featured in the portrait and is told it was handed down. Roger asks why he blew into Collinsport. Barnabas says since there's no more family in England, he came to America and plans to go into business there, eventually.

In the foyer, Vicki and Carolyn, blah, blah, Barnabas. The men join them and Barnabas leaves for a meeting. Once he's gone, Roger gives the thumbs-up —

he likes their distant cousin. He mentions the ring and the three gather round the portrait, commenting on the uncanny resemblance. Out in the woods, new arrival Barnabas is just standing there, as dogs howl in the distance.

What's Ailing Willie?

Episode #215 – For some reason, there is a crappy, cheesetastic picture of the Blue Whale exterior. Anyway, Burke walks into the bar and joins Maggie, who's waiting for Joe. She refers to Burke's "victory" over Willie and I gag, remembering that ridiculously retarded fight scene. They wonder where Loomis went (where *is* Willie? If it's faux five episode Willie, good riddance, but not real Willie, I like him). McGuire steps in, looking around. Burke approaches him and blah, blah, Willie, is he gone? Jason admits he doesn't know where his friend is. More blah, blah. McGuire seems concerned and Burke issues a threat if Willie comes back. Prick. McGuire leaves, Burke goes back to Maggie and blah, blah. Joe finally arrives, looking glum. He tells them he was out at his uncle's farm, looking for a missing calf. They finally found it on the other side of town — dead from blood loss, completely exsanguinated. Since there was no blood near the body, they figure it was stolen, drained and dumped. And, oh, yeah, there were two puncture wounds on its throat. They wonder aloud who'd want the blood, what would you do with it? Blah, blah, stolen cow. Hey, Willie's back! He quietly shambles to the bar and orders a drink. Burke approaches him. Willie seems either half-asleep or half-dead, he's not even touching his drink. He won't make eye contact either. Tough guy Burke acts like a shit and Willie says he won't make trouble and that he's sorry. Since that is highly unusual, Burke asks if he's all right, thinking he may be hurt. He suggests Willie take a sip of his drink and the poor son-of-a-bitch can't even raise the glass without shaking. Willie insists Burke just leave him alone. Jason comes back and Burke catches him and tells him Willie's in bad shape, something's wrong, his whole personality has changed. Burke suspects internal or head injuries. McGuire goes to the bar and Burke goes back to his table.

McGuire asks Willie where he's been and what he's been doing. Willie says nothing, don't ask, and is evasive. Jason mentions the cemetery trip and finding the cigarette butt. McGuire chastises Willie for "sinking so low as to rob a stiff" (great line, delivered well). Jason wants to go outside to give Willie the five hundred bucks, but Willie refuses it, saying he's staying in town. At the table, Burke is telling Maggie and Joe about Willie, but Joe's preoccupied, thinking about that poor little bloodless calf — camera cuts back to Willie (no clues there, at all). To say Willie is a hot mess is an understatement. Jason notices blood on Willie's coat sleeve and our Mr. Loomis looks like he's about to suffer a nervous breakdown.

Episode #216 — The Blue Whale and — gah! Someone really caked the eyeliner on Willie today. Yeesh. McGuire's asking about the blood on the sleeve. Willie claims it's not blood and he doesn't even want to look at it. In fact, he begs not to be forced to (oh, Willie, what has befallen you? You're completely broken). Willie asks to be left alone. Jason brings up the cemetery again and knows Willie was there because of the cigarette butt. Hmm, seems Willie's partial to foreign cigs, who knew? McGuire says Willie has to go and now Willie seems eager to get out of town, but Jason says he has to go to Collinwood first. That is the *last* place Willie wants to go. Burke wanders over and acts a prick. When he hears that McGuire wants Willie to apologize to Liz, Burke objects. Devlin suddenly shows concern and says Loomis should be in a hospital. Then Asshole Burke resurfaces, bids farewell, and says he hopes he never sees Loomis again (unlike unstable Carolyn in the early days, who should have been on meds, Burke is just a jerk). Burke leaves and McGuire is confused when Willie refuses a drink.

At Collinwood, Carolyn and Liz are arguing about Carolyn going out so late, with Liz assuring her daughter there's no need to worry about Willie anymore. Guess who arrives? In the foyer, half-dazed Willie apologizes in a way that can be read as either sincere or not, since he needs a little prompting from Jason. Liz isn't impressed, but Carolyn seems to believe him. McGuire asks to speak with Liz and they go to the drawing room. Carolyn is about to leave the house, when Willie stops her by apologizing again for scaring her and saying he understands if she doesn't believe him. She asks him if he's all right, since he doesn't seem to be. He says, yeah, sure, and she leaves. Willie starts moving away from the Barnabas portrait.

McGuire and Liz are arguing in the drawing room and Liz finally breaks down and says, yeah, okay, she accepts the apology. Out in the foyer, Willie is cowering near the stairs. As if against his will, he moves back towards the portrait, turns and looks at it. In the drawing room, Liz and Jason hear Willie cry out. They rush out to the foyer and find Willie passed out on the floor.

Willie's asleep in his room and when Jason reaches to loosen his collar, Willie wakes with a scream and grabs Jason's hands. He asks what happened and where he is (God, there is some fantastic noir/Grand Guignol lighting in this scene. Absolutely beautiful). Willie inquires where he was when he fainted. When told the foyer, he says he remembers and is desperate to leave. Jason tells him he's sure he can convince Liz to let him stay. Willie asks Jason to tell Liz again that he's sorry. McGuire's perplexed, like you don't have to sell me, kid. Jason leaves and Willie cowers on the bed, repeating over and over again that he's sorry.

In the drawing room, Liz isn't buying that Willie is sick, it's just another con. McGuire tells her to call a doctor, then. More bickering, McGuire insinuates about the dead hubby in the basement, then back to Willie staying. Liz finally consents (I usually hate Jason, but at least he sees his friend is really ill). McGuire leaves the room. A short while later, Carolyn has joined Liz in the drawing room and Dame Stoddard is telling her daughter that Willie is sick and will be staying on. Carolyn isn't upset and says she thinks something is serious- ly wrong with Willie. She mentions their conversation in the foyer and says he seemed numb or in pain, either emotionally or spiritually (this is incredibly perceptive and profound). She says he's either very sick or something *very* strange has happened to him and she doesn't want to know what it was.

McGuire enters Willie's room and wakes him. When he tells Willie he can stay, Willie doesn't want to. Jason helps Willie take off his jacket and sees that one sleeve of Willie's shirt is torn to the elbow and a crude bandage is wrapped around part of his forearm. Willie won't let Jason look at or touch it, claiming it doesn't hurt. Terrified and traumatized in some way, he repeats, over and over again, that no one can see it.

Episode #217 — Late afternoon and Willie tosses and turns in bed. He wakes up suddenly and finds Jason there. He asks the time, nearly four. Willie an- nounces he has to go, but McGuire says he's going to call a doctor and wants to see under the bandage. Willie weakly protests, saying it's nothing, but is so physically drained he can't fight. Jason removes the bandage and finds a small, barely perceptible cut, but comments how Willie's arm looks strange, very gray, no visible veins and seemingly drained of blood. Willie, looking like shit, tells Jason he was in a bar fight and got cut with a razor. He then starts mum- bling and falls asleep.

In the foyer, with the Barnabas portrait conspicuously in the background between them, Carolyn fills Vicki in on Willie being ill and remaining in the house. Vicki doesn't like it. Carolyn says Willie frightens her in a whole different way, like he's become a totally different person. She offers more incredibly insightful commentary on Willie. Jason comes downstairs and gives a vague update, saying Willie doesn't want a doctor, but if he worsens, he'll call one. He asks Vicki to have Mrs. Johnson fix a tray for Willie — he needs the nourishment. Vicki heads to the kitchen and Carolyn and Jason go to the drawing room. Carolyn asks where Willie's been, but McGuire can't really give her an answer. She then confronts him about his comment about getting Liz in trouble and questions if he's really a friend of her mother's. She tells him she doesn't like him and she knows something weird happened to Willie.

Upstairs, Willie's talking in his sleep, frightened about it getting dark again and not wanting "it" to happen again (whatever "it" is). Vicki comes in and slams the tray down on a table, waking him (what a bitch). He's surprised it's dinner time and asks if it's dark yet. Almost, she tells him. She moves the tray to the bedside table and he gets a bit edgy, insisting that she leave, he's all right. Once she goes, he gets out of bed and puts on his coat. Jason walks in and Willie tells him he has to get out of the house, he's not wanted there and he feels okay. McGuire says he's too sick and forces him back to bed. Willie lies down and admits he's tired and wants to sleep. Blah, blah, Willie drops off and Jason leaves the room. Ah, Willie pulled a fake-out. He gets out of bed and goes to the window. Looking out, he cries out, saying it's dark and it's too late. He hears that strange heartbeat and says, "I know. I hear you, I'm coming."

Willie drags himself downstairs, his legs buckling under him on the way down. He goes to the portrait of Barnabas and hears the heartbeat again. From the drawing room, Jason sees Willie heading for the door. Willie tries to bolt, but McGuire stops him. Willie, desperate, begs to leave. Weakened and broken, Willie sobs, falling against McGuire. They start up the stairs and Willie shoves Jason, then dashes out the front door. A car is heard driving off a few seconds later and Jason runs out, too.

Willie is creeping through the cemetery, with Jason not far behind. Willie goes to the Collins mausoleum and reluctantly pulls the ring to open the secret panel. Hearing the heartbeat, he walks into the secret room. McGuire goes into the crypt; the panel is closed and there's no sign of Willie. McGuire leaves.

Episode #218 — A redo of Jason's crypt visit, only as he leaves the cemetery, Barnabas emerges from nearby and watches him go.

At Collinwood, Roger's on the phone to the inn. Hanging up, he asks Liz if she's talked to Barnabas. Seems he isn't registered at the inn and we learn that, per Roger at least, any other place in town is a flophouse. (Really? We've seen Burke's shitty motel room; if that's the best in town, it makes you wonder). Liz suggests maybe Barnabas is staying with friends. Roger brings up having him stay at Collinwood, screw the two "sea tramps" lodging there. Liz says she gets the feeling Barnabas wants privacy. Blah, blah, Barnabas may settle and start a business. Someone knocks and Roger answers the door — speak of the devil. Roger mentions having called the inn and Barnabas conveniently avoids revealing where he's staying. Going to the drawing room, Roger extends the offer to stay in the homestead. Barnabas asks if he can instead move into the Old House. Roger think he's crazy, the house is decaying. Barnabas says it's just neglected and he feels he belongs there. Somewhat apropos of nothing, Liz mentions that the first Barnabas was supposed to have died in England, unmarried, but Barnabas assures her he's the "product of a proper marriage." (Side note: I'm loving Liz's loungewear). Blah, blah, Barnabas says there was bad blood way back in the family tree and some wished the first Barnabas dead. Back to the Old House, Roger points out that it's filthy and lacks electricity. Barnabas says he'll get it cleaned, doesn't care about the power and will pay rent. Roger nixes the offer of money, as he's family. Roger and Liz both express concern about anyone staying in the house. Barnabas backs off, not wanting to push Liz, but asks her to consider the request. She says she will and leaves the room. Roger says he gets where Barnabas is coming from with the Old House and says he'll talk to Liz.

Liz goes to the study, where she finds Jason helping himself to the liquor. She demands to know where Willie is; wasn't he too sick to leave? They bicker and bitch about Loomis. Liz says to kick him out or call a doctor. Jason responds with a veiled threat.

Roger and Barnabas are in the foyer. Roger goes to get a business contact's address for him. Jason comes along and, seeing Barnabas, asks if they've met before. Nope. Yes, we have. Barnabas' expression reveals that he knows Jason is full of shit. Barnabas points to the portrait and McGuire mentions the jewels and how the first Barnabas was buried with them (really? First I've heard of it; these writers change things at the drop of a hat). Jason gets on a vague grave robbing theory and the back-and-forth between the two makes for a fun scene.

Roger joins Liz in the study, announces Barnabas has gone, and that he saw McGuire trying to work him. They discuss Barnabas' request and Roger says if Willie and Jason can stay at the main house, surely a blood relative can stay at the old one. Liz isn't ready to make that decision and I wonder what bug has nestled in her posterior. He asks Liz to think it over, then remembers asking Barnabas for a phone number, but not getting it. Where is he staying? he wonders. Meanwhile, Barnabas is taking a stroll through the graveyard and goes to the family crypt.

Episode #219 — It's five a.m. and Willie, looking like death warmed over, drags himself in from the back foyer door. Jason darts out of the drawing room and starts bitching at him, knowing he went to the cemetery. What was he doing there? Willie looks about ready to drop, the poor bastard, and says he doesn't feel well, he wants to sleep. Jason doesn't believe he's sick and says he knows Willie went to Eagle Hill for the jewels. Willie says yeah, sure, the jewels and no, he won't look for them anymore. McGuire's ready to boot Willie from the house and heaps on the sarcasm and disdain. Willie pleads to go to bed and sleep and collapses to his knees. McGuire hauls him up and Willie, with a sob, begs for help. Jason says he shouldn't have looked at the Barnabas painting, with all the jewels. Willie says he won't ever go out again for the pretty, shiny gems.

Back in bed, Willie is restlessly sleeping. Roger comes in and wakes him. Willie begs to be left alone to sleep, he's sick. Roger tells him to get out and when he makes a move toward him, Willie cowers, then asks for help getting out of bed. Now it's Roger's turn to drip sarcasm and disdain. Willie collapses onto the bed again and Roger storms out.

In the drawing room, Roger and McGuire argue over whether Willie is really ill. Roger's about to call a doctor when the phone rings. It's the sheriff, wanting Roger to come into town to discuss some important matter. Roger hands a phonebook to Jason and tells him to call a doctor. As he leaves, he says he hopes Willie's gone by the time he returns.

At the sheriff's office, Patterson tells Roger that the cattle on the family farms (how does that work? Do the Collinses pay people to farm for them?) are mysteriously dying from loss of blood; they're completely drained. He tells Roger other farms have experienced the same and the two wonder who would do such a thing?

The doctor has finished an exam of the still sleeping Willie. He tells Jason there's no infection, but that Willie's heart rate is thready; he's lost a lot of blood.

Patterson and Roger, blah, blah. Roger leaves.

In the foyer, the doctor and McGuire discuss Willie's arm wound and the physician admits to being puzzled. Roger comes back and is told that Willie is suffering from severe blood loss. That strikes a chord with Roger, obviously. The doctor says Willie will recover with rest and a good diet.

Upstairs, the sleeping Willie is tossing, turning and talking in his sleep, saying he won't go back there (wherever "there" is).

Episode #220 — Willie wakes with a start — hey, did he get a haircut? — and seems to feel better. He gets out of bed, walks to the window and is seemingly pained to see that it's dark. He starts putting on his shoes when Jason walks in and wonders what he's doing. Willie states the obvious, getting dressed, as he feels better and McGuire says he looks it, which is hard to believe, seeing as how Willie could barely stand a few hours ago. Jason questions how Willie could suffer from blood loss, but seem so markedly improved. Willie has no answer, as he's not a doctor, and is talking the way he used to. McGuire blah, blah Liz/doctor. Jason believes Willie has his own scam or plan going and is supremely hurt that he's not a part of it. Why, that's a betrayal (like you not telling Willie *why* you're blackmailing Liz? Hypocrite). Willie says he has no plan afoot. Jason says he'll lose everything if he sticks with Willie; the partnership is over, which Willie quietly accepts. McGuire comments that his friend seems empty and suddenly sensitive (which just seems to be pouring salt in the wounds), and wishes he knew what happened to him in that cemetery (don't we all?). Jason leaves the room and a short while later, Vicki comes in with some food. She tells him that Mrs. Johnson thinks that, under his exterior, Willie is a good person (will we ever know, one way or another?). She comments on his whole demeanor changing and encourages him to eat. He says he doesn't want to eat, he can't. Vicki turns to go and he follows her, announcing that he's leaving and apologizing for his treatment of her. She snaps at him a little, but he says he understands. She's surprised at him showing remorse.

In the drawing room, Jason is telling Liz that Willie will be out in a few minutes. Blah, blah, and man, Liz is an unpleasant bitch. Willie politely interrupts and is adamant about speaking to Liz about something important. McGuire tries to hustle him out and Liz snottily turns her back on him. Defeated, Willie walks with McGuire to the front door. Jason's convinced Willie was going to drop a dime on him. Willie assures him he wasn't. McGuire gives Willie the five hundred dollars and says he'll stop by his motel before he leaves town. Willie wonders what's going to happen to him; Jason says it's up to him, but

Willie counters that's not the case — not anymore.

By the foyer clock, it's seven-thirty and Barnabas has stopped by Collinwood to ask Liz about the Old House. Though she was hobbled with indecision just the other day, she's now totally fine with him moving in. Barnabas is thrilled. She offers to have Mrs. Johnson go over to clean, but Barnabas says he's already made arrangements. Liz heads off to get the keys and, meeting up with Vicki, relays the news about their new neighbor. Barnabas and Vicki talk Old House, with Barnabas explaining he hopes to restore the mansion to its original condition. Liz comes back with the keys and Barnabas leaves. Liz and Vicki briefly discuss Barnabas and the house, then Willie being gone, as well as the change in him. Liz thinks it's temporary, but Vicki believes it's permanent.

Barnabas enters the Old House and calls to someone outside to come in. Willie somewhat reluctantly enters and is told that the Old House is their new home and there's much to be done. Barnabas then tells Willie to go out, knowing what he has to do. Willie shudders, turns away, and says he can't. Barnabas reminds him that he has no say in what he does anymore, then orders him to go. Willie complies.

(Quick note: in these last six episodes, John Karlen, as Willie, has been giving a master class in acting. The first actor, I believe, was too young and unseasoned for the role. His interpretation of the character was all over the map; hothead, petulant whiner, easily cowed, not very bright, then full-on pervert. Karlen's hitting all the right notes, with a lot of nuance, and where I *loathed* the faux Willie, I'm enjoying the hell out of the real one)

Episode # 221 — The coffee shop and Maggie is closing up for the night. As she puts on her coat in the motel lobby, she's startled by Barnabas, who's come in looking for a cup of coffee. She re-opens for him and after pouring two cups of day old, bottom of the pot mud, she sits with him and chats. He tells her he's newly arrived in town and, oh, yes, is a Collins, who'll be staying in the Old House. Maggie tells him some folks say the place is haunted. She notices his silver wolf's head cane, which he explains is an heirloom and his most prized possession. As she goes to refill his coffee, he sets the cane down on a vacant chair. Dogs suddenly start howling, for no discernible reason, which makes her nervous. Barnabas watches her with a slightly malevolent expression. As he readies to leave, she tells him her name and mentions her father is an artist. Barnabas bids goodnight and leaves via the motel lobby. A couple of seconds later, Joe strolls in, having left work early (must have pulled a night shift, or some overtime). He was concerned for Maggie, as a young woman was attacked a little earlier that night. The woman wasn't hurt, but the man got away without her getting a good look at him. Maggie mentions she had a customer who just left and Joe said he didn't see anyone. She fills him in on the newest Collins, proclaiming that he seemed somewhat sad and lonely, but she likes him. She notices the cane on the chair and wants to return it right away, as it's valuable. Joe offers to drive her out to Collinwood before they hit the Blue Whale. Dogs start howling again as Maggie locks up.

The couple knock on the Old House door, but receive no answer. Turning to go, the front door mysteriously opens on its own (oh, like the Stockbridge crypt). They walk in and find the parlor has been made habitable (how much time has passed? That's some mighty speedy rehabbing) and ablaze with candles. Joe goes to see if anyone is upstairs. Nervous Maggie waits in the parlor and is startled once again when Barnabas suddenly appears out of nowhere. She explains about bringing the cane and mentions Joe, who comes downstairs. After introductions are made, Joe says they have to split. Once they leave, Willie comes from somewhere in the house, asking what they were doing there. Barnabas replies that Willie shouldn't be there, as he has a job to do. With suspicion, Willie asks where he met the girl and what does he want with her? (is it possible our Mr. Loomis has truly reformed, or is he jealous?).

Joe takes Maggie home and she offers him a nightcap. A man after my own heart, Joe doesn't say no. They discuss Barnabas; polite, but odd. Maggie admits to being momentarily afraid of him when they were alone in the parlor.

At the Old House, our Mr. Loomis is grilling Barnabas, knowing his employer has something planned. Barnabas tells Willie to go out and do his job. Willie begs not to go, as the task, whatever it is, will make him lose his mind, but eventually he goes. Dogs start howling again as Barnabas peers out a window.

At the Evans cottage, Maggie is flaking out, staring out the window as Joe's talking to her. Snapping out of it, she tells him she has the feeling she's being watched.

Mr. Loomis, Reformed Reprobate

Episode #222 — Willie's lighting candles in the Old House parlor (may I note that Willie looks good in that white shirt and unbuttoned vest). Someone knocks and he freezes, then decides to hide alongside a column in the room. Vicki comes in, looking for Barnabas, and I'm thinking maybe some new locks should be installed on those doors. Anyway, she sees Willie and asks him what he's doing there and why did he hide? He gives a vague answer, then tells her to leave. Vicki gets a bit terse and refuses, saying she's come to visit someone who lives there. Willie drops Barnabas' name and says he knows him; he helped him change a flat tire, and now works for him, fixing the house. Vicki still seems a tad bitchy, then says the reason she's there is to deliver a dinner invitation from Liz. Willie says Barnabas is out and snaps that he doesn't know when he'll be back, but then apologizes. Vicki compliments his work in repairing the parlor. When she mentions the approaching sunset, Willie gets jittery and insists she go. He finally convinces her and she leaves, much to his relief. Barnabas emerges from wherever he was and makes some snide comments about Willie's concern for Vicki. What a dick.

Maggie rushes into the cottage, in a bit of a nervous panic. She's out of breath and seems spooked. Someone knocks and when she inquires who's come calling, discovers it's Barnabas. She partially opens the door, still scared. She reluctantly lets him in, however, and reveals that she's convinced she was being followed. Barnabas is all charm. Maggie relates the story of the woman who was attacked the other night and mentions that all the dead animals are freaking people out (has no one made the damn connection yet? They were pretty quick to realize weird things started when Laura blew into town). Maggie's calmed down and Barnabas says he's there to see some of Sam's work. He starts browsing when Sam comes home, glad his daughter is okay, as another girl was attacked an hour ago; jumped from behind, but a car scared the attacker off. Just as with the first victim, there's no description of the perpetrator. As Sam relates all this, Barnabas is sort of fondling and glancing at the head of his walking cane. The talk then turns to paintings. Sam thinks Barnabas is there to buy, but turns out, he wants to commission a portrait, for a cool thousand dollars. Of course, Sam accepts, and tells Barnabas to come over the next morning. Oh, but Barnabas wants to start right away, at the Old House — and, oh, his schedule is such a bitch, all the sittings will have to be done at night. Sam is easily persuaded (sure, a grand can do that for an old lush). Barnabas shovels some b.s. compliments, then leaves.

Since the Evans family station wagon (Sam mentioned it earlier) is a magical transporter, Sam is setting up his gear at the Old House. Barnabas tells him he'll arrange a ride home for him and Maggie leaves (hey, where's Josette's painting? It's gone). Barnabas sits in front of the fireplace and Sam starts to sketching.

Vicki answers a knock at Collinwood proper; it's Maggie, dropping in to say hello. She explains why she's there and Vicki shows her the first Barnabas' portrait.

Wow, Sam works fast; almost a third of that painting is done. Anyway, he takes a break as the cock crows. When Sam notices a facial detail that he wants to add to the canvas, Barnabas gets snippy, saying the sitting is over, but Sam is in full-on artist mode and rushes to the easel. Having captured whatever intrigued him, he looks and finds Barnabas is gone. Willie is suddenly in the hall and quietly tells Sam that he's to take him home. Confused Sam wonders where his patron is and when he should come back. Willie tells him to return at sundown.

Episode #223 — In the drawing room, Vicki is telling Liz that Willie is still in the vicinity and Liz wants to vacate him from the premises. Vicki mentions that she saw him at the Old House — oh, Liz interrupts, Barnabas will take care of him, in short order. Ah, not so fast, Dame Stoddard, Vicki goes on, Willie's *working* for Barnabas. Liz decides to talk to her cousin post-haste about Willie. David comes by and wants to go to the Old House with his aunt, but she says no and takes off alone. A disappointed David tells Vicki he's mad at Barnabas for changing the Old House and he doesn't want him living there.

Having received no answer to her knock, Liz waltzes into the Old House, noticing the unfinished canvas as she looks around the parlor. The front door slams shut, but it's only David. He comments on the house being different, that he can feel the change (damn, this kid continues to grow before our very eyes). Perceptive David notices Josette's portrait is missing — as is Josette. He immediately starts upstairs to look for the painting. Liz stops him, saying it's his cousin's house now and to get over it. David laments that Josette herself is gone and not watching over them anymore.

In the Collinwood foyer, Burke and Vicki are examining the portrait of the first Barnabas, when Burke opines that present Barnabas is none-too-bright if he has Willie working for him (asshole). Vicki defends the new Collins. Burke walks into the drawing room and Vicki asks if Liz was really expecting him. Of course not, Burke says, but she likes when he visits from time-to-time (this jerk). He goes on to say that he wants to talk to Liz because she's done something very out of character.

Must be a little later, as Liz and Burke are walking into the study. He inquires why she sold some prime real estate to someone named Hackett, who apparently is a hack that will ruin the seafront property. Burke susses out that she needed fast cash and says he would have purchased the property, stating she was somehow forced to sell the land. Tough-as-nails Liz says she wasn't forced, but Burke (and we) know better — that McGuire is somehow responsible. Burke lets the matter drop, then brings up Willie working at the Old House. He offers to help Barnabas get rid of him, but Liz says that won't be necessary; Barnabas is a Collins.

In the foyer, Burke finds David sitting on the stairs, looking down. Blah, blah, change to Old House/Josette painting (I complain about Devlin, the character, a lot, but Mitch Ryan is especially good in scenes with David). Burke suggests David ask for Josette's portrait. David thinks that's a swell idea and heads off to do just that.

Just like the main house, Barnabas doesn't lock the damn doors, so David strolls right in. Suddenly, dogs start howling and he calls out to Josette, afraid. The doors slam shut and frightened David can't open them. The dogs continue their yowling.

Episode #224 — In tears, frightened, panicked David pounds on the door, calling to be let out. The dogs suddenly stop and — guess who's there? David explains to his cousin how he couldn't open the door, which Barnabas does with ease. David mentions the bizarre pack of howling dogs, never before heard in the area, then asks about Josette's portrait. Barnabas explains he's going to hang his over the mantel and that hers has been moved to another room. David asks for it, but Barnabas says it belongs in the Old House. However, he'll hang it someplace special and David can come to see it anytime. Willie walks in from another room and David walks up to him and says hello. Willie explains that he works there now and very protectively tells David to go home as it's getting dark, shooting Barnabas knowing glances the whole time. David leaves and Barnabas chides Willie that he worries too much, then calls after David to wait up, he'll walk with him.

Liz saunters into the drawing room to talk Willie with McGuire, revealing that his buddy is working at the Old House. Jason says he'll take care of it a.s.a.p., then asks about a financial arrangement — a Swiss bank account in his name (this piece of shit). Hearing one is being set up, he goes upstairs (what about going to take care of the Willie issue?). David and Barnabas come in and blah, blah, Josette painting. David's worked up an appetite, so he heads to the kitchen. Liz asks Barnabas to give Willie the boot; he's trouble. Barnabas says he knows all about Willie and his past doesn't bother him; in fact, Mr. Loomis is working out quite well. Liz still wants him gone, but Barnabas says Willie is completely under his control, there will be no trouble. Cautiously, Liz agrees to let him stay and give him a chance to prove he's reformed (Liz is wearing those enormous earrings again; I think they're also emerald and diamonds).

Oh, I guess McGuire did go to the Old House. Anyway, when Willie answers the door (who'd have thought McGuire to be the one to have the good manners to knock?). Jason immediately starts giving him shit and pushes his way inside. Willie says he can't talk, he's got stuff to do, and that he is, indeed, employed there, doing whatever's needed in the restoration (guess Willie is a master plumber, carpenter and mason, but non-union). McGuire acts a total a-hole, wanting to know what Willie is really up to. Willie says he's just trying to live a different kind of life. McGuire grabs him and yells at him when Barnabas arrives back home and tells Brogue Blarney he can answer all of his questions. Barnabas sends Willie on a task. Jason tries to warn Barnabas about Willie and offers to get involved if trouble arises.

At the Evans cottage, Sam goes to Maggie's room, ready to leave for more painting. She wishes he didn't have to go and, sensing she's uneasy, he offers to stay. She tells him to go on ahead, and he leaves. A nervous Maggie goes to bed. At the Old House, Sam and Barnabas chat as Sam works. The conversation works around to Maggie and Barnabas looks a bit — crafty. Meanwhile, sleeping Maggie tosses and turns. The picture starts to go wavy, then blurry, to indicate she's dreaming. She's running around the foggy woods in a nightgown when she comes across a coffin. It opens of its own volition and she sees herself in it, dead. Then — what the hell? — Maggie's head is a skull. Maggie wakes up screaming.

Episode #225/226 — It's a Maggie nightmare redo; roll yesterday's tape! She stops screaming and calls Joe (now, the Evanses are far from rich, but she has a phone in her bedroom. The super wealthy Collinses have to haul ass downstairs to use a phone. Something's amiss here). Frightened, she asks Joe to come over and where the hell has Joe been that necessitated him wearing a jacket and tie?

Joe and Maggie enter the Blue Whale and Joe orders a couple of drinks (huh, now Joe's wearing one of his usual sweaters; I'm confused). Maggie eventually gets around to describing her dream — that she saw herself dead. Joe prescribes another sip of alcohol to calm her down. Logical Joe logically applies logic in an attempt to decipher her dream. The recent attacks, perchance? Sam and Barnabas walk in and Maggie asks that Sam not be told about her nightmare. Maggie seems unnerved by Barnabas, so much so that she knocks over a drink. Sam jokes that he raised her better than that. The quartet start talking and Barnabas mentions the night and its influence on people. Maggie asks Joe to dance and beats a hasty retreat to the dance floor. Barnabas shovels compliments Sam's way regarding his fetching daughter, while Maggie and Joe slow dance. When the song ends, Maggie prefers to stay at the bar; she's obviously afraid of one Mr. Collins. Burke walks in and says hello. Hearing that Barnabas is there, he strolls over to the table and horns in. Joe questions Maggie on why she's acting so strange and they get a little edgy with each other. Burke and Barnabas talk Willie, with Sam saying Loomis is a changed man and Barnabas intoning that he detests violence and won't abide it from his hired man. Now Maggie's feeling better (must be the booze), but maybe not, as she refuses to say goodnight to the men. She and Joe start arguing again, but Maggie toughs it out and says goodnight to Sam and the others.

Back home, Maggie wants to go to bed, but is afraid to. Sam comes home, asking what's wrong and says she's acting like she did as a little girl after having a nightmare. She says she's okay and Sam leaves the room. Maggie goes to bed and the dogs start howling. At the bar, Burke and Barnabas are talking about Barnabas' cane. As Burke inspects it and asks a question, Barnabas is really preoccupied. Mr. Collins suddenly apologizes and hurries out. Meanwhile, Maggie's tossing and turning and the dogs are still at it. Barnabas creeps in through the French doors (locks, people!), approaches the foot of her bed, gazes down at her and — snarls at her? (I really don't know what he's supposed to be doing, so snarl it is)

Episode #227 — Redo (I should differentiate between replays, using previous day's footage, and an actual redo, which this is). Maggie's clutching her throat. Barnabas creeps, gazes, malevolently grins (?) — is he sporting fangs? Hard to tell. The next morning, dumbass Barnabas has left the French doors open (way to cover your tracks). Sam knocks, calling to Maggie that she's overslept, and walks in. She doesn't feel well, is cold and has zero energy. Sam notices that she looks pale. Maggie struggles to get up and he tells her to forget about work. She relays that she had bad dreams and wants to go to work, she's all right, and then starts yelling at Sam. She apologizes and says she'll have some coffee, admitting that she doesn't want to spend the day in her room.

Well, Maggie's made it to work and is sporting a scarf around her neck. Joe comes in. As she tries to get him a cup of coffee, she drops it, then shrieks at him when he makes a joke about sweeping up. She tries again, first pouring too little, then overfilling. Joe asks what's wrong, did she sleep okay? Nope, bad dreams. Jovial Sam walks in and as she gets him a cup of java, she nearly collapses. Sam says he'll phone the doctor; Maggie says no, then passes out.

Early evening and Maggie's home in bed, seeming her old self and talking with Joe, who's wearing different clothes again — oh, he's going out with the boys for the night. Joe says he'll bring her flowers and she freaks out, saying that's what he did in her dream, brought flowers to her grave and I'm wondering when was this? We never saw that or heard her talk about it. She calms down and Joe leaves. Over at the Old House, Barnabas strolls into the parlor and goes to the window. Maggie momentarily hovers by her French doors before starting to brush her hair. Sam comes in and notes she looks better and she says she does feel improved and wants to drive him to the Old House. Hmm, she seems slightly…vixenish.

Barnabas is waiting for them when they arrive. He and Maggie exchange rather knowing glances. She looks *very* vixenish and their conversation is, let's call it interesting by what's *not* said, but rather, non-verbally communicated (this was done well). Barnabas says Willie will take Sam home and Maggie leaves. Sam gets to work and tells Barnabas that Maggie hasn't been feeling well. Back at home, Maggie goes to bed, quite at ease. Barnabas walks to the parlor window and Maggie is suddenly restless. Sam announces he's tired and wants to knock off for the night. Barnabas convinces him to work through the night and take the next off. He decides to go for a walk while Sam finishes up (what the hell time is it? Two, three a.m.?). Maggie wakes up, opens the French doors, loosens her scarf, and lies back down (for some reason, I found this episode boring; maybe the repetition).

27

Episode #228 — Liz and Jason are arguing in the drawing room; people are starting to talk, he claims (which makes no sense; it's not like Liz lives there alone, there's five other people around). He wants in on the family business, but Liz is (rightfully) adamantly opposed and calls it for what it is — black-mail. The mangy leprechaun wants to do public relations for the company; that will 'explain' the money she's giving him. Liz is fed up with his constant demands. The toad claims he cares for her and hates to see her upset. Robe attired Carolyn (is this morning or evening?) interrupts and immediately senses her mother is upset. McGuire spews malarkey, which Carolyn ignores. She exits, with anger visible on her face. Jason decides to head to work and expects his office to be ready for him by the time he gets there (this worthless sack of crap). He leaves and after a few moments, Liz makes a phone call.

What I'm assuming is later in the day, Roger and Liz are in the study, discussing the new PR director and he knows McGuire put Liz up to it. Roger's concerned and wants answers, but none are forthcoming. He tells her she's making a mistake. Meanwhile, in the drawing room, the now clothed and still perceptive Carolyn is telling Vicki what a worthless, phony shit McGuire is. He happens along and she asks him how long he's staying. He replies that Liz asked him to stay and, furthermore, to help with the business. Carolyn is shocked and doesn't believe a goddamn word of it (somebody kill the ingrate). A short time later, Carolyn, Roger and Vicki are now in the study, talking McGuire. Roger says he never laid eyes on him before, despite the claim that he and Liz are old friends. Ah, he was at school during the Paul Stoddard days and didn't know him much, either. Carolyn wants to know more about deadbeat daddy. Roger says some of his things are locked in the basement. She gets excited, but Uncle Rog can't give her any details. A concerned Vicki is listening to the exchange and thinks they should drop the subject. Liz sails in and Roger snarks about McGuire. Carolyn asks for the key to the locked room. Liz says there's nothing in it, and besides, she lost the key, then gets testy when her daughter suggests they break the door down. Absolutely not, Dame Stoddard decrees, and stop talking about that damn room! Needless to say, Liz storms out, leaving everyone puzzled.

Liz is pacing the drawing room when Vicki enters, having been summoned. Liz apologizes for her outburst; the room is of no importance and won't she help her convince Carolyn of that? Smart Vicki says the room is somehow a part of Liz's current woes, but Liz says that's not the case at all. Of course, Vicki doesn't believe her. Blah, blah, room/Carolyn/Paul and Vicki knows Liz is lying.

Carolyn is searching the study when Vicki comes back and tells her to stop looking for the key. Vicki theorizes that maybe something other than Paul's belongings are in that locked room (is Vicki onto something regarding dead Paul?). Carolyn continues searching.

Whatever It Is, It Must Be Catching

Episode #229 — Maggie's in bed, with the French doors open again. Sam quietly comes in, checks on her, then goes out and calls the coffee shop, telling them she won't be in. Maggie stirs, rubbing her throat. Extremely weak, she struggles to get out of bed, but collapses. Post opening credits, Maggie is back in bed, sleeping. Sam brings in some coffee and wakes her. Blah, blah, slept late/ill/work. Wanting to care for her, Sam offers to make her tea or soup, but Maggie doesn't want anything. He notes that the doors were open again and says he wants to call the doctor. She protests, loudly, but Sam is firm. Maggie forlornly cries that the doctor can't help her (I liked Willie's malaise better for some reason).

At the Blue Whale — hey, a different jazzy tune — Burke and Vicki are on a date (still a cheapskate, I see). Vicki tells him things have gotten a might strange at Collinwood. Burke asks why Willie is still around and Vicki fills him in (hasn't this been explained to him already? Why the continuing hard-on, big man? I think Loomis got under Burke's skin because he wasn't afraid of him and that bruised his ego). Burke asks if he's over his illness and Vicki says he seems to be. Well, if that's so, then he needs to leave town (it's not up to you, jackass, and this isn't the wild west when the mayor or sheriff could run somebody out of town). Vicki then mentions that McGuire is working for Collins Enterprises. Burke gets off a good line about the unemployment going down in town.

Joe arrives at the cottage and Sam fills him in while the doctor is checking Maggie. The doc comes out and says that Maggie is very sick, suffering from — can you guess? — blood loss. Blah, blah, he's going to run some blood tests. He prescribes diet, rest and some medication (hey, why didn't Willie get an

Rx?). The doctor leaves and Sam stops himself from pouring a drink. Joe tells him to get out for a bit, go to the bar, he'll stay with Maggie. Sam takes him up on the offer and Joe settles on the couch with a magazine. Once it's dark, our girl wakes up to howling dogs. Opening the bedroom door, she coldly asks Joe where her father is. She's in full-on bitch mode and insults him, demands he leave, and throws his coat at him. Stunned, but remaining calm, Joe says he'll go, against his better judgment, so as not to upset her anymore. Once he's gone, Maggie's expression is a combination of evil and whorishness.

At the Blue Whale, Vicki and Burke are discussing the attacks and bizarre animal mutilations. Sam wanders in and joins them, explaining Maggie's illness and doctor's visit. Smart Vicki connects the dots to Willie's illness and even Burke concurs. Joe comes in and tells a surprised Sam that Maggie threw him out of the house, amid much bitching. Sam runs off and rushes into the house, calling for his daughter. Going into her room, he discovers that she's gone.

Episode # 230 — Worried Sam is pacing when Joe, Vicki and Burke show up. Could Maggie have gone for a walk? Nah, Joe and Sam say Maggie's been acting strangely all week. Where could she be? Turns out Maggie's taking a late night promenade in the graveyard and she looks like hell (and I thought Willie looked bad when he first fell ill). Sam informs the group that the sheriff is looking for Maggie and he, Joe and Burke decide to canvas the area as well, leaving Vicki behind in case Maggie comes home. A little over an hour later, someone knocks at the cottage and Vicki answers to find Willie, with a message for Sam from Barnabas. Vicki says Sam won't be able to paint, as Maggie is missing and he's searching for her. Willie seems upset to hear the news and leaves in a hurry.

Looking like a zombie, Maggie wanders the woods accompanied by the howling of canines. At the Evans cottage, the phone rings and we find out it's Willie calling from a payphone. He pulls the old handkerchief over the mouthpiece trick and tells Vicki that Maggie is in danger, but he knows where to find her. Vicki asks who it is (either that hankie must work great or she's too stupid to recognize that distinctive voice). He tells her to go immediately to Eagle Hill Cemetery. He quickly hangs up, but for a few seconds, we can still hear her, asking who it is (unintentionally hilarious). Vicki then dials the operator and asks for the sheriff, but there's no answer (guess if you're about to be murdered, you're out of luck). Burke returns and blah, blah, phone call/Eagle Hill. He decides to go check it out and Vicki says she's coming with, but he tells her a cemetery is no place for her to be at night (really? What about the two visits with Frank to the Stockbridge crypt? And what the hell happened to Frank, anyway? Where is he?). Burke then relents and off they go.

In the cemetery, Maggie's just standing around in the fog, listening to the dogs — oh, Barnabas emerges from some nearby shrubbery. He approaches her, looking very creepy and evil, and says that they have to go. Willie suddenly runs up, telling Barnabas they have to leave, Maggie's friends are coming for her. Barnabas inquires as to how they know she's there. Willie says he doesn't know and let's book. We hear Burke calling for Maggie. Barnabas insists she come with him and she suddenly faints. Desperate Willie says let's boogie on out of here. Meanwhile, Vicki comes across one of Maggie's slippers and she and Burke start calling her name again. Dumbass Barnabas just keeps gazing at the unconscious Magster and Willie says let's get the fuck out of here already. They finally depart, leaving Maggie with her head pillowed on a large rock, which seems really uncomfortable. Burke and Vicki find Maggie just as she starts to come to; she can't remember anything. Burke thinks he sees someone in the distance and goes to check it out, leaving the two women alone (isn't there some perv attacking young women at night?).

Willie and Barnabas go to the Collins mausoleum secret room. Burke enters the crypt, but finds nothing, naturally. Willie and Barnabas listen from the secret room and I wonder how they manage that through all that thick concrete and/or brick. Burke leaves. Vicki's consoling Maggie as Burke returns and the three depart, with Burke carrying the weakened Maggie. Willie exits the secret room and takes a look around, then goes back and tells Barnabas the coast is clear. Barnabas begins interrogating him; how did Burke know where to find Maggie? Willie doesn't know, then says when he went to deliver the message for Sam, he heard them talking about checking the cemetery. Barnabas doesn't believe him and claims he's lying and has betrayed him, so he must be punished — and then proceeds to beat the holy hell out of him with his cane (loathsome, sadistic bastard. Didn't he recently say he abhorred violence? Fucking hypocrite.)

At the Evans cottage, Sam and Joe are about to phone the state troopers to get in on the search, when Burke, Vicki and Maggie come in. Setting Maggie down on the sofa, she snarls when they try to remove her scarf. She complains of not being able to breathe, then passes out. When they remove her scarf, they discover two puncture wounds on her neck.

Episode #231 — Burke and Vicki have left the cottage, leaving Sam and Joe to discuss the marks on Maggie's neck. Dogs howl, sleeping Maggie moans. Sam closes the French doors and blah, blah, doors/dogs. Maggie moans and writhes, then wakes up, asking what happened. Sam and Joe blame themselves and fill her in on the nocturnal doings and it's boring as hell. Maggie asks if she was alone when she was found, then complains of being cold. A bit later, the doctor has shown up (new actor as Dr. Woodard). Maggie's temperature is five degrees below normal, but we don't find out about her pulse or blood pressure, though he goes through the motions. Sam anxiously watches it all while puffing on a cancer stick. I will say this Woodard has a pretty good beside manner, but Maggie's a bit frosty towards him. He inquires if she's ever sleepwalked and if she's been having bad dreams. Sam mentions her recent nightmare, much to her dismay. Woodard thinks she walked in her sleep to the cemetery because of the dream. She tries to hide the marks on her neck, but Woodard sees them. As he treats them with what is presumably disinfectant, Maggie cries that they have to be left alone and I liked this shit better when it was Willie. Blah, blah, puncture wounds. Also, bitchy Maggie is an unlikable Maggie.

Joe is waiting in the living room as Sam and Woodard come in. The doc says Maggie needs a blood transfusion right away. As luck would have it, Joe has the same blood type. As the procedure takes place, Maggie moans and whimpers. Dogs start howling and Maggie whines some more (and this is irritating beyond belief). Maggie suddenly starts screaming "don't take his blood!" and tries to rip the needle out of her arm.

Later, Woodard writes out a prescription for a tranquilizer and tells Sam his daughter must be watched at all times. Sam smokes and the doctor leaves. Joe is sitting with Maggie. She wakes up and asks where her father is. Filling her prescription, it turns out, and I'm wondering where and what freaking time is it? Does a tiny village like Collinsport have an all night pharmacy? Joe looks in fine health, even after the transfusion. Sam comes back and tells Joe to take off and, having found the key, locks the French doors. Joe goes home and Sam takes a seat in Maggie's room and fires up yet another cig. Later, as he dozes in the chair, the canines are at it again. Maggie groans, then gets out of bed. She tries to open the French doors. The racket wakes up Sam who grabs her and she shrieks to be let out (please, let this be over soon, it's annoying).

Episode #232 — Maggie's sleeping, with Joe keeping watch (must be the next day). Maggie wakes up, worried she may have gone sleepwalking, but Joe tells her she slept fairly well, after sunrise. He fills her in on the previous night that she can't remember. Maggie's well enough to have some coffee and is behaving and talking like her usual self. Joe tries to get her to remember, but she can't and complains of exhaustion. Puncture would talk ensues. Aw, crap the dogs start again and Maggie gets bitchy (I really can't take this). She tells Joe to leave — for good, it's over. From the living room, Joe calls Vicki and asks her to relieve him as he's got to get to work (he took a half day). A wicked storm is rolling in, but Vicki says sure. McGuire walks into the foyer and catches the tail end of her conversation. Once Vicki hangs up, he puts in his two cents about going out in the storm, then tries to charm her. It only succeeds in aggravating our Miss Winters. She relays Maggie's sleepwalking incident and Eagle Hill and that catches McGuire's attention. She mentions the strange phone call and the unexplained marks on Maggie's neck. McGuire finally let's her go, then grabs his coat and leaves, too.

Jason's gone to the Old House and pulls the knock, then walk in routine. Willie comes downstairs, trying to hide his battered face, and McGuire starts giving him shit. When Jason sees the injuries, he shrugs it off like the humanitarian he is (some friend; if I saw a friend with a messed up face, I sure as hell would ask how it happened). Anyway, McGuire starts asking about Maggie and Eagle Hill and promises he'll get to the bottom of it. He connects Willie's wound to Maggie's; good deductive reasoning, too bad he's an asshole. Willie insists he wouldn't hurt Maggie, in fact he'd — he stops and Jason asks if he protected her by placing the mystery phone call. Willie denies and tries to get back to work. Jason says *he's* letting Willie stay because it seems like he's reformed (*he's* letting him stay? This arrogant schmuck), but if he does anything illegal that gets the cops involved — well, don't interfere with his plans. Willie yells at him that maybe he should *forget* his plans. McGuire asks if that's a threat. Willie calmly, and like his wily, crafty old self, says, oh, no, take it as a warning. Jason again asks if Willie made the call; now why would heI do something like that? our Mr. Loomis responds.

Vicki's arrived at the Evans' and relieves Joe. Maggie's asleep, calling for her man. Vicki comes in and Maggie wakes, asking if it's night yet. The storm rattles on. Maggie starts talking about liking the darkness. Vicki asks her about dumping Joe and Maggie repeats that she never wants to see him again. She then gets out of bed, but Vicki convinces her to go back. Maggie gets bitchy. Vicki takes a seat and Maggie dozes off, but is restless. Later, Maggie sits up and Vicki asks her what's wrong. The French doors suddenly blow open and, in a flash of lightning, the silhouette of a man in an Inverness coat is seen outside (weren't the doors locked?). Vicki screams and with the next lightning flash, the man is gone. As Vicki goes to close the doors, Maggie initially protests, then says everything is all right.

Episode #233 — Replay of the Vicki/Maggie/interloper stuff. Or is it a redo? Seems slightly different at first, but then the same.

At Collinwood, Carolyn, attired in a satiny looking lounging robe, is in the drawing room with a book. Vicki rushes in, with the storm still raging. As they chat, the power temporarily goes out and they talk about the strangeness of the storm. The power eventually goes out completely and Carolyn is scared (where are Liz, Roger, et al?). As the ladies light some candles, Vicki is startled, thinking she sees something at the window. She explains having seen a figure outside Maggie's room. Carolyn thinks she imagined it. Both scream at observing a silhouetted figure of a man in an Inverness coat in the drawing room doorway. It's just Barnabas, who claims he knocked, but the storm must have drowned it out (and, pray, tell, why would he be out walking in a raging thunderstorm? He's not even wet, nor is Vicki for that matter). He asks after Miss Evans, having heard she was unwell. Carolyn invites him to stay a while and he starts babbling about past storms that both houses weathered, shipwrecks and the wailing of the widows in the wind. He then starts to tell a story that would probably be a good place to start a new paragraph.

Barnabas spins a yarn about a young woman who died on such a night as this. She had quarreled with her lover and ran away from him. He followed and she headed for the cliff. He caught up with her and kissed her neck (uh-huh). She broke free and took a deliberate header off the cliff, smashing onto the jagged rocks below. He went down to the beach and found her bloodless body, but her face was tranquil. Well, that's enough for Carolyn, who finds it all just a bit too creepy. She dashes off to bed. Vicki, however, is intrigued, having caught the 'bloodless' reference. She mentions the animals, Willie and Maggie having a similar problem to varying degrees. She mentions Maggie's sleepwalking and the phone call she received on where to find her. Barnabas asks who it was, but Vicki doesn't know. She goes on to posit that logic will not explain what's going on with Maggie. Barnabas says she should make sure the same doesn't happen to *her*.

With flashlight in hand, McGuire comes in, (honestly, I forgot about him) and he mentions Liz (huh, guess she is home; she probably decided a power outage in the middle of the night wasn't worth getting out of bed for). Vicki heads on up to bed. Jason tells Barnabas that Willie is up to no good and he should get rid of him. There's something going on with that cemetery. Barnabas tries to brush it off, but McGuire asks how do you explain Maggie ending up there? McGuire thinks Willie is involved and says he's changed. He then mentions Willie's battered face. Barnabas tells him Willie fell off a ladder (oh, please), then leaves. Arriving back at the Old House, Barnabas is ticked and yelling for Willie, ready to beat the snot out of him again.

Episode #234 — Willie's on the floor of the parlor, having apparently suffered yet another beating, to "loosen his tongue." He denies having made the phone call and gets to his feet. Barnabas threatens another beat-down by brandishing his cane and whines about broken trust. Willie maintains his innocence (and good for him. Also, he must have truly changed, as he's taking some serious physical abuse to protect someone else; or was that a latent quality in him that only surfaced after *he* suffered?). He promises not to do anything wrong and Barnabas tells him to keep McGuire from coming to the house and asking questions. Willie wonders how the fuck he's supposed to manage that, but says he'll do what he can. Barnabas dismisses him as he wants to "meditate" (this asshole). Willie walks out, his body language conveying he'd like nothing more than to kill the son-of-a-bitch. Meanwhile, Barnabas is at the window.

Maggie goes to the French doors in her room. The storm is over and she and Sam talk about Vicki's story of seeing someone. Sam then tells normal acting Maggie to get some sleep. She goes to bed and pipe smoking Sam sits nearby. Finally, it's the next morning (it had been another one of those interminably long nights) and Dr. Woodard is paying a call. Maggie wants to go to work. Woodard asks about the marks on her neck, which she'd completely forgotten about. The doc prescribes lots of rest and leaves the room with Sam. In the living room, Woodard reveals that he's awaiting blood test results, but is cautiously optimistic. He goes on to say that Maggie needs to be watched, as serious harm could befall her from the sleepwalking. Sam wonders if the problem is psychological, Woodard is baffled by the puncture marks and I'm bored.

Later, Vicki is at the cottage, as Sam needs to work on the portrait at the Old House. He tells her Maggie is resentful and can get a bit unpleasant about having people stay with her; just ignore it. Sam leaves and Vicki goes to Maggie, who's glad to have the company. Then she doesn't want the company. Back and forth about being left alone (for the love of God, make this shit stop already).

At the Old House, Barnabas is posing for the portrait. Sam's stuck on color scheme or something and wants to take a break, but then quickly changes his mind and tells Barnabas he doesn't need him at the moment. Mr. Collins mentions that it's a ~~marvelous night for a moon dance~~ nice night for a walk and goes out as Sam paints on. Willie comes along a short time later, inquiring where his employer might have gone. Sam doesn't know and is testy in his replies to Willie's perfectly legitimate questions. Willie then tries asking about Maggie and Sam angrily shouts not to ever mention her name again — and don't bother me when I'm working! (Look, I get it; the old Willie's impertinent question if Maggie ever posed nude, pissed off Sam. Now add that to the 'artistic temperament' cliché. But, really, shut the fuck up).

At the Evans cottage, restless Maggie wakes up and acts a proper, full on cunt to Vicki. Dogs howl and Maggie bitches (Vicki, slap this cow — *hard*). Vicki is unnerved by the howling. More bitchiness, with Maggie claiming she doesn't hear a thing. The French doors start shaking, Vicki screams, then runs out, terrified. In the living room, she places an hysterical call to Burke (wait, there was a phone next to Maggie's bed a couple of episodes ago. What happened to it?). The bedroom door suddenly slams shut. Vicki rushes over, but is mysteriously unable to gain egress, prompting her to pound on the door and screech in a sort of obnoxious hysteria. (This episode was pretty irritating, except for the brief appearance of Willie)

Episode #235 — Vicki is still hysterical when Burke shows up and breaks open the bedroom door. They find the unconscious Maggie lying on the bed, blood dripping from the wounds on her neck. The French doors are wide open. A little while later, Woodard is checking on Maggie; more blood loss. Woodard has a wild theory; the bite marks might have been caused by a large animal. He asks where a telephone might be and Vicki points him in the direction of the living room (because either Maggie's phone is for Maggie only or New England Telephone retrieved their property; it's true, back in the day you didn't own your phone, you leased it from the phone company). Woodard is putting in a call for an ambulance to take the Magster to the hospital just as Sam comes home with Burke. Sam rushes to Maggie's room and he and Vicki blah, blah. The doc comes back in and announces an ambulance is on the way, then kicks them out to continue his examination of the patient.

In the living room, Burke's into the liquor and Sam (gasp!) refuses a belt. Vicki recounts what happened and she and Burke console Sam (and I wonder how long does an ambulance take? Collinsport is a tiny burg, they could have driven Maggie to the hospital by now). Woodard joins them and says Maggie needs another transfusion and he and Sam discuss her chances. The siren indicates the ambulance has finally arrived.

At the hospital, Maggie is getting treatment. Joe comes in and Maggie regains consciousness. It's a struggle for her to speak, as she's very weak. Woodard leaves the room to give them some time alone. Sam asks her what happened. All she says is she had a nightmare. She apologizes to Joe for the fighting, Sam promises to stay dry and Maggie pronounces that she's going to die. Woodard and the nurse come back in and tell Joe and Sam they'll have to leave, Maggie needs her rest. They opt to hang out in the waiting area.

A little after midnight, Maggie is sleeping and Woodard instructs the nurse not to leave her alone and keep the window closed and locked at all times. Joe and Sam sit in the waiting area for a couple of hours. Sam is broken up and smok-ing, of course, saying he sat in that same hospital when Maggie was born and now he's waiting for her to die. Some time later, the patient wakes and asks the nurse to open the window. Blah, blah, ~~Lucy Westenra~~ can't breath, so please open the window and the dumbass nurse complies. Sam and Joe continue to wait for Maggie to die. Maggie sits up, takes her last, labored, wracking breath and flops back on the bed. The nurse does a quick check of vitals, then goes out to call for Woodard, who conveniently emerges from a nearby room. They go back into Maggie's room and — she's gone and the window is wide open. The nurse insists the patient was dead, there was no heartbeat. Outside, dogs howl. (Can something more interesting happen now? Maggie's illness was a bit of a bore, although on one level, it was interesting to see the different effect it had on its victims; it brought out the bitch in Maggie, but compassion from Willie).

The Comely Corpse Vanishes

Episode #236 — It's a Maggie death redo. Woodard tells Joe and Sam that Maggie is "gone" — as in missing. Puzzlement all around, but doc has the cops looking for her. Joe wants to search the cemetery, but Woodard says she was too weak to walk that far; he thinks she was taken from her room. Joe leaves anyway. Sam is worked up, asking if his daughter is dead. Blah, blah, grief. In case you were wondering, Maggie is wandering the woods in her nightgown, looking very much in the pink.

Woodard is pushing a sedative on Sam, who refuses. Burke rushes in, blah, blah. Joe returns; no luck. Burke mentions the phone call about Maggie that Vicki had received and her hunch that it was Willie (a hunch which was never mentioned before). Burke doubts Loomis knows anything, but decides to talk to him anyway. He and Joe head to the Old House.

Dogs yowl as Burke knocks on the Old House door. Barnabas answers. They ask for Willie, but he's up in Bangor until tomorrow evening, attending to some matters for Mr. Collins. Blah, blah, phone call. Barnabas says Willie was with him immediately after delivering the message for Sam and as they don't have a phone, he couldn't *possibly* have made the call. He further asks if they think Willie abducted Miss Evans, which they don't. As Burke and Joe start to leave, Burke thinks he hears a floorboard creak, which Barnabas dismisses as just a random noise the house makes. Burke and Joe leave. A mesmerized Maggie emerges from a room off the parlor and goes to Barnabas.

Ooh, a new set; a large, fancy bedroom, with Josette's painting hanging above the mantel. Barnabas enters with Maggie and tells her it's *her* room, just as she left it (Maggie's in a kind of trance and her hair is different, done up in some curls, which begs the question; who did her hair? She seems a bit too spacey to manage a new coiffure herself and supposedly Willie's not home, which leaves the master of the house). He calls her Josette and informs her she will come to think, act and become her (oh, that's not creepy *at all*). He waxes rhapsodic about them being together and Maggie parrots his words in a spaced-out way. He says he's forgiven Josette for her suicide and that the life he wanted to give her, he'll give to Maggie. Our Miss Evans begins to remember Eagle Hill, but he's able to redirect her attention. He takes Josette's wedding gown from a trousseau and tells her she'll be his bride. He then gifts her a music box, the melody of which entrances her.

Episode #237 — The next morning at Collinwood, Jason comes downstairs as Vicki talks to Sam on the foyer telephone. Once she hangs up, he inquires why so many phones calls. Why, Maggie's disappeared from the hospital, Vicki informs him, whilst they stand near the ancestral portrait. Burke and Patterson then show up, with Devlin introducing McGuire to the lawman. They all engage in rehash filler talk in the drawing room, mystified as to how Maggie got out of the hospital. Burke brings up the anonymous phone call Vicki received and Jason listens with great interest, whereas I would prefer a merciful death. Patterson wants to talk to Willie and Jason seems quite concerned; so much so, he walks Patterson to the door and says he thinks the sheriff is accusing Mr. Loomis a bit prematurely. Patterson reminds McGuire that Willie caused trouble in town and has a record (big fucking deal, so does Burke, yet you kiss his ass). Minor offenses, Jason rejoins. Patterson asks if *he* has a record; seemingly not, which is hard to believe. Regardless, Sheriff George Patterson doesn't buy McGuire's crap. That's something, I guess. Meanwhile, in the drawing room, Burke and Vicki blah, blah Maggie. They decide to go see Dr. Woodard.

For some odd reason, the front door to the Old House is wide open. Patterson strolls in and starts wandering around. Willie comes downstairs and is startled by the sheriff. He busies himself replacing candles while answering questions, informing Patterson that Barnabas is out and won't be back until late. Willie says he was in Bangor overnight and got back that morning, Mr. Collins can verify it. Patterson asks about the Eagle Hill/Maggie incident. Willie denies making the phone call and Patterson badgers and harasses him — hey, George, why the hard-on? Sheriff P says lots of strange things happened after Loomis hit town (seriously? What about Laura and Barnabas? Prick). Ooh, Patterson then threatens that he's going to watch Willie (uh, that's harassment) and if Maggie turns up dead, he'll arrest our man Loomis on suspicion (for real? Hey, Willie, call the M.I.A. attorney Frank Garner and file a lawsuit). Patterson finally leaves.

Burke and Vicki are at Woodard's office talking Maggie's illness and how she seemingly died (and it's all so boring). The doctor is stymied by the case and is awaiting blood test results, which I suspect have been outsourced to Indochina, given how freaking long it's taking. Blah, blah, puncture wounds.

Willie's in the parlor, repairing some furniture, when Jason shows up wanting to talk. Willie tells him he's busy, but the lout forces his way in. The asshole accuses Willie of being responsible for Maggie's disappearance, because it's all about him — cops snooping around will ruin *his* illegal plans. This dick. He tells Willie to quit his job and get out of town. Willie tells him to get out, stay out and leave him the fuck alone and threatens him with the hammer. McGuire laughs at him and — oh, for fuck's sake — *slaps* him, knocks the hammer out of his hand and beats him up, just like the retarded Burke fight scene (these writers suck, McGuire slap-fights like a seven year old girl and why the hell is Willie Loomis everyone's favorite whipping boy?). McGuire threatens worse if Willie doesn't leave town and even alludes to murdering him, then walks out. Our Mr. Loomis picks himself up off the floor and tends to his bloody lip. Out in the woods, McGuire hears dogs a-howling and looks ready to soil his pants.

Episode #238 — Collinwood drawing room and Carolyn's just hanging out. Vicki brings in the late edition newspaper, which is all about Maggie's disappearing act, and shows it to Liz and Carolyn. Liz says she doesn't want either of them to go out after dark alone, in the off-chance Miss Evans was kidnapped. Liz's further hunch is correct; she thinks Maggie was abducted and is being held captive. Liz leaves the room and Vicki asks Carolyn to go for a walk with her, before it gets dark. How 'bout the Old House, to check the progress of the restoration?

Once at the Old House, they receive no answer to their knock and Carolyn wants to leave. The Magi-Door ™ opens on its own and they walk in, Vicki calling for Barnabas. Carolyn wants to book, saying they shouldn't just wander in. Vicki, it seems, has lost some of her manners and says it's okay. Carolyn joins her in the parlor and they're amazed at the quality of Willie the factotum's work. After checking the progress of the portrait, Vicki wants to go upstairs, but Carolyn tells her the house isn't a museum, but selfish Vicki wins out again. They go upstairs to the bedroom and are all agog. They ooh and aah over Josette's toiletries and dressing table — ooh, even jasmine perfume! Suddenly, the door slams shut. Vicki opens it to find our man Willie, who asks them why they're there, as they shouldn't be. Both ladies compliment him on his work. Willie doesn't care and asks if they touched anything, then notices the toiletries have been moved and he begins to rearrange them, just so. As he tries to hustle them out, Carolyn asks what the room will be used for, whose is it? Nothing and nobody, he replies. He gruffly tells them to leave as it's getting dark. They walk out and he meticulously checks items in the room before exiting himself.

As the three reach the bottom of the stairs, they find Barnabas in the parlor. The girls gush over the restoration, especially the feminine bedroom. Watchful Willie interrupts to say they should get going and he looks torn up about something. Barnabas asks for a Maggie update and Willie seems particularly troubled by that. Vicki asks Barnabas who the suicide woman was in the story he told. Josette, he replies. Carolyn admits she found the story disturbing. Vicki asks who the lover was. Oh, his name is lost to history, Barnabas intones (yeah, sure). The two finally leave and oh-so-polite Barnabas tells Willie that was a nice visit, but he seems to not like people talking to him (gee, wonder why?). Mr. Collins then tells his man to finish the arrangements for their dinner guest.

Back at Collinwood, Liz bitches about Vicki and Carolyn going to the Old House, what with that Willie Loomis character still around. They tell her about the restoration of Josette's room — so fab! Liz seems troubled by the news for some reason, wondering why Barnabas would bother.

At the Old House, a small table has been set for an intimate dinner before the fireplace. Barnabas sends Willie upstairs to get their 'guest.' Maggie comes down, wearing Josette's bridal gown and veil and carrying the playing music box.

Episode #239 — Sam's at the Blue Whale when Joe comes in; no news from the cops in the search for Maggie. Blah, blah, where could she be? A little redo of Maggie coming downstairs at the Old House. She sits with Barnabas at the table and Barnabas calls Willie in to light the candles. Loomis asks why she's being called Josette and Barnabas insists that she only be referred to by that name, as that's who she is (I think 'ole Barney is a bit delusional — or just flat-out evil). He then lays on the sweet soft talk to Magsette and explains that the music box was his gift to her, play it and she'll stay with him forever. Willie returns and sets a dish of something (soup, perhaps) in front of Maggie (is he a master chef, too?) and Barnabas tells her to tell Willie her name. "Josette," she dreamily replies.

At the bar, Sam's trying to get drunk, but can't, no matter how much he drinks. Joe suggests he work, but Sam's not feeling it; in fact, he'd like to tell Collins he's postponing the work on the portrait. Joe offers to drive Sam to the Old House.

Barnabas continues his creepy mind-rape of Maggie as the music box plays. When Barnabas kisses her hand, Maggie recoils, but then the brainwashing kicks back in. We discover through Barnabas' blathering that he met Josette when she was eighteen and he was to teach her English, as she could only speak French. He's interrupted by a knock on the front door. Willie is instructed to tell whoever it is that Mr. Collins is not available. Willie answers the door and tells Sam that Barnabas can't be disturbed, but Evans insists on seeing him. A slightly panicked Willie goes back inside and explains that Maggie's father and Joe are outside. That rings a bell with Maggie. Barnabas tells Willie to take her upstairs and stay with her while he talks to Sam and Joe (Willie is incredibly gentle with her, taking her hand and walking at her pace; there's something very sweet about it). Blah, blah, Barnabas talks to Sam and Joe about Maggie and the portrait delay. Mr. Collins understands completely.

In Josette's room, Maggie is walking around in a dreamy daze. Willie guides her to a chair and tells her to sit quietly. Downstairs, Joe is gathering up Sam's paints to take to the car and, as he's walking out, calls to Sam about taking the easel, too. Maggie hears and starts to shake off the brainwashing. Willie tries to calm her down. She asks whose room she's in. He tells her it's hers, but she says no and wants to leave. Willie tells her to calm down or she'll get into trouble (listen to him, he's taken a couple of brutal beatings for you). Sam makes a comment on the cozy table setting and how they interrupted Barnabas' evening. Having a moment of clarity, Maggie realizes she heard Pop and Joe; Willie tells her she can't go to them and reiterates that something terrible will happen. Joe and Sam are about to leave when Maggie breaks free of Willie and rushes to the bedroom door, knocking a vase over in the process. The three men downstairs hear the noise and Barnabas says Willie must have dropped something. Upstairs — boy, Willie sure does have a hold on Maggie, one arm around her waist, and a hand clamped over her mouth (is it just me, or is there a sexual subtext going on here? Damn you, Willie!). Hearing the front door close, Willie loosens his grasp somewhat, Maggie breaks free and runs to the window, calling for Sam and Joe. At the sound of a car driving off, Willie says it's too late, they're gone. Barnabas slowly mounts the stairs.

Sam and Joe are driving home, briefly slowing down at the sight of a woman on the road — nope, not Maggie. Sam says the worst part is not knowing if she's dead or alive. Joe admits to having the feeling that Maggie is nearby, they just can't find her.

Barnabas enters the bedroom and tells Willie to get out. Willie immediately claims responsibility for knocking over the vase. Again, Barnabas tells him to leave and Willie says it was him who screwed up and asks him not to hurt Maggie. Barnabas ain't buying it and Willie reluctantly leaves. Barnabas asks Maggie why she's crying, why she lied and why she tried to leave (how about you kidnapped her, are holding her captive, are psychologically raping her and attempting to erase her identity? Asshole). He states that she's never going to leave him and advances on her. Maggie, understandably, screams.

(Once again, I'm loving Willie; he has a lot of layers, which makes him one of the more interesting characters on the show).

Episode #240 — In the drawing room, Roger's reading the paper about the talk of the town. Walking into the foyer, he meets up with David and Vicki and the boy excitedly tells dad that Vicki found Josette's portrait, so that means she's still at the Old House. Roger's a little tired of the ghost talk and David goes out to play, with a warning from Vicki to stay away from the Old House.

David immediately goes to the Old House and it looks like Willie locked the doors. David knocks and, getting no answer, takes a peek inside through the window, just in time to see Maggie wander through the parlor. Naturally, he thinks it's Josette and starts knocking on the door asking her to let him in. The door magically opens on its own and David enters, calling for his ancestor. He goes upstairs to the bedroom and starts talking to the portrait, asking why it feels like she's gone. Barnabas walks in and asks why he's there and to whom is he talking? David admits to talking to the portrait and says he saw her downstairs. Nah, you just imagined it, Barnabas proclaims. Blah, blah, Barnabas gives David a talking to about peering through windows and whatnot. The boy claims Josette opened the door for him. Barnabas says it's an old house and can act strangely, what with warping wood and the like. Back to boring Josette talk and Barnabas finally convinces David that her spirit is gone from the house.

Back in the Collinwood foyer, Roger is reprimanding David and tells him to apologize to Barnabas. Oh, the boy meant no harm, Barnabas replies. The two men go into the drawing room, while Vicki and David remain in the foyer. David tells his governess that Josette is different somehow. In the drawing room, Roger apologizes for David and says he understands Barnabas' desire for privacy. Barnabas would prefer if there wasn't a repeat occurrence. Roger then explains a theory; Maggie's disappearance has upset the family and is something David picked up on, hence his renewed interest in Josette. Blah, blah, Maggie and Roger hopes for the best. He mentions that Woodard is running some blood tests (which are being shuttled about by Pony Express it seems). Barnabas is quite interested in that news.

On the stairs, David is still pondering over Josette — and even Vicki is getting annoyed. She finally yells at him to knock the shit off and go have his dinner. She disappears upstairs and David fakes going to the kitchen. After a moment, he grabs his coat and heads out of the house (where, oh, where, could he be going?).

In another time hiccup, Barnabas is gone, but Vicki is now in the drawing room telling Roger that David sneaked out. Roger bitches at her for being too lenient with the lad. She says she'll go to the Old House and find him. Roger asks her to hide her feelings about Maggie when around David. The two argue and she's a bit overly emotional, telling Roger he's unfeeling. They settle things rather quickly, with both apologizing. Roger tells her he'll accompany her on her trek to the Old House.

Back at his favorite haunt, David strolls in through the front door, which suddenly is *not* locked. He goes to the parlor, looking for Josette, when Maggie comes downstairs, carrying the music box. David's thrilled (where's Barnabas? And Willie? They just leave Maggie alone? What the hell time is it?).

Episode #241 — Redo. Maggie comes downstairs and asks David who he is. Veiled Maggie calmly crazy talks about having been away to a place of death. David and Magsette talk and she gets confused. He comments that it's the longest she's spoken to him. When he brings up her portrait, she becomes confused even more. He shows her Barnabas' portrait and says it's the work of Mr. Evans. Maggie starts to remember and becomes frightened by the name of her captor. Vicki and Roger knock, distracting David long enough so Maggie can go…somewhere. David opens the door and he's asked if Barnabas or Willie is home. Roger, obviously indulging the boy's imagination, asks if he saw Josette. The lad gives a quick nope, but Vicki suspects otherwise. Barnabas comes in to find his front hall filled with uninvited people. Roger tries to make light of the situation; though Barnabas is miffed, he hides it. Blah, blah, Josette. David lies when questioned. Roger starts talking about the Barnabas portrait and his son suddenly wants to go home right away. Roger, David and Vicki leave and I wonder if Willie's going to get a beating even though he didn't do anything.

Maggie's in Josette's room, listening to the music box. Barnabas comes in and slams it shut, then asks if she saw people in the house. He tells her she has to lie low, no one can see her because she looks like someone else. Maggie parrots and asks questions in a spaced-out way. He continues brainwashing and it's boring. George Patterson shows up. Barnabas acts all polite, asking for an update on Maggie. Patterson wants to talk Willie, who, it turns out, is in Bangor (guess he won't get a beat down). The lawman mentions Willie's record (but Burke is pure as the driven snow, right, copper?) and wants to know where he was both times Maggie disappeared. Barnabas backs Willie's stories. As he's leaving, Patterson hears the music box playing upstairs. Barnabas lies, saying he restores them and obviously needs to tweak the mechanism on the one he was just working on. Patterson is stupid enough to believe it and leaves.

In the Collinwood drawing room, Roger's bitching at David for disobeying and he instructs Vicki to have David write the word 'honest' and its definition fifty times as punishment. Moving to the foyer, Vicki asks David for the truth about seeing Josette, as she smelled the jasmine perfume in the Old House. David 'fesses up about the long conversation with her and how different she was (this makes me wonder how corporeal the real phantom Josette appeared, since he is unable to tell the damn difference). Vicki sends him up to bed and promises mum's the word. Patterson stops in, with bad news; the cops are pulling back on manpower. Oh, boo-hoo, his main suspect is cleared (God, he's really got a fixation on our Mr. Loomis). Clown Patterson says they'll have to call off the search soon, Maggie's probably dead anyway.

At the Old House, Maggie comes downstairs looking for the little boy and that music box plays on and on.

Episode #242 — In his office, Woodard is checking slides on a microscope when Burke shows up, wanting help for Sam — he's on the edge. Woodard's out of ideas, as the tranquilizers/sedatives haven't helped (what a waste of good pharmaceuticals). Blah, blah, Sam. Woodard says he's prepared slides for another doctor, a man named Hoffman, to look at. Seems this Hoffman is quite the expert. Woodard says the slides are unusual, something strange is in the blood, but he'll have to wait for his colleague's input (frankly, this scene is kind of boring). Burke says something about looking at the blood samples under the *microphone* and I think, that's one helluva feat, I didn't think that was possible. Woodard says he and Hoffman could discover something frightening, terrifying or impossible.

In the Collinwood study, Liz is bitching at Roger about some employee named Peterson, who was questioning the business accounts. Liz haughtily tells her brother that she's not about to discuss financials with *him*; never has, never will. Roger says large sums of money have been withdrawn and he wants to know why. She replies she'll get the books in order for the audit. Roger says great, but he won't let the subject drop, and says he knows the money's going to McGuire. He tries a different tack, saying he knows how it feels to have something held over you (the old hit-and-run manslaughter thing) and he wants to help. He brings up the locked room in the basement; is her secret there? Impassioned Roger talks a lot of sense and is slowly peeling back layers of the mystery. Liz doesn't want his help and rushes out.

The ne'er-do-well known as McGuire is having a drink in the drawing room. Liz comes in, wanting to talk business. The jackass starts talking about some picnic they were on and tries to remember a toast over wine that was made. He says he knows there's complaints from work as he hasn't been in the office lately. Liz brings up the money transfers and the smug miscreant rambles on about that damn toast, talking over her as she bitches about the money, saying the well's run dry. God, he's infuriating. Liz suspects he's up to something and says she's *not* his darling (hilarious). She starts to walk out and the Irish piece of shit recites the toast.

Liz returns to the study and tells Roger the accounts are straightened out with Peterson (some time must have passed). Still angry Roger says swell, then gets up to leave. Liz apologizes for the earlier quarrel and understands that he's concerned. He quietly asks if he can help her. She says no, just stand by her as she's frightened and lonely.

Woodard and Burke enter Woodard's office to find the place ransacked. Someone broke in through the window and stole the slides with the blood samples. Woodard says a madman must be responsible, one with incredible strength, because the bars on the window are twisted (that leaves Willie out, though he'll probably get blamed anyway). Gee, wonder who it could have been?

Episode #243 — Woodard goes to the Old House. Willie answers and the doc asks how he's feeling. Dandy, Willie replies. Woodard asks if he can examine those wounds and oh, yeah, take a blood sample. Screw you, our Mr. Loomis replies and tries to close the door, but Woodard forces his way in (what is it with some of these people?). Woodard says Willie may not be as well as he thinks. You see, he has another patient, with similar, but worse symptoms; Maggie. Willie cringes a bit at the name mention. Woodard wants to do a finger prink blood sample, but Willie backs away, refusing. The two argue a bit, then Willie stops, as if he senses something, then tells Woodard he should leave, as it's getting dark. Barnabas is suddenly just sort of there and Woodard explains wanting to examine Willie. At first, Barnabas says no need, as his man is fine, then changes his mind. Willie begs to go to his room without submitting. Barnabas let's him go, then apologizes to Woodard, saying Willie just may not like doctors.

Liz is in the drawing room when Jason comes home, bearing flowers for her (violets, I believe). Bicker and bitch. Someone knocks and Liz answers; it's Woodard, wanting info on Willie during the time he was ill. The three talk in the drawing room, focusing some on the day/night aspect of the illness. Liz says she thought Willie was faking being sick. Woodard says both Willie and Maggie suffered the same symptoms and is afraid of an epidemic (really, after only two people and one is functioning normally again?). Blah, blah, stolen samples and getting Willie to consent to an exam. Jesus, more rehash filler and now something about Eagle Hill Cemetery.

McGuire heads to the Old House. Barnabas answers and informs the lout that Willie is out doing something, you know, useful. McGuire, blah, blah, doctor, with Barnabas promising to try to convince Loomis. Then, both talk about how Willie and Barnabas met and the job offer. Eventually, Jason gets around to mentioning Eagle Hill; it's obvious he's fishing, but, getting nothing, he leaves (can't Barnabas kill him? Please?).

Jason goes back to the main house and starts asking Liz questions about her rather eccentric cousin (McGuire's instincts about Barnabas are correct; too bad he's an insufferable asshole). The two go back to fighting over the usual and the Irish toad brings up that people are talking about him living there (this shit again? Five other people also live there, including Liz's brother; story-wise, this doesn't really fly). Liz suspects he wants more money. Oh, Heavens, no, the oily leprechaun replies — we're getting married (gag).

Episode #244 — Liz outright laughs at Not-So-Lucky Charms' marriage suggestion. She also flat-out refuses. Brogue Boy brings up Paul and all the nastiness an investigation would bring. Well, we learn that Liz killed Paul right there in the drawing room, though she says it wasn't premeditated. Verbose McGuire keeps talking about how great he was for helping her. Liz says Roger's onto the blackmail — why, that's why we should marry, he explains. She refuses and he goes to the phone and pressures her to call the sheriff. Liz starts to dial, but then Jason hangs up (right out of Burke's playbook, remember?). Now the slimy Irish troll brings Carolyn into the argument. God, he is truly loathsome; I mean, beyond the pale, resorting to both monetary and emotional blackmail. Liz says she'll tell Carolyn the truth, so McGuire goes to fetch her.

Carolyn's in the study, reading. Jason comes in and tells her Liz wants to see her. He spews some manure, saying Liz is upset and can't differentiate between reality and fantasy (where the hell did that come from? Oh, desperation; nice try). Carolyn exits and McGuire is concerned.

Carolyn goes to the drawing room and Liz starts telling her about what a gallant her father was; domineering, never loved anyone, never wanted children and never held or looked much at his own daughter (uh, because he was gone *before* she was born; see episode #5!). Carolyn becomes upset and runs from the room (Paul Stoddard sounds like a real piece of shit, just like his old buddy, McGuire. Birds of a feather, I suppose).

Carolyn goes back to the study. McGuire asks her about the discussion and she reveals she only found out what a cad her father was, nothing more. Then she says, oh, you told me good things, Mother told me bad — who to believe? Did Daddy talk about her? Oh, sure, the brogued one replies, why, he carried a picture of you around, showed it off to everybody (God, what bullshit he spreads) and she believes it, of course (have I mentioned this is a rather sluggish episode?). His work done, McGuire returns to the drawing room where he finds a dejected Liz — who folds like a cheap lawn chair on the marriage issue.

Episode #245 — In the Old House, Willie dashes downstairs, followed by Barnabas, the latter of whom promised Dr. Woodard that Willie would give blood. Willie's pleading not to, but Barnabas is a sadistic s.o.b.; besides, the doc is on his way.

Burke's at Woodard's office, having a confab. Woodard tells him that if Willie won't give up the blood, he could be compelled to via court order and, get this, be charged with harboring a dangerous disease! (What dumbass writer came up with that? I almost spilled my cocktail with that one. Besides, Willie ain't no 'Typhoid Mary' Mallon.) Blah, blah, Maggie/blood samples (and since when do physicians discuss cases with an ex-con?). Burke asks if a rabid dog or wolf could be responsible for the puncture marks on Maggie, then blames Willie for stealing the samples (oh, please). Woodard says it couldn't have been Loomis, as he doesn't possess the superhuman strength to bend iron bars. Burke asks to be informed of how things go; he'll be at the Blue Whale.

Woodard's at the Old House and Barnabas is plying him with booze. Collins then calls for Willie, who's very timid about giving blood. As Woodard conducts the test, Barnabas starts psychologically tormenting poor Willie, talking about how losing blood can be like surrendering a part of yourself (dick). The finger prick test completed (honestly, wouldn't you have to draw a vial or two?), the sadist then tells Willie to pour some more wine for the doctor. When Woodard says something about how he understands Willie's fear of doctors, Willie, pissed off, starts to mouth off a bit. Barnabas shoos Willie out of the room. Woodard then allows Barnabas to look at the slide of Willie's blood. Blah, blah, disease/Maggie/Willie (where *is* Maggie during all this, locked in a closet?) and Barnabas feigns concern, hoping Willie isn't involved. Woodard asks him to basically quarantine Willie until he can check the sample. Blah, blah, madman on loose; Barnabas claims to loathe him(self).

Burke and Vicki are at the Blue Whale, talking about how people are staying home since there's a crazy man running around. They hit the dance floor, but Vicki's tense and wants to go home. Burke wants to wait for Woodard. Vicki thinks she hears a dog howling, but it seems she's imagining things. Burke selects another tune on the jukebox and as they start dancing a dog is heard.

Woodard's in his office, at his microscope. He momentarily stops his work as he hears the howling, too.

At the Old House, Willie is beseeching Barnabas to let him leave town. He's terrified of the police coming after him after the blood test results come back. Barnabas says he (Loomis) has sympathy for Maggie, but Willie denies it (liar) and says he won't tell anyone anything, even if they hurt him (Barnabas brought up that last part). Betrayal comes up again and Barnabas shoves Willie to the floor. Willie asks why the blood test was allowed and Barnabas acts all fucking high-and-mighty saying he's loyal to Willie and switched the slides with one acquired after 'visiting' the doctor's office. Barney plays head games with Willie about protecting him — or not. Jackass.

Woodard enters the Blue Whale and tells Burke and Vicki that Willie's blood is perfectly normal. Blah, blah, Maggie's blood was weird, something foreign is in it (a whole lot of words are used to say basically nothing). A dog starts howling and they all listen.

Wedding Bell Blues

Episode #246 — Collinwood the next morning and Liz is pacing the drawing room. She answers the front door just as Carolyn is coming downstairs. It's Richard Garner — hey, where's Frank? (Richard drove down from Bangor, when Frank supposedly mans the branch office in Collinsport? What gives?) Liz and Richard go to the drawing room. Vicki comes into the foyer and asks if that was Richard Garner and doesn't say a word about Frank. Who she dated. (Honestly, it's like Frank never existed. Maybe he's still trying to track down B. Hanscombe, although Vicki seems to have forgotten all about that). Carolyn worries that something awful is about to happen.

In the drawing room, Liz is having problems talking to Garner. She finally tells him to file for divorce. No problem, he says, it could be over and done with in three months (seriously, wasn't *Frank* the divorce expert? Yes, see episode #136). He asks if she's getting married again. She says no and then McGuire barges in. After brief introductions, Garner leaves, and my, Liz has quite the dilemma, having to marry the Irish toad she despises so. A bit later, Liz is alone in the drawing room when Roger comes home from work. He pours drinks (I'll have one, thanks) and says most of the female staff stayed home out of wandering madman fear, so they were shorthanded and very busy. Everyone pitched in — except for Jason, he wasn't in at all. Liz asks if Maggie's been found. Roger opines that Patterson is clueless. She then tells him she's thinking of filing for divorce. Roger is very supportive, then comments that they both had back luck in marriage, maybe they're not meant to be wed. Liz says she may marry again. Roger susses out that she's hinting. She denies it and McGuire walks in and says something about being part of the family. Roger's like, the hell you are. Jason tells him to ask Liz about that. Liz decides to go check on dinner.

Vicki's in the study when Carolyn comes in and asks if Vicki will drive into town with her. Blah, blah, Maggie, who will be next? Roger joins them and pours another libation. He apprises them of the divorce and his suspicion that Liz was hinting about marrying again — marrying McGuire. Carolyn doesn't believe and they're all in agreement that Jason has something on her. Roger says it has to be connected to the room in the basement. Carolyn wants to find the key and Roger tells her Liz wears it on a chain around her neck. Carolyn's determined to get it.

In the drawing room, Liz and Jason quarrel over the marriage. Carolyn interrupts and bluntly asks for the key. Liz lies, of course, and becomes distressed. They argue basement and Liz lies, very badly. Carolyn says, okay, I'll just break in. Distraught Liz rushes out of the room. McGuire asks why Carolyn causes her mother so much trouble, then says he agrees she should go into the room. He tells her that *he'll* get the key. Carolyn calls him a liar and wants him gone (why hasn't anyone killed this bastard yet?).

Episode #247 — At the Evans cottage, Sam tries to work, but decides to hit the sauce instead. Patterson shows up with no news (so why bother?); heck, even the FBI can't figure it out (geniuses, one and all). Sorry, she may be dead, but we'll keep at it (what?). Burke shows up and Patterson leaves. More blah, blah, she's dead/she'll be found. Burke invites Sam out to dinner, then asks about painting. Sam can't work and doesn't feel much like eating. Sam reconsiders working on the Collins portrait, to take his mind off things. The two leave.

Willie's working on some more furniture when Sam shows up. No, Mr. Collins is not home. Sam asks to see the painting and Willie informs him that he can't work on it, what with all the repairs going on in the house. Furthermore, Willie isn't supposed to let anyone into the manse. Sam won't let up (at least he's polite) and Willie allows him inside, with a nervous glance up the stairs. He tells Sam to take the painting home and finish it there. Sam sets his pipe down on a table and carries out the canvas, with Willie helping by carrying the easel out to the car. Maggie floats down, dazed and confused. She wanders around the parlor for a moment, then finds the pipe. She picks it up, knowing it's familiar, then returns upstairs, just before Willie and Sam come in, looking for the pipe. Not finding it, Willie suggests maybe it was dropped outside. Sam leaves and Willie, again glancing upstairs, is suspicious. Maggie comes back down and he tells her to do as she's told and stay the hell upstairs, but she doesn't want to stay in that room. Asking who she is, Willie tells her Josette, but she thinks she's someone else. Willie tells her Barnabas will be back soon, so she better get where she belongs and a frightened Maggie goes back up.

A new set! Willie goes down some stairs to what I presume is a basement. A coffin is there. It opens to reveal Barnabas. From his prone position, he asks Willie what he wants, reaches up, and grabs him by the throat, all of which is unintentionally hilarious. Willie tells him about Sam showing up. After pushing Willie away, Barnabas clambers (unseen) out of the box. After muttering some threats, he goes upstairs.

Maggie, Sam's pipe in hand, comes down to the parlor. Via voice-over, she's thinking she's someone else, recognizes the pipe and casually walks out the front door (and she didn't do this sooner because…?).

At the cottage, Sam's working on the portrait when Burke arrives with dinner; a ham and swiss sandwich. The big spender strikes again! (And the writers fail again; he couldn't have picked up Chinese or meatloaf with mashed potatoes? This is like Vicki's grilled cheese in episode #92. Hell, I'm betting Sam could whip up that sandwich in his own kitchen). They discuss the portrait and we get a close-up of the work (and whoever does these portraits is quite good).

At the Old House, Barnabas is sitting in the parlor, complaining about David and Willie promises to keep him away from the house (good luck with that). Barnabas then asks after 'Josette' (if she's so goddamn precious, why didn't he look in on her first thing?). Willie explains that she came downstairs and that the brainwashing isn't fully taking. Barnabas sends him up to get her. Discovering she's taken a powder, the two men rush outside.

Sam takes a break from painting and Burke goes to the kitchen to make some coffee. Outside, Maggie wanders up to the window, rather ghost-like. Sam sees her and he and Burke race outside, but she's vanished just as suddenly and mysteriously as she appeared.

Episode #248 — Back inside, while they wait for the sheriff, Sam tells Burke that he saw Maggie. As for the Magster, it seems she's meandered to the cemetery, serenaded by howling canines. Barnabas is there. Ever the gentleman, he reaches out and grabs her by the throat.

Sam's smoking and pacing, then decides to go look for his daughter. Patterson shows up; the search is on! Blah, blah — and then I saw Maggie! Sam describes what she was wearing, an antique gown and — why did the lights suddenly dim? For effect or a gaffe? Anyway, George asks Sam if he's been drinking, which Evans doesn't appreciate. Patterson leaves.

Barnabas leads Maggie to the family crypt. He opens the secret room and she tries to run, but he grabs her and twists her arm, intoning that he *has* to punish her (this psychotic asshole). Maggie begs not to go into the room, but then either the brainwashing kicks in or she starts faking it is. He decides not to punish her. When he goes to close the panel, she pulls Sam's pipe from, I don't know where, a fold in her dress? (I don't think it has pockets) He sees it and tries to wrest it away from her and Maggie starts screaming (I knew she was appeasing him). She screams for her pop, then passes out. Sadistic psycho Barnabas carries her to the secret room and closes the door. Maggie comes to lying in a coffin (guess he has a spare). He closes the lid, ignoring her terrified screams. Later, the shit has sent Willie to retrieve her and what a contrast. Willie's voice is soft, his touch gentle as he helps her up and reminds her that he won't hurt her. He takes her back to Josette's bedroom, advising she lie down and rest. Still traumatized, she becomes understandably hysterical. Willie tells her that Barnabas can be cruel (and he should know) and she has to do what Barnabas says; she has to become Josette, as she'll never escape. He then plays the music box, to both calm and convince her, telling her to listen to the music if she's afraid.

Sam and Burke play the waiting game. Patterson shows up, proving to be useless; he's calling off the search. Sam suggests the graveyard, which they checked. All they saw was a large, ugly dog (Barnabas?). Both Patterson and Burke think Sam imagined the whole thing and now he thinks so, too.

Maggie wakes with a start, then plays the music box. She goes to the dressing table, saying that she's Josette Collins. Looking into the mirror, she slams the box shut and states she's Maggie Evans. She tries the door, but it's locked, then goes to the window, yelling for Joe and her father. She goes back to the dressing table and repeats her true name several times. (Maggie is proving to be a pretty smart, and tough, cookie. With all she's been through, she's a fighter and good for her).

Episode #249 — Carolyn's in the drawing room, looking determined. She informs Roger and Vicki that she's getting into that padlocked room that night. Roger's all for it, Vicki, not so much. Carolyn decides to break in and Roger offers to help. Out in the foyer, we see the oily leprechaun has been eavesdropping — big surprise.

Liz is in the study. Jason comes in and tells her about Carolyn's plan. Liz's giant up-do coif is distracting from a particular camera angle. Anyway, McGuire talks a whole lot to basically say, give Carolyn the key and let her in the room, after he checks it out first, of course. Liz relinquishes the key to him.

On her way upstairs, Carolyn is stopped by McGuire, who bullshits about Liz. Carolyn calls him out as a hypocrite and that gets his ire up. Basement talk ensues and he says he'll make sure she gets the key (and I have an epiphany during this scene; McGuire *detests* women who stand up to him, misogynistic piece of shit).

The basement set has been resurrected. McGuire goes down to the room and we see it for the first time; a couple of pieces of old furniture and some trunks and suitcases, one of which contains some men's clothing. McGuire checks the mortar and stones of the floor. This is nothing but non-suspenseful filler. Back in the study, Jason tells Liz everything's fine. He then suggests that she show up Carolyn and Roger by taking them into the room herself.

In the drawing room, Carolyn and Roger talk Jason/Liz/Paul. Vicki inserts her two cents. Liz and Jason come along and blah, blah locked room. Liz makes the announcement she's going to open the room — hey, Carolyn's rather loose fitting cardigan sweater is hiding a cast on her right forearm. I wonder what happened? Anyway, they all file down to the basement; unlock, open and enter to find a whole lot of nothing. To drive home the point of Paul Stoddard's final resting place, the camera pans down a bit toward the floor and we're treated to practically every character trodding over Paul's grave. McGuire chides them a bit, then Carolyn and Roger apologize before going back upstairs with Vicki. Jason then spews bullshit and presses Liz to announce their engagement to the family. Ass.

In the drawing room, Roger's into the liquor, feeling foolish. Carolyn is guilt-tripping. McGuire and Liz come in and she eventually spits out news of the impending nuptials.

Episode #250 — Old House, Josette's bedroom. Maggie's at the dressing table, looking at her reflection and repeating her name over and over, intent on remembering. She knocks over the music box. As it plays, she slips into Josette mode, however, the slams the box shut and says her real name. Willie comes along and Maggie craftily responds to, and refers to herself as, Josette. Mr. Collins want to see her. She responds that she'll be down in a minute, then gives herself a reminder to remember.

Downstairs, Willie tells Barnabas that Maggie referred to herself as Josette. The Evil One is pleased. The Magster drifts down and proceeds to play 'ole

Barnabas for a fool, pretending to be Josette and saying how much she enjoys that infernal music box. Barnabas sends Willie off to finish some task, then gifts her some extravagant necklace as a wedding gift, telling her they're about to be joined together for all eternity (so I guess Willie is a wedding planner, too. Does he also DJ?). Maggie refuses to wear the necklace, not until she's his bride. He gives her the jewel case and as she's heading back for the stairs, he calls her Maggie. Clever Miss Evans asks why he called her that, as it sounds like a servant's name and she can't recall one by that moniker ever being there (very clever). Barnabas apologizes, saying there *was* a Maggie there, briefly, but she's gone now (how wrong you are). Maggie goes upstairs. Barnabas looks ecstatic, Maggie looks concerned.

Back in the bedroom, Maggie hears some banging or hammering noises and her voice-over memory recalls Barnabas sending Willie to do something. She goes downstairs, following the noise. In the basement somewhere, Barnabas is commending carpenter Willie on his excellent work, which hammerin' Willie doesn't seem to care too much about. Maggie creeps nearer. The conversation is now about how both she and Willie are under Barnabas' control, and for as long as he's alive (shouldn't that be 'exist?' Oh, need I mention that he's a freaking vampire? Have you not figured that out yet?) they'll never be completely free. He goes on to say that after that night, Maggie will never recover (well, if you kill her via vampirism, duh) and will always be Josette (don't bet on it). Barnabas then waxes rhapsodic on the beauty of whatever craftsman Willie is working on. Willie doesn't see the beauty in it (of course not, it's not a pretty girl or a beautiful gemstone) and never wants to — as it's a coffin. Maggie, peeking around the corner, gets a glimpse.

Later, Willie's alone in the basement and catches Maggie, who plays at being Josette, but he's suspicious; in fact, good old crafty Willie surfaces and catches her out. She begs him to help her, but he's going to lock her upstairs. She holds out the jewel case with the necklace and entices him (how, exactly, does she know about his jewel fetish/obsession?). Our Mr. Loomis is mesmerized, but fights it. She tells him it's his after they've both gone and Barnabas is de-stroyed. He says he can't do it (kill Barnabas); she rejoins that *she* can. Willie's conflicted, Maggie tells him he'll be free. She gives him the box and he starts to go upstairs, pausing when he hears the heartbeat. Maggie picks up a metal awl or chisel or something. Willie comes after her and wrestles the tool from her grasp, saying he has to protect Barnabas.

A bit later, Maggie's in the bedroom, dressed in bridal gown, veil and wearing the necklace. Blah, blah, remember name. Willie comes along and apologizes for having to take her to Barnabas and advises her to give in, it will be easier. Willie, as father of the bride, I suppose, reluctantly takes her to the basement. It's almost sunset, she's to wait there. When she asks him to stay, he tells her he's been instructed not to. He goes upstairs. Maggie is no shrinking violet. She picks up the awl/chisel from the floor. Even though the heartbeat sounds, she opens the coffin. About to bury that awl into the bastard's chest, Barnabas opens his eyes. Maggie screams, drops the tool and he bares his fangs.

Episode #251 — It's a Maggie in the basement, trying to stake Barnabas redo. Barnabas is out of the coffin, holding the tool and asking Maggie what she was doing. He advances on her, blathering. She tries to convince him she's his precious Josette, but it doesn't work. Rejected psycho Barnabas starts to strangle her. Maggie manages to get out a scream and — fucking A — Willie comes flying down the stairs, shouting for Barnabas to stop, saying he can't kill her. Willie then proves to be even more awe-inspiring by physically positioning himself between the two, stating that if Barnabas wants to kill Maggie, he'll have to kill him, too (it's official; Willie Loomis has fully redeemed himself and is aces in my book). Barnabas says, okay, but Willie counters that if he goes missing, too, people are going to wonder, McGuire for instance. Arrogant Barnabas thinks he's smarter than everyone else. Willie again challenges him to kill him, but says he has to do it *before* killing Maggie. Loomis then notices someone knocking and relays that he left the door unlocked. Barnabas reminds him that he was instructed to keep the door locked at all times (right, how many people have wandered in?). Anyway, Barnabas tells Willie to stay with Maggie and if she makes a sound or tries to flee, he'll kill them both. Collins heads upstairs. Willie takes a few steps and — ha, his hand ever so lightly brushes across Maggie's waist (damn subtext, or was it an actor's choice?).

Barnabas answers the door; it's Vicki with a message from Liz. Patterson has issued a curfew; no women out alone at night. The talk turns to Maggie and Barnabas is a lying piece of shit. Down in the basement, meantime, Willie's got the hand over the mouth/waist clasp going on. He releases Maggie and she thanks him for, you know, saving her life, then tells him she tried to off the big bad vampire. Willie reveals that he would have done the same, a long time ago, if he could. He tells her she has a chance if Barnabas decides he doesn't want her and somehow, something happens to her favor in the interim. He then tells her to let him do all the talking when Barnabas comes back.

Upstairs, Vicki says Liz is wondering why Big Bad Barney hasn't been to the main house lately. She notices the music box on the hall table. Oh, she thinks it's just lovely, a reminder of the past. Need I say he liked her reaction? Vicki leaves and Barnabas, I do believe, is onto plan B, as it were.

Barnabas comes downstairs, ready for some killin'. The conceited ass basically calls Maggie common and plans on inflicting a slow, painful death. Willie intervenes, (including physically) again, and this time, his hand is on Maggie's hip, straying down to her thigh and this oh-so-subtle sexual stuff is slaying me. Willie reminds Barnabas he's needed to protect him during the day. Sly Willie does some fast talking, pointing out Maggie's beauty and that he still wants her. Having obviously been read by a street savvy skel, Barnabas grabs Maggie and begins to lead her away, despite her protestations. He takes her to another part of the basement and locks her in a cell with a steel door and small, barred window. She'll stay there until he decides what to do with her (he's not a very good villain, is he? Never follows through on threats and never has an alternate plan).

Barnabas goes to Collinwood. Vicki answers the door. He's there to drop off a small gift for Liz, an antique handkerchief that belonged to Josette. Well, Miss Winters is simply *charmed* by the heirloom and reveals that she's an orphan (oh you *know* Barnabas loves that). As he's leaving, he invites her to come to the Old House and he'll tell her all about the past.

Maggie's in the dungeon, lying on a cot and crying. Barnabas comes in and tells her he wants to kill her. She says go ahead. Then he says he wants her as his bride (this vacillating asshole cannot make up his mind). Maggie's all what-the-fuck? He says she must come to him of her own free will (*this* shit again? Laura pulled this crap, too, episode #177. Seems the writers pull this out to prolong a story arc). When Maggie comes to him as Josette, he'll kill her (what?). He's going to keep her locked up, like a good serial killer sociopath. Maggie says she'll go mad. He walks out, ignoring her pleas.

Episode #252 — Carolyn goes down to the drawing room and hears Liz on the phone to — Frank! (He's still alive!). Divorce talk and Liz is in a hurry. After hanging up, Carolyn snarks about Jason, which upsets Liz. Carolyn wants to help, blah, blah, and she's absolutely correct on everything she says about the Irish toad. Liz either stonewalls or lies and it's irritating. She tells Carolyn to stay out of her life and do something about her own. Teed off daughter says, you bet, Mama, and rushes out.

In the study, Roger and Vicki are discussing David's schoolwork. Carolyn comes along and mentions her conversation with Liz. Lots of blah, blah between the three of them. Carolyn then grabs a phonebook, looks up a number and makes a call, saying she's going to do something with her life and find love in the process. She calls some motorcycling cat named Buzz and makes a date.

At the Blue Whale, another jazzy new tune is playing that sounds vaguely Latin, in that Herb Alpert kind of way. Vicki and Joe are having drinks. Joe explains having seen an entourage of bikers, with Carolyn on the back of the lead bike. He then asks Vicki about the Liz marriage rumor. Carolyn and a leather jacketed, sunglasses wearing, bearded hippie biker waltz in. Loaded Carolyn wants more booze. She orders two Stingers, but Buzz wants to stick with beer (I'll take his cocktail). Joe and Vicki watch in disappointment. Carolyn drags the disinterested Buzz over to meet her friends, Vicki and 'Joey' (is Buzz wearing an earring? Indeed he is, left ear) and tells them they had a real 'gas' that afternoon. Carolyn tries to get Vicki to go for a ride with Buzz, but Miss Winters passes. Miss Stoddard just starts making out with her new beau.

The foyer clock at Collinwood says it's two fifty. Buzz's motorcycle sounds like a hedge trimmer. Outside the front door, more making out, with Buzz actually pushing Carolyn away, as she's a little *too* enthusiastic. They go inside (did I mention she's wearing cigarette pants?). Buzz makes a joking comment about riding his bike up the stairs. Carolyn wants him to go for it, man, and he shushes her, saying he'd wake up the whole house and he doesn't want to get kicked out (not so wild, this one). They go to the drawing room, where Carolyn turns on her little transistor radio (I kind of miss those things) and pours some drinks. Carolyn then begins to dance a spirited Pony (one of her faves, along with the Jerk and the Shimmy) that must be seen to be appreciated. Robed Liz comes in. Carolyn calls her 'mommy.' Perturbed Liz points out that it's three in the morning. Buzz and Carolyn refer to Liz as 'mommy' a couple of times. Liz snaps off the radio and tells Buzz to beat it. He calls her Mrs. Stoddard and Carolyn drunk babbles that no, her name is *Mrs. McGuire*. She then starts angry drunk screaming at Liz, who leaves the room. Carolyn follows her out, screaming and almost crying as Liz climbs the stairs. Buzz comes out, to see the commotion, I suppose. Carolyn turns to her man and throws herself at him, while poor Joan Bennett can't open the door at the top of the stairs, despite her valiant efforts.

(Buzz is an interesting character already. Though supposedly a bad boy, he seems to have his head on straight. He doesn't drink too much, told Carolyn to cool it when she was out of control with the kissing, wasn't about to wake the whole house and when seeing that Liz meant business, respectfully called her Mrs. Stoddard. I hope we see more of him)

Episode #253 — Maggie's in her cell, now wearing a shapeless black thing, kind of like a monk's cassock. She's trying to figure a way out when she thinks she hears Willie coming. Unfortunately, it's Barnabas. Blah, blah, the whole I'm Maggie/you're Josette thing. He brought the music box and Maggie threatens to break it (please do!). She then changes tune and says to leave it, but she's just buying time. She asks if she can send her ring (which is completely different than the one she was initially wearing) to Sam, as a keepsake for him when she's gone. First, Barnabas says no, then, sure — *after* she becomes his bride.

In the foyer, Vicki tells David he can't go out, as it's getting dark. He promises to stay by the main house and then mentions Maggie, saying he hopes they find her.

Willie's in the cell, tsk-tsking that Maggie didn't eat and I don't like his shirt, he looks better in solids. We discover that he's not supposed to talk to her, but does anyway. She offers her ring to him and his obsession takes over. Outside, David tries to get into the house, but smartest denizen of Collinsport, Willie, has locked the doors. David proceeds to climb in through the parlor window (the brat needs some major discipline for that stunt). He starts calling for Josette and begins to go upstairs, but is caught by Willie, who scolds him for being there. Willie manhandles the kid and is about to shove him outside, when David says he knows what they're doing there. Blah, blah, Josette. Fed up, Willie then picks David up, literally *throws* him out of the house and locks the door (this whole thing is a laugh riot). They yell at each other through the door for more hilarity. David finds Maggie's ring (must have fallen out of Willie's pocket) and tries to tell Willie that he found something, but Willie won't open the door, thinking it's a ruse. David says fine, he'll keep it.

Back at Collinwood, Vicki scolds David for straying too far from the house. Noticing the ring, she asks about it. Barnabas conveniently shows up and David wants to make a quick getaway upstairs. Barnabas apologizes to the lad for Willie's rude behavior. Vicki asks if that's where David found the ring and blah, blah. Barnabas says it's an heirloom he wants to sell.

In the Old House basement, Barnabas pays a visit to Maggie, who fakes that she's enjoying the music box. He plays head games, before showing her the ring (is he going to pummel Willie again? Maybe not, he didn't after Loomis prevented him from killing her, which was a pretty ballsy stance for Willie to take).

Wild, Mild and Reviled

Episode #254 — Carolyn and Liz are arguing in the drawing room about going out while there's a madman on the loose. Pants wearing Carolyn doesn't care and storms out of the house. Liz is genuinely concerned, what with the loon lurking about town. Vicki and Liz talk Carolyn a little later. Liz knows calling off the wedding is the only way to reign her daughter in. Blah, blah, McGuire and blackmail. Vicki goes up to see David.

At the Blue Whale — huh, Willie and Jason walk in together. Ah, Willie would rather not be there. McGuire asks Willie what he was doing at the bank with some jewelry earlier in the day (this is vaguely reminiscent of Mr. Twissel dogging Colonel Deverill in *Varney the Vampire*). Willie explains he was selling the jewelry for Barnabas, feel free to ask him. A typical asshole, McGuire says he has no intention of asking (this is because he knows Willie is telling the truth and he wants to ignore the facts). Brogue Blarney announces his upcoming marriage to Liz and Willie's incredulous at first, then suspicious. Man, I love it when crafty, street-wise Willie comes to the fore. Oh, now McGuire's angling to get a piece of the action, convinced Willie is stealing from Barnabas. Willie says he has to leave. McGuire repeats that he wants in on the scam. Loomis wisely advises him to be satisfied with Liz's money and to leave him and Barnabas alone (McGuire is the true lowlife). Buzz and Carolyn come in and she makes some snide, rude comments (all true) to McGuire. Buzz says nothing, but listens attentively (he's a fascinating character under the grunge). Willie and Jason leave and Buzz drops some hippie talk. Later, after a drink or two, Buzz reveals that he's not that dumb; "all drinking makes you feel is drunk," he declares (he seems dissatisfied, so is always looking out for the next adventure). Carolyn wants to dance. She limits herself to a modest Shimmy while he watches. They decide to hit the road. As they're leaving, Joe walks in and he and Carolyn exchange strained hellos. Buzz opines on Carolyn's ex. She tells him to wait outside and she approaches young Haskell. She says a few words about Maggie; Joe's upset and would rather not talk about her. The subject then moves to Buzz and Carolyn's crazy behavior of late, then onward to Liz's marriage. Hah, Joe tells her she's throwing a temper tantrum. Carolyn leaves with the impatient Buzz.

In the drawing room, Liz and Jason are talking wedding. He wants to set a date; two weeks. Buzz and a tanked Carolyn stumble in. McGuire delights in telling her when the wedding will take place. Buzz twirls a small twig, which he's holding for no discernible reason. Liz tries sending Carolyn to her room (for the second time and futile if you ask me, Carolyn's what, twenty?). Our wild child turns to Buzz and says — let's get married! In two weeks! Right on! the bearded one replies. By their expressions, neither McGuire nor Liz approves.

Episode #255 — Maggie's in her cell, languishing. Barnabas and Willie are in Josette's room, with the latter inquiring if Maggie is being given a second chance, noting that she'll go mad if she stays locked up in the dungeon. Barney says if the mind-rape hasn't worked this time, he'll kill her.

Sam's drinking at the Blue Whale when Joe comes in. No updates from the useless cops. Sam has finished the portrait and is going to deliver it and collect his cash.

In the basement, Maggie is happy to see Willie. He advises her to let Barnabas think he's won the day. Collins is fussing over things in the bedroom when Willie delivers Maggie. Barnabas acts a haughty prick. Blah, blah, Josette talk, music box and brainwashing. Maggie fakes it, but can't help recoiling from him, which gives her away (I've come to realize Barnabas is an obsessive coward; he keeps threatening to kill her, but never follows through). Maggie, bless her, stands up to him. Willie dashes in, saying Maggie's old man is at the door. She tries to run, but quick Willie grabs her and applies the patented Loomis Hold. Handing him a handkerchief, Barnabas instructs Willie to gag Maggie and take her onto the landing so she can hear the conversation with Sam. If she does anything stupid, Barnabas will kill both Evanses.

Barnabas answers the door and Willie holds onto Maggie on the landing (observation; Willie has much more physical contact with her than Barnabas). Sam hands off the portrait and Barnabas is pleased with it. He asks about Maggie. Sams tells him the search has been called off. Joe strolls in and tells Sam that a girl's body was found a few towns over, washed up on the beach. They think it's Maggie and need an I.D. Cold as ice Barnabas offers condolences and the two men leave.

Back in Josette's room, Barnabas torments Maggie by saying she's considered dead and will be forgotten quickly; Joe will marry someone else and no one will care about her (such a prince, this one). Willie hangs back, listening. Our Maggie is determined to hold onto her identity (more power to her). Barnabas then tells Willie to take her back to her cell. Gentle Willie, a quasi model of chivalry, tries to console her as he leads her out. Locked up again, Maggie begs him to stay with her for a while. He can't and reluctantly leaves. A short time later, Maggie suddenly hears a little girl singing *London Bridge*. Looking out the barred window of her cell door, she sees a child sitting with an old fashioned doll.

Episode #256 — Redo. Maggie hears the singing, only this time, the little girl, in a long dress and cap, is playing with a ball. Maggie calls to her, but the girl doesn't answer; is Maggie losing her mind? Maggie tells the girl to go get help. The kid finally stops singing and walks away. Willie comes along with some sustenance and asks the Magster if she's okay and who was she talking to? Maggie wants his help in escaping, they'll go together. Willie reveals that he's tried, several times, but Barnabas has fucked up his mind so badly he can't succeed. Willie says *he's* doomed, but that she still has a chance. Maggie gets upset that he's not helping her and, to his credit, he doesn't get offended. Once he leaves, the girl is back outside the cell door.

In the drawing room at Collinwood, a school lesson is winding down when Carolyn comes along. David goes out to play. Vicki doesn't believe Carolyn will go through with the marriage to Buzz. Blah, blah, Liz/Jason marriage. Angry, upset Carolyn says Buzz is far better than Paul or Jason (this is actually true).

David's out playing by the Old House. The mysterious little girl is outside now and, seeing him, calls him over, wanting to play. She tells him she lives nearby, but can't find her friends. Her name is Sarah. They play catch and she sings *London Bridge*. She then says that everyone went away and left her and she can't find them. David promises to play with her again and she wanders off to find whoever. Willie steps outside and David says he was talking to some kid. Willie says they shouldn't play there and David heads off.

David enters Collinwood to the sound of a motorcycle outside. He meets his cousin in the foyer and tells her the bike is cool. Carolyn leaves on her date. He goes back to the drawing room to hit the books (guess he took a recess). He tells Vicki about meeting Sarah at the Old House and her unusual, old fashioned clothes.

Willie's gone to check on Maggie, concerned about her. He takes the untouched food and leaves. Maggie starts to play the music box when she hears Sarah singing again. Maggie talks to her again through the bars and this time Sarah responds, asking not to tell her big brother that she was there, he doesn't like people in the basement. Having made that cryptic pronouncement, she skips off (if David also saw and interacted with Sarah, Maggie's not loco).

Episode #257 — Buzz arrives at Collinwood. Liz answers the door and refuses him entrance. Carolyn comes downstairs and the two argue over Buzz (I think Liz was in the wrong and uncharacteristically rude). Outside, Buzz smokes a stogie. Carolyn steps out and Buzz complains about the cold reception. Carolyn goes to the drawing room to read Mother the riot act, while Buzz sits on the stairs (hmm, he's wearing a black kerchief today). I get why Liz is concerned, but she has no place to talk, or threaten an annulment; she's grasping. Carolyn taunts Mater with a double wedding. Meanwhile, McGuire tries to get down the stairs, but is blocked by Buzz. McGuire threatens to step on, and break, Buzz's shin if he doesn't move (and I wish Buzz would shank him). He then spreads malarkey. Huh, Buzz is also wearing a huge, chunky pendant. McGuire goes to the drawing room, Carolyn rushes upstairs, and Buzz waits in the foyer. Liz wants to back out of the wedding for her daughter's sake. Jason says he'll handle it by having a talk with the girl.

McGuire stops by Carolyn's room, wanting to offer 'fatherly' advice. She basically tells him to go to hell. He bullshits, blah, blah she's just like her father, stubborn. More McGuire bullshit (you have no idea how I long for this asshole's death). Carolyn states that he makes her sick. Misogynistic McGuire gets *pissed off* at her for standing up to him and leaves.

Back in the drawing room, McGuire lies to Liz about how things went, but she knows bullshit when she smells it and calls him out for failing. McGuire's next step is to talk to Buzz.

At the Blue Whale, Carolyn and Buzz are dancing (she's doing her favorite, the Pony, he's just sort of groovin'). They sit at a table and decide it's too dead, so they'll book on over to Logansport where it's swingin' (is that where Burke is? We haven't seen him lately). Carolyn goes to powder her nose. Jason walks in and approaches Buzz. He starts asking about him and Carolyn. Buzz says he's from a wealthy family (the Hacketts that bought Collins property a while back?). Brogue Blarney tries to tell him that Carolyn is just using him to stop Liz's marriage. Buzz says so what, he's got it pretty good. McGuire wants him to break up with Carolyn and savvy Buzz asks for how much. Oh, the price of another motorbike. Buzz replies with a firm no. Carolyn comes back and Buzz fills her in. Both enjoy poking fun at the unsuccessful McGuire and amid laughter leave (it's great to see Jason taken down a few notches. Gotta love that Buzz!).

Episode #258 — Maggie calls for the little girl and — damn, she's barefoot. Willie, get her some shoes! Anyway, Sarah is suddenly *in* the cell, playing with her ball and singing. How could that be? Maggie wonders, but no answer is forthcoming. Sarah just says she came back because she heard Maggie crying and assures the captive that no one saw her. Maggie's acting a little squirrelly and the fact that Sarah doesn't answer questions and talks vaguely doesn't help. Sarah complains about not being able to find people. Maggie says she'll be her friend and they start to play catch and sing *London Bridge* (and I ask which is more annoying; that song or the music box melody?). Maggie turns her back for a second and guess who disappears? It's obvious now that the once rock-solid Maggie is cracking. Need proof? Now *she* starts singing that damn song. Barnabas comes in and wow, Maggie has gone off the deep end. She tells him that her secret friend knows she's alive and they play together when she visits. Maggie is now speaking in a child-like manner. Nice going, Barnabas, you heartless bastard. Wait, is that a tear I see in his eye? Too bad, his soupcon of emotion (most likely for himself) doesn't move me.

In the parlor, Barnabas tells Willie that Maggie has gone nuts. Our man Loomis tries to talk him out of killing her. When Willie asks Barnabas to have mercy on her, the selfish asshole begins to wangst that nobody had mercy on *him*. Fuck you. For good measure, he puts the choke hold on Willie to drive home the point that Maggie has to go.

In the basement, Maggie's calling for Sarah as Willie comes down with a bowl of something. As she starts eating whatever slop he brought, he tells her to drop the imaginary friend bit. He's worried by the way she's acting. Getting angry, he insists she act normal, but she doesn't. Unable to convince her, he leaves. Maggie begins to cry, then finds Sarah's doll on the floor, which gives her hope. (Kathryn Leigh Scott is doing a good job conveying the slow mental breakdown of Maggie)

Episode #259 — In the drawing room, Liz is on the blower. Hanging up, she goes into the foyer and calls for Roger. Vicki comes along and tells her Roger's left and gone into town. Liz apprises the governess that the sheriff just called; Carolyn's been arrested for almost killing someone. Like Uncle Roger, Carolyn was driving drunk and, unlike Uncle Roger, *almost* ran over a pedestrian. Vicki offers to go pick up the blonde menace, but apparently a family member has to. Liz decides to call Roger at the club (what the hell kind of club could a backwater town like Collinsport have?) and have him pick her up. Dame Stoddard is quite distraught, what should she do? Seems Carolyn acted a real bitch after the accident and, like a true drunk, only suffered a sprained wrist (now they can explain the cast they've been trying to hide). Vicki suggests Liz go, as it will show daughter dear how much mommy cares for her. Recluse Liz doesn't want to go (which makes me wonder just how iron-willed she really is; in the roost, yes, but when it comes to the outside world, not so much). Vicki drops the subject. Liz reconsiders and asks Miss Winters to drive her into town.

At the sheriff's office, sullen and snotty Carolyn gives Patterson some lip. Man, Patterson is suddenly sporting a moustache and needs to lose it, it looks terrible. Carolyn continues to mouth off and he's had enough, he's taking her to a cell. A little while later, Liz walks in and Patterson is surprised to see her out of her millieu. He goes to get Carolyn. A tense Liz waits. Carolyn bounds in alone and is genuinely surprised to see her mother; for a moment, at least. Ungrateful Carolyn asks the *real* reason she's there. Because she cares. Bitchy Carolyn then starts screeching at Liz and we find out the whole reason she's acting up is daddy issues. Liz remarrying means she forgot Paul (may I slap this bitch, please? Your deadbeat father abandoned you; get over it). Carolyn then starts yelling for Patterson to lock her up again. George comes in and tells her to go the fuck home with her mother. Liz tells Patterson to forget it and triumphant Carolyn heads back to her cell. Liz takes off.

Back home in the drawing room, Liz informs Jason of the cop shop incident. Liz wants to tell the truth about Paul. The woman hating McGuire yells at her to settle down. Asshole then tells Liz to forget about Carolyn. Liz is near tears out of sheer frustration.

Later that night, Liz is on a crying jag in her bedroom. Vicki checks on her. Blah, blah Carolyn and Vicki says she doesn't feel too sorry for the blonde; she is an adult after all (right on, Vicki!). More blah, blah Carolyn/marriage and Liz is in knots. Suddenly, Liz blurts out that she killed her husband.

Episode #260 — Willie's doing some work in the parlor and notices the time.

Via his voice-over thoughts, we learn he's agonizing over Maggie only having a couple of more hours to live. Addressing the new Barnabas portrait, Willie says *he's* the one who should die and that he, Willie, should do the deed (if only). Willie then second guesses himself, because Barnabas has scrambled his head too much. Poor Willie wants to help Maggie, but is unable.

Willie takes a tray of food down to Maggie. Initially, she's unresponsive to him. When he asks about the doll she's holding, she becomes very possessive and won't let him see it. She tells him she's not hungry and Willie convinces her to at least drink the milk he brought. Just before she takes a sip, he stops her, admitting the beverage is poisoned. He explains that he wanted her to have an easy death, because Barnabas is going to kill her and it'll be harsh. He starts to leave, saying he'll leave it to her to decide her manner of death (yes, I'll admit that Willie was about to commit premeditated murder, but under the circumstances, I can understand why. Misguided, but he was trying to prevent her suffering). Maggie again asks for his help in escaping, but he can't and it visibly tears him up. She pleads with him and he rushes out, tormented.

Some time later, Maggie hears *London Bridge* being played on the flute and — surprise! — Sarah's in the cell (with a recorder rather than a flute). Maggie tells Sarah her father's name and begs her to tell him where she is. Maggie asks how to get out of the room. Sarah talks in her obscure way, which is annoying. She tells Maggie an incredibly convoluted riddle on how to get out of the room. Sarah then pulls the disappearing act.

At the Evans cottage, Sam's painting and Sarah is just sort of there in his living room. She says she's looking for Sam Evans and he's like, you found him. She asks him if he'll do a painting of her and he offers to do a drawing instead. They sit down and get to chatting while he sketches (David Ford is good in scenes with kids). Sarah asks if he has a little girl. He says yes, Maggie, only she's a grown-up and she went away and he doesn't know where she is. Sarah asks if he looked on the beach under Widows' Hill. If he looks there tonight, he'll probably find her. Well, this intrigues our resident artist. Sarah takes a powder.

In the basement, Maggie is starting to figure out the riddle as the sun sets and Barnabas wakes from his siesta — why is he 'sleeping' in his Inverness coat? How could he be chilly, he's dead. Maggie hears him coming and geez, that Old House basement is as cavernous as the Paris catacombs. Maggie finds a secret latch in the brickwork of the wall, which I assume triggers a counterweight that opens a panel. Miss Evans high-tails it out of there. Barnabas enters a moment later and sees that his precious is gone. Clutching Sarah's doll, Maggie walks the labyrinth, followed by ~~Minotaur~~ Barnabas. She tries a couple of doors along the way, to no avail. Barnabas calls out that she can never escape. (I sincerely hope she does; it would be nice to see this bastard thwarted).

Episode #261 — Maggie escape replay to start; hey, Maggie's wearing shoes now. One of the doors she couldn't open suddenly does, on its own, and she hears a flute playing *London Bridge*. She follows the tune as predator Barnabas tracks her. She eventually sees light and heads toward it. Barnabas opens a different door leading to another corridor. Well, whattaya know, Maggie made it to the outside world and heads for the beach, where she collapses (although I ask how in the hell did her clothing get all torn and tattered in the space of ten seconds?). Barnabas catches up to her and tosses out some typical, overly-confident villain smarm. Maggie screams and Sam, searching nearby, hears her and calls out in response. That pillar of valor, Barnabas, hides behind some large rocks. Sam finds Maggie, but she's unresponsive to his questions. Creepy Barnabas watches from his hiding place. (In *Varney the Vampire*, there is a mansion, Anderbury-on-the-Mount, set atop a cliff overlooking the sea. It has an underground passage hewn into the cliff, which leads out to the beach. Just saying.)

The unconscious Maggie is at the hospital with Sam and Woodard. Joe comes in and she recoils at his touch, as she does when anyone touches her. Sam recounts the story of Sarah's visit and suggestion to check the beach. Maggie starts mumbling the girl's name, then wakes up and asks for her doll. Maggie's asking Sam about some event from her childhood; seems she's regressed, poor thing. Joe tries talking to her; she doesn't recognize him, but allows him to hold her doll (Sarah's). The men then step out into the hall. Woodard explains that, as a coping mechanism, Maggie has 'retrogressed.' Woodard thinks the kidnapper will try again and then proposes the most ludicrous, fraudulent and illegal counter-measure; fake Maggie's death, including a death certificate and all necessary records. They'll just tell everyone that she died and that'll fix that kidnapper! Logical Joe asks how the hell are they going to keep the hospital staff from finding out she's alive? Woodard intends to send Maggie to a private facility a hundred miles away, run by Dr. Julia Hoffman — you remember, the blood expert? (Sure, I remember, *when he was a man!* Either Hoffman pulled a Christine Jorgensen or Woodard needs to brush up on his basic anatomy. Oh, by the way, Woodard's license would be pulled for this stunt). Anyway, Joe and Sam agree to the lunacy. The two go back into the room and tell Maggie she's going on a trip, to a place where she'll be safe.

Out in the hall, Barnabas strolls up to the desk. The clock on the wall shows it is three twenty-six a.m. (because he can't go out during the day). He asks after Miss Evans (this is hilarious, because back then, hospitals had strict visiting hours. It's not like now when you can wander in whenever, or even stay in the room with the patient overnight). Woodard happens by and Barnabas tells him he heard in town that Maggie was there, why, *everyone's* talking about it (at three-thirty in the morning? Try again, moron). Woodard says he's not surprised (I sure as hell am, because — *three thirty a.m.!*) and tells him Maggie died from shock, having never regained consciousness. The sociopath is so pleased he's safe and offers phony condolences. Jerk.

Episode #262 — Drawing room next morning. Vicki hangs up the phone just as Liz walks in. After some unnecessary hemming and hawing, Vicki spits out that Maggie is dead. Over coffee (or perhaps tea) Vicki and Liz talk Maggie, with Vicki fondly remembering their first meeting (oh, when the Magster called you a 'jerk?'). Vicki relays there will be no funeral, as Sam wants to avoid curiosity seekers. Moving on to a new subject, Liz struggles to ask Miss Winters a favor — will she be the witness at her unholy union to McGuire? Vicki says she wasn't planning on attending, as she'd want to object. Blah, blah Carolyn/Paul. Vicki's sure Liz had a perfectly good reason to off her old man, so why not tell Carolyn and avoid marrying Jason? She agrees to think over the request. Walking into the foyer, Vicki meets Carolyn, who's still dressing like a beatnik and spouting attitude. Vicki tells her Maggie's dead. Carolyn is truly bummed and wonders how Joe is doing. The ladies then argue over Carolyn's upcoming wedding. Vicki tries to insinuate McGuire's still blackmailing Liz. She stops herself from saying something disparaging about deadbeat daddy and they quarrel over whether Liz is courageous or not.

Later, Vicki and some guy are walking on the cliffs, talking. Oh, this is a new Burke; Squarejaw is out then? Burke and Vicki discuss Maggie and the lunatic who kidnapped her. Oh, geez, Vicki has some sympathy, if the kidnapper/killer is mad. Burke's like, for real? The subject turns to Liz/Jason/Carolyn (I'm not sure about this new Burke; his voice, and manner, is too gentle and passive).

At Collinwood, Buzz brings Carolyn home and isn't happy about it. They meet up with Liz in the foyer. The couple squabble — he made the day's plans for her. Vicki comes home and Carolyn tells Buzz to make like a bee and buzz off. He's *not* happy and tears off. Carolyn gets snippy with Vicki, then calms down, saying she saw Joe on the road and suddenly didn't feel like being out having a good time. After a few words with Liz, Carolyn goes upstairs. Liz is surprised her daughter felt sympathy for another human being. Vicki presses Liz to tell

Carolyn the truth about Paul. Vicki then agrees to be the witness at the wedding. Self-aware Liz acknowledges that she's a coward; Vicki says she's not.

Episode #263 — Next day (?) Carolyn's in the drawing room, reading the paper when Vicki comes in. The news of the day is that another woman was attacked. Carolyn says she had a dream that she'd be the next victim. Blah, blah, Maggie. Vicki says she's going to see Sam and Carolyn decides to see Joe and be a friend to him as he's been to her. Carolyn says she doesn't want to fight with Vicki, but then Vicki tells her about being a witness to the upcoming nuptials. Miss Stoddard gets bitchy and, like a twelve year old, says they're not friends anymore and to leave her alone!

Sam's on the phone to Woodard, asking for a Maggie update, insisting on seeing her soon. Vicki shows up, offering any assistance he may need. She struggles to express herself and he tells her not to try, it's enough that she's paid the call. He apologizes for not having her at the 'funeral.' Vicki offers to get rid of Maggie's things. Sam says thanks, but he wants to keep them and he almost spills the truth.

On the docks, Joe's having a quiet lunch, looking out to sea, when Carolyn walks up. Now it's her turn to not know how to express her sympathy. Joe appreciates her trying. They briefly discuss Maggie, before Joe brings up her upcoming marriage. Carolyn feigns happiness, then tries to stir things up, saying he disapproves. Wise Joe doesn't bite and simply states that she should marry Buzz if he makes her happy. Carolyn apologizes for treating good guy Joe like shit a year ago (man, I love level-headed Joe; Carolyn really screwed herself out of a decent guy). She tells him to call if he needs anything and leaves.

Later, Vicki and Carolyn are in the drawing room, discussing their visits. Miss Stoddard sings Joe's praises — too, late, Princess, that ship has sailed — then tries to figure out why she's such a neurotic mess. Carolyn then notices a vase of violets on the piano and gets angry again. Kitten decides to go out.

Joe is with Sam at the cottage, getting a Maggie update. Sam wants to reveal the truth to Vicki, as he trusts her, but Joe talks him out of it. Sam wants to find the maniac responsible for kidnapping Maggie.

Episode #264 — Evening and McGuire goes down to the drawing room for a drink. Roger's there, reading the paper, and ignores the oleaginous oaf's greeting. McGuire repeats himself, in that threatening tone. Roger offers a dry retort, then gets up to leave the room (like the honey badger, Roger don't give a shit). McGuire fills a glass, to the brim, and laughs at Roger wanting to stop the marriage. Roger stands up to the shamrock huffer and butthurt McGuire threatens. Honey badger don't care and is taking steps to protect the family money and business. Once Roger walks out, the Irish toad laughs.

At the Old House, Barnabas is staring out the window. Willie comes along and tells him the basement is cleaned up, there's no sign Maggie was ever there. Barnabas says he may have seen a child outside, but not David. Willie asks what they'll do now. He goes on to reveal he has a conscience by saying they're responsible for Maggie's death and he hates himself for it. Oh, and Barnabas, too. Willie stands up to him and Barnabas, Mr. Never-Follows-Through threatens him. He tells him to forget Maggie, then sends him outside to look around. Willie says, sure, he'll go and he won't think about Barney's next victim. Roger shows up, needing to vent about Jason. He tells Barnabas that McGuire has something on Liz, but they don't know what; he's obviously a fortune hunter. Barnabas offers to talk to Liz, but Roger says it will be no use. As Lucky Charms wants to get his corned beef and cabbage stained fingers on all things Collins, Barnabas offers to talk to him.

Out in the woods, Willie runs across Sarah, who's looking for someone to play with. She says she can't find her parents. Willie asks if she's the girl David was talking about, then tells her they can't play there. Willie tells her to go home and asks where she lives. She points to the Old House and is adamant that she lives *there*. He figures she's lost and will take her back into town. Naturally, she disappears (that surprised you?).

Roger and Barnabas arrive at Collinwood. Roger goes upstairs to look for some paperwork regarding the Old House while Barnabas goes to the drawing room, finding McGuire playing lord of the manor. Blah, blah, marriage (Barnabas, please prove useful and bash McGuire's skull in with your cane). Mr. Collins says he may have McGuire sussed out (I don't mind Barnabas giving McGuire shit, he deserves it). Jason tries to get the upper hand and resorts to his usual, oily tactics. Smarmy McGuire wonders where Barnabas gets his money and where the hell he goes during the day (smart, but I still hate this boggy bastard). Back at the Old House, Barnabas tells Willie that he spoke with McGuire. Our man Loomis says to chill, he's bluffing, then says that he did find a little girl in the woods who, damnedest thing, kept saying she lived there, in the Old House.

Episode #265 — Maggie is being hypnotized by a woman with a pen light. Oh, Dr. Hoffman, I presume? (So much for him being a...him.) When asked what her name is, Maggie becomes distraught.

Woodard is at the Evans homestead and Sam is bitching that he can't see his daughter. Apparently, Hoffman isn't forthcoming with info and, per Woodard, is 'unusual.' Lots of Maggie blah, blah and we learn the facility she's in is called Windcliffe. Sam is suspicious, thinking Woodard's trying to hide some-thing and announces he's driving up there with Joe. Woodard decides to go as well. In the car, a driving Joe tells Sam he's having second thoughts. Blah, blah Maggie (Woodard must be taking his own car, or they have him in the trunk).

In Hoffman's office, the good lady doctor is bitching at Woodard, Sam and Joe, for showing up unannounced. She does allow them to see Maggie, but warns that anything can happen. Sam and Joe go to see the patient. (Julia seems a tough-minded type, confident and dedicated to her work. Also a bit of a 'my way or the highway' kind of person).

Maggie's in her room, sitting with her doll, looking lost. Sam and Joe come in. Maggie doesn't respond to them, just looks forlornly out at nothing. She sud-denly drops the doll and goes to the grated window. Sam gives her the doll and asks her about one she had as a child that she called Cassandra. It doesn't ring a bell and Maggie starts singing *London Bridge*. She then completely loses her shit, screaming to be let out and rushing to the door. The nurse comes in, shoos the men out, and comforts Maggie (how the hell is broke Sam paying for this private care?).

Still in the office, Woodard and Julia are discussing differences in methodolo-gy. Julia seems a bit cagey. The talk turns to the blood anomaly and she's tight lipped. Sam and Joe come back in, bummed out. Julia says it may take a long time for Maggie to recover and it's best not to see her until she allows it. The men leave. Julia has another hypno session with Maggie, who just keeps singing the 'lock her up' portion of *London Bridge*.

Suicide is Painless

Episode #266 — Night at Collinwood and Liz is having a dream. She's walking the cliffs and hears women (the widows?) calling to her. She then jumps from the cliff and three widows appear near where she was standing. One a.m. and Vicki is still up and dressed. She goes to Liz's room and she's up now, too — oh, it's one in the afternoon. Uncharacteristically, Liz slept in late. She declines lunch and is obviously in a major funk. She pulls a Greta Garbo. Vicki talks about McGuire/Carolyn/Buzz and Liz is low-energy apathetic about everything. Vicki leaves, but is very concerned.

A little later, Liz, now dressed and desiring a walk, comes downstairs. She's met by McGuire, who wants a word. They go to the drawing room and the linty leprechaun wants the wedding to take place at Collinwood. Dead inside Liz doesn't care. In fact, she agrees to everything he asks for. He wants a reception, too. He's surprised by her attitude, but is too stupid to figure out something is seriously wrong. Oh, now he's puzzled and suspects something's afoot. Liz says there's only one way out of the marriage. She leaves for her walk and he smugly smiles.

On Widows' Hill, Liz is looking down into the drink. Mrs. Johnson comes along looking for her, as she's been out there for hours. It's getting dark and she should come home. Mrs. J asks about the reception plans and the two women start talking the legend of the widows. Liz relates the death stories of each and it seems they're waiting for another. Mrs. Johnson declares a header off the cliff and dashed to bits on the rocks below is a terrible way to die (just ask Bill Malloy; remember Mrs. J had a thing for him). Liz suddenly comes over dizzy and Mrs. Johnson grabs hold of her and takes her home.

McGuire corners Liz for yet another confab in the drawing room, where Vicki happens to be. Jason gives Liz a wedding present; a pin that supposedly belonged to his mother (I'll wager it's stolen, but probably belonged to *somebody's* mother). Liz dully accepts the gift, then goes upstairs, while McGuire goes off to read the paper or something. Mrs. Johnson comes in and tells Vicki about finding Liz on Widows' Hill and how she almost fainted and fell.

In her room, the resting Liz, in yet another delightful bit of loungewear, hears the widows calling from the cliff.

Episode #267 — Liz is back on Widows' Hill and Barnabas is lurking in the shrubbery. He creeps up on her and grabs her, concerned she might fall. She talks about looking for serenity or something, but he pretty much suspects her true motives. They discuss life and death. She admits to being tormented and he offers to help. More veiled suicide talk from Liz.

Arriving at Collinwood, Liz heads upstairs, ignoring David, who politely says hello. Barnabas and David start chatting and Barnabas brings up Sarah. David affirms he met the girl and that she sings *London Bridge* a lot, which for some reason grabs Barnabas' attention. Barnabas asks David to tell his friend not to play at the Old House. David heads to the kitchen and Barnabas joins Vicki in the drawing room. He schmoozes her for a bit, then tells her about finding Liz on Widows' Hill, about to take the leap. Blah, blah, depressed Liz, then back to schmoozing. Barnabas readies to leave. Vicki's going out, too, for dinner with Burke. Barnabas doesn't seem to like that very much.

At the Blue Whale, NewBurke waits as a new tune plays on the jukebox and he gets a refill from Not-Bob the Bartender (it's like bizarro world, what's going on?). Some guy in a suit is 'dancing' in the background, herking and jerking to the music, which provides unintentional comic relief. NewBurke heads to the payphone and is about to call Vicki when she walks in. Mr. Moneybags complains about losing his dime in the phone (I remember those days). The couple starts to slow dance and when finished, take a table, have a drink and start conversing. Burke isn't keen on her working at Collinwood (give it a rest, she's a fixture there now) and offers her a job with him (why? You never do anything at your rival business in Logansport. Also, I'm still not sold on this passive, milquetoast Burke. Who'd have thought I'd miss the blustering, bellowing Burke?). Vicki is loyal to the Collinses, then tells him about Liz's odd behavior and the Widows' Hill incidents. Burke reveals he's having McGuire checked out and asks Vicki if she knows more than she's letting on. Vicki suddenly leaves, wanting to check on Liz.

Liz is in the drawing room, wearing that fabulous loungewear I liked so much a while back. David comes in. Liz exits and heads upstairs just as Vicki comes home. Vicki goes to the drawing room and finds David looking at the family Bible that Liz was reading. The book is open to the page recording the date of Liz's birth. Vicki seems somewhat alarmed.

Episode #268 — Depressed Liz now has the family Bible in her room. She seems confused, then hears the widows calling to her again through the open windows. Vicki comes along and wants to take David on a shopping trip to Bangor. Liz prefers she delays it until tomorrow — oops, that's her wedding day. Liz asks if she can postpone the trip and gives her the day off so she can spend the day with her nephew. Roger comes along, asking for a word, and Vicki heads out. Roger asks Liz what's up with her will, Garner called. Roger suspects she's changing it and she assures him that's not the case; David and Carolyn will inherit. Roger's relieved and encourages her to back out of the marriage. He notices the Bible and asks why she has it out. More marriage talk before Roger leaves. David comes in a while later, disappointed he can't go to Bangor. Liz tells him he can, if it's that important to him, but he says nah, he'll hang with her. She says they can do whatever he wants and he suggests a walk on the beach — he'll show her a secret place he's found. The perceptive boy notices she seems sad. Liz says she's not, so how about that walk?

Later that evening, Liz is in the drawing room when Carolyn, full of attitude, comes home from a date with Buzz. Liz doesn't take the bait and says she just wants to talk. Carolyn continues bitching. Liz, in gentle tones, tries to tell her daughter how much she means to her. Carolyn remains an overgrown brat. She notices, however, that her mother is acting strangely and suggests she go to bed.

In her room, Liz writes the current date in the Bible as her date of death (for trivia's sake, we also learn that Roger is eight years younger than her).

Carolyn is still in the drawing room and hears Vicki come home from a date with NewBurke. Blah, blah, Liz acting weird, to which Vicki says don't worry about it. Vicki goes to Liz's room to find Dame Stoddard is not there. Vicki glances at the open page of the Bible and looks concerned.

Liz is on Widows' Hill. The widows cry out her name and she prepares to take a header (a rather slow and uneventful episode).

Episode #269 — Liz is still on the cliff (wearing big, pearl earrings — hey, if you're going to suicide, suicide in *style*). There's a redo/replay of Vicki finding the Bible entry and Liz hearing the widows calling. Damn it, Liz, jump already, third time's the charm and all. Instead, Liz paces, then *finally* takes a running start to the edge when Vicki arrives and stops her. Liz wangsts about betraying the family and Vicki says she's courageous (man, that is a leap of logic). Liz says she deserves to be punished for killing Paul and Vicki reveals that, if she likes you, she's very flexible with morality. After thinking it over, Liz embraces the governess and the two head for home.

Back at Collinwood (oh, Liz was also wearing a pearl necklace for that suicide; darling, one *must* accessorize properly for the coroner), Liz and Vicki talk in the drawing room. Vicki offers to tell Carolyn the truth about the upcoming wedding, but is shot down. More blah, blah and Liz asks Vicki not to mention the cliff incident. Vicki says she'll erase the death date from the Bible (she should get a job in government). The toad comes in, looking for his affianced. Jason wants Vicki to leave, but Liz wants her to stay. McGuire shows Liz the wedding band he bought (either with her money, or it's stolen, I'm sure). She refuses to try it on and McGuire again asks Vicki to leave. Liz says it's all right, she can handle the leprechaun. Jason asks Liz if she told Vicki anything. Liz, having some of her fire back, insults him and exits.

At the Blue Whale, NewBurke is on the phone, confirming receipt of a report on McGuire. Vicki rushes in. Burke informs her of Jason's activities; smuggling, extortion, fraud, but there was never enough proof to nail him (told you he was a piece of shit). Burke wants to apprise Liz. At first, Vicki says don't bother, then changes her mind.

At Collinwood, Vicki persuades Liz to see Burke (what the hell time is it? Isn't it kind of late?). Burke offers Liz the report (sorry, this new Burke isn't working; he lacks the swagger needed for the character. Old Burke was a bull, new Burke is a steer). McGuire saunters in and smarms at Burke (why didn't tough guy Burke ever punch out McGuire?). Devlin shows him the report. The Irish irritant says he can explain all that. He smarms some more, then invites Burke to the wedding. Kissing Liz's cheek, he walks out of the room (and I feel like I need a shower).

Episode #270 — Carolyn's rifling through suitcases and drawers in McGuire's room. She finds a locked diary, slices through the flap and gets to reading. The Kilkenny kill-joy walks in and, misogynist that he is, menacingly threatens her. He *orders* her to pick up the dropped book. She tries to flee, but he grabs her arm and makes the demand again (another seventh century Barbarian). Carolyn complies and hands the diary to him. She tries to leave, but he blocks her and spews crap. She calls him a fake (she should have stabbed him in the eye with that letter opener). He asks her why she's not getting married, then says he expects her to marry and vacate *his* house — he's *Mister* McGuire! (sorry, that only works with *Mister* Tibbs). After manhandling her, the woman hater issues the edict that she leave her own house; if she's not gone by nightfall, he'll have Liz banish her and his wife will do whatever he wants (there are no words to accurately express how vile this character is).

At the Blue Whale, Carolyn is drinking alone and I mean the place is dead. She asks Bob where everyone is. He speaks (!) and advises her to go home. Joe comes in and seeing how plastered she is, wants to take her someplace to sober up. Drunk Carolyn says she's waiting for her man, so she can get married. She drunk babbles about Liz and Jason in a vague way that confuses Joe. She whines and logical Joe says there's nothing she can do about it. The blonde gets an idea and Joe offers to take her home.

At Collinwood, Carolyn pulls a revolver from a desk drawer. Vicki's in Liz's room, helping her dress for the ceremony. Liz recalls how happy she was when she married Paul, who turned out to be a worthless s.o.b.. Blah, blah, marrying McGuire sucks and Paul sucked, too. Liz worries about Carolyn/Buzz, then back to Paul and damn, that is one ugly, shapeless dress she's wearing (if she were marrying someone she truly loved, I think Liz would care more about her attire). She sends Vicki out, wanting to be alone.

In the drawing room, Roger tells Burke he's surprised he was invited. McGuire strolls in. Carolyn comes downstairs, carrying a beaded clutch and all are surprised she's there. The judge arrives and filler ensues. Vicki walks in and while the others are all milling together, Carolyn stands apart. The reluctant bride finally enters. Carolyn checks the contents of her purse — she's packing heat. The ceremony starts and Carolyn readies to shoot McGuire through her evening bag. Liz hesitates on the "I do" part, then says, fuck this and drops the mother of all truth bombs — she killed Paul Stoddard and Jason was her accomplice. Carolyn's so stunned, she drops both her bag *and* gun.

Episode #271 — Wedding bombshell replay. McGuire then tries some fast talking, but NewBurke tells him to shut the fuck up and let Liz talk. The judge decides to beat a hasty retreat, not wanting to be involved, in case there's, you know, a trial. Roger demands a lawyer be called. Liz says screw that, I want to talk to Carolyn. The judge offers any help he can because, cronyism, then departs. The blonde admits she almost killed McGuire and Burke picks up the gun. Jason claims Liz is hysterical. Carolyn wants to know why mommy killed daddy. McGuire tries walking out, but armed Burke warns against it. Liz starts to tell the story of the night Paul Stoddard was killed. We go to flashback, with a little bit of voice-over (a call-back to Joan Bennett's noir days) to set things up.

Paul's in the drawing room, having a last drink before abandoning his family. He's about to take off with a suitcase full of stocks, bonds, money and jewelry; wow, he's just like McGuire — a worthless piece of shit. He's ready to steal from his own daughter (which, according to episode #5, hasn't been born yet, damn it). Stoddard is waiting for his pal to show up. Liz threatens to call the cops and there's McGuire type bullshit from Paul. He picks up the suitcase and Liz picks up a fireplace poker. More arguing ensues and when Paul turns to leave — ha! Liz cracks him but good on the head with that fire poker. Sweet, now do it to Jason. (Note: Paul's face is never seen, his back is always to the camera). Disturbed, she goes into the foyer and guess who waltzes right in? Liz begs McGuire to check Paul and call a doctor. He goes into the drawing room and comes back out a minute later, saying Paul is dead. Liz is mortified and jackass McGuire sees his opening. No need to call the police, it was an accident. Furthermore, he offers to dispose of Paul's mortal remains in the basement (McGuire is different in this episode, not smug or smarmy, so he's tolerable. I gather that at this point, his scams are small potatoes, hence the lack of over-confidence and self-satisfaction). We're told via voice-over that they destroyed all evidence (and where the hell are the servants? In episode #6, Matthew Morgan told Vicki that Liz fired them all the day Paul left. Did she fire them earlier that day? If so, it looks like premeditation. I wish there was more continuity). Anyway, McGuire insists Liz see where Paul is buried before they lock up the room.

Episode #272 — Replay of the room locking. Back to the present in the drawing room. It's a lie! McGuire bleats. He says there is no body in the basement, go ahead and start digging. Liz wants to call the sheriff, but Roger says not so fast. McGuire insists he's done nothing wrong. Bicker and bitch, there's no body. Liz calls the cop shop and reports a murder. Jason then applies a karate chop to distracted NewBurke's arm, causing him to drop the gun (*now* someone gets the upper hand on Burke, when he's milquetoast?). Pushing Burke aside, the toad from Tipperary then runs away like a little pussy. Burke and Roger give chase and gunshots are heard outside (oh, please, *please* let McGuire be dead).

Out in the woods, Burke is armed with the hand gun and Roger, in another area, is toting a rifle (be vewy, vewy quiet, they'we hunting wepwechaun). The men meet up and NewBurke tries to act like OldBurke, complaining about having served time for manslaughter (give it a fucking rest already).

At Collinwood, Carolyn continues to stare like a doe in headlights because daddy's been mouldering in the basement all these years. Liz asks her for forgiveness. Princess still has loads of daddy issues and won't talk to or look at her mother. Her wangsting becomes annoying (she's in denial that he was about to abandon her; sorry, but your mother did you a *huge* favor offing the caitiff). When asked by Vicki, Liz admits to being responsible for the sobbing heard in the dead of night. Carolyn turns and glances at her mother, then boo-hoos and runs from the room.

Later, Patterson's at Collinwood, saying they'll find McGuire. Roger walks in, wanting to know what happens next. Patterson wants to dig up 'ole Paul. Liz mentions McGuire saying that there's no stiff in the basement and Patterson is interested. Burke comes back, saying the cops think they have McGuire cornered somewhere. George asks Burke to help with the digging and Liz hands over the key to the locked room. The two men head downstairs with a shovel and get to work. Patterson admits to believing McGuire. Meanwhile, Vicki and Liz wait it out in the drawing room. Liz wants to see Carolyn and is told that she left the building and nobody knows where she is. In the basement, after digging about a foot deep, out of shape Patterson is ready to quit, but then, (miraculously) Burke strikes pay dirt — a trunk!

Episode #273 — Burke and the sheriff pull up the trunk and brace themselves for the putrid mess they're about to find. They open the lid, take a glance, then look at each other in surprise.

In the drawing room, Liz is fretting. Roger asks why she never told him and she replies that it was pride. Roger concedes that, although he wouldn't have told anyone, he would have used the knowledge to his advantage. Blah, blah Carolyn. Patterson and Burke walk in, just as the phone rings. It's for George; McGuire's been found and the lawman says to drag his sorry ass back to the house, he has some questions. Hanging up, Patterson says a lot of nothing to the point where even Burke suggests he just tell Liz whatever he's *not* telling her. The non-suspenseful build up has led up to — the trunk is empty.

Liz, Roger and Patterson go down to the room. Liz gets wound up; I guess eighteen years of pent-up fear is finally being released. Patterson asks her if she's sure Paul was dead. Blah, blah. Burke, McGuire and a deputy come in.

The coward from Cork smarms that he doesn't know a thing (this fucker; at least Patterson isn't buying his shit). Roger brings up the blackmail and the Swiss bank account. The linty leprechaun wants to talk to Liz alone. Roger and Burke try to dissuade her, but she agrees.

Patterson, Roger and Burke are waiting in the foyer, with Roger convinced McGuire will worm something out of Liz. In order to build suspense (and failing spectacularly), we don't get to see what Liz and Jason talk about. Instead, they have the others come into the drawing room. Liz has McGuire tell the truth; she only knocked Paul unconscious. Jason convinced Stoddard to fake his death and split the money with him. McGuire lost touch with Paul a decade ago, but he was very much alive. Story told, the Dublin dick attempts to saunter out. Patterson is prepared to arrest him, but Liz won't press charges; it's what Jason weaseled out of her in exchange for the truth (this cocksucker). Roger insists he be arrested for extortion and fraud, but Liz wants to avoid a scandal. Burke puts in his two cents, thinking it best to let things go and Roger reluctantly agrees. Patterson gives McGuire until sundown to drag his carcass out of Collinsport and milquetoast NewBurke issues a weak threat. Brogue Boy blarneys his way into staying until sundown the next evening (for the love of God, why hasn't anyone killed him yet?) McGuire finally exits with an escort from Patterson.

Having somehow mystically changed out of his bridegroom togs without retrieving his clothing from Collinwood, McGuire is now lurking around outside the Old House, no doubt preparing to annoy and irritate our Mr. Loomis. At least the not-that-engaging mystery of the padlocked room is solved.

Episode #274 — McGuire is lurking in the woods, looking at the Old House from afar. Inside, Barnabas comes down to the parlor as Willie is lighting candles. Emo Barnabas angsts, saying Josette's room must be occupied again, and soon. He reveals that he's chosen his next victim. Willie doesn't much care for the news and says maybe it won't work out, 'cause, ya know, Maggie. Barnabas makes excuses for his failure by throwing Maggie under the bus (so, having a strong will is a defect?). Barnabas sends Willie to get the "jewel chest" as he wants to gift his next victim something shiny. McGuire creeps up and stations himself outside the parlor window and peers in. Willie brings the jewelry box and asks Barnabas if he thinks baubles can buy the next girl. Barnabas haughtily mocks Willie for wanting to help Maggie. Though Barney plays chary by not naming names, street savvy Willie says he knows Vicki is the one. Somehow, McGuire manages to overhear everything, which suggests that Barnabas skimped on the glazing for the parlor windows.

Later, Willie is walking through the woods and comes across McGuire, who says his farewells, as he's leaving town. Willie asks if he got married. Jason tries to bullshit, but the old, pre-Barnabas Willie surfaces to ridicule the plan backfiring. McGuire says he's got some schemes cooking in other states and asks Willie if he wants to come along. Willie's staying put, thanks. Scumbag Jason hits his old buddy up for money, lots of it (uh, what about that bank account in Switzerland?). The s.o.b. with the shit-eating grin tells Willie to steal the jewels from the chest in the Old House. Willie plays stupid, then says he can't. McGuire pressures him by mentioning Vicki and Maggie. Willie agrees to meet with him the next afternoon at the Blue Whale.

The next day, McGuire's at the bar when Vicki comes in and asks Bob if Miss Stoddard has been in. Jason insists on talking to her, but Vicki would rather avoid the shamrock pestilence. She gives him a piece of her mind and he bullshits, trying to insult her. Misogynist asshole makes veiled threats (playing off the Barnabas plan, of which he knows nothing), then intimates that he may know something about her identity, having been in town eighteen years ago (yeah, like what? Vicki is older than Carolyn; you know jack). Vicki knows he's just trying to screw with her and leaves. Willie walks in and McGuire immediately gives him lip. He insists Willie have a farewell drink with him then prolixly talks out of his ass. Our man Loomis hands over a handkerchief. Greedy McGuire opens it and is teed off to find a single brooch. Willie says he's got to boogie and McGuire threatens him. Willie says fuck you, this is all you're getting, and leaves. Aw, boo-hoo, McGuire, you malcontent.

At the Old House, presumably later, McGuire breaks in through the parlor window and inexplicably misses the open jewel chest sitting on a table that he just walked past.

Episode #275 — Early morning and a sedated Liz is mumbling in her sleep, worrying about Carolyn. The concern is needless, as she is merely strolling the beach. Returning home, Carolyn goes to her mother's room and wakes her. Turns out, she's fine with mom having offed daddy and we'll get the best lawyers for the trial! Liz tells her McGuire lied and that Paul isn't dead, he just took a powder. You, mean…daddy might still be alive?! Go back to sleep, Mom (all this was painfully dull). Later on, Liz is awake and Carolyn brings her some java. Blah, blah, Liz hopes her worthless ex-husband never comes back. The talk turns to McGuire and Liz assures Carolyn he's gone, having been kicked out of town.

Jason's in the Old House parlor (I guess it's the same day as the previous episode, but the timeline is non-linear) and — hey, where's the jewelry box? Anyway, he skulks around the parlor, searching, and is caught by Willie, who tells him to get the hell out, he's not safe there. Willie warns that Barnabas is in the house. Asshole McGuire rifles through drawers, saying he wants all the jewels, so where's the box? Willie won't tell and McGuire gets seven year old girl slappy again, then literally twists Willie's arm behind his back to give up the info. The box is in the basement and then our Mr. Loomis breaks the vampire/victim code by actually telling McGuire the truth; Barnabas isn't alive. Of course, Jason laughs at him as if he's crazy and heads to the basement. Panicked Willie follows.

McGuire finds the coffin and won't listen to Willie's warning not to open it (and isn't Willie something of an authority on coffins better left closed?). Loomis grabs a few pieces of jewelry from a small table, but avaricious McGuire, like Oliver Twist and gruel, wants *more*. Willie says he doesn't have time to get the rest, as they're sealed in the wall (and please, *please* bash McGuire's skull *against* the wall; repeatedly). Willie warns the infuriatingly loathsome and repellent McGuire to no avail, then gives up, saying, okay, cocksucker, *open it* (and reap what you sow) and backs away. Practically drooling at the thought of riches, McGuire opens the coffin and is treated to the one-handed throat grab.

Episode #276 — It's a replay of the Willie warning/McGuire coffin opening scene. Barnabas is then up and about and I grudgingly applaud his first truly useful action — for Jason McGuire is dead on the floor. Guess Not-So-Lucky Charms' luck ran out. Willie is in shock. He tells Barnabas how McGuire broke in and Barnabas loses the minuscule amount of respect I had mustered for him by bitching at Willie; he put him in danger, he should punish him! (Fuck off, you managed, didn't you?). He then says they have to dispose of McGuire; they'll bury him in the hidden room of the mausoleum, which has remained secret for two centuries (just dump him in the landfill with the rest of the trash). Willie can't touch McGuire, as they were good friends once. Barnabas derides our man Loomis for being too sentimental (I think it speaks volumes of the inherent goodness in him). Willie counters by asking if he ever had a good friend who died. Barney says yes, someone who died very young, whom he mourned for a long time. Willie, trying not to retch, helps Barnabas pick up the body and carry it upstairs. Sarah is standing by the wall, playing with her ball.

Woodard's at Windcliffe, with Sam's sketch of Sarah, inquiring of Dr. Hoffman if Maggie has seen it yet. That would be no. Woodard blusters and Julia feeds her fish. Woodard decides to show Maggie the picture. Maggie is brought in and Julia wants to administer a Rorschach test, but Woodard interrupts, show-ing the sketch instead and asking Maggie if she knows the little girl. At first, Maggie seems confused, but then says the girl's name is Sarah and she came to play with her when she was in the room. Woodard pushes, against Julia's warn-ing. Maggie begins to remember more, including the riddle. Agitated Maggie stands up and starts miming pushing bricks while reciting the riddle. Woodard keeps badgering, Julia tells him to shut the fuck up and Maggie starts singing *London Bridge.* Hoffman calls for a nurse and Maggie is led out, screaming the lock her up bit. Nice going, Woodard, you jackass. Julia rightfully reams him out. But we've made progress! The little girl is the key! he insists.

Willie and Barnabas carry the corpse of the Shillelagh Shamrock King to the mausoleum. Hmm, either Barnabas knows some hocus-pocus to crack open the stone flooring or Willie is superhuman, as he has buried his former acquain-tance in record time with merely a shovel (Barnabas, of course, isn't about to get a speck of dirt on his Saville Row suit). Barnabas makes a sarcastic, but truthful, comment about McGuire's final resting place. Willie looks like he's fighting to keep from crying *and* vomiting. He quietly states that he wants to leave. Surprisingly, Barnabas agrees it's time to go. After closing the secret room, but lingering in the main section of the crypt, Barnabas discusses his mother, father and sister, Sarah, who died when she was nine. He recounts a sob story about how she had broken her doll the day before and he fixed it for her and that she died holding it. They depart and guess who's in the crypt, hold-ing her doll? (Wait, doesn't Maggie have the doll? What gives?)

(Good riddance to Jason McGuire. Dennis Patrick did a fine job of imbuing the character with all the loathsome, repugnant, vile and oily traits needed to make him truly insufferable. Rot in hell, Not-So-Lucky Charms, rot in hell)

HJ Peterson

A Droll Divertissement

Episode #277 — Barnabas is in Josette's room, pining. Willie walks in with news that as far as the sheriff is concerned, Jason left town. Barnabas threatens Willie to remember what happened to him (empty threat; Barney won't kill Willie, he needs him far too much). Willie changes the subject by mentioning that Barnabas has been spending a lot of time in that room. Barnabas says it must be occupied soon. Willie points out that another kidnapping will rouse suspicion and Barnabas brings up that 'come of her own free will' bullshit and threatens Willie again. Then Barnabas decides to throw a party for the family to see the restoration. Fondling Josette's dress, he says it'll be a costume party and Vicki will come as Josette. Willie just looks at him like he's nuts.

Liz is in the drawing room, going over some paperwork. Roger strolls in and asks why she does it at home, she should come to the office as there's no need to be a recluse anymore. They talk it over a bit and it's really rather sweet how encouraging he is. The ascotted and dressing gowned Roger wonders where their former houseguest is, as all the expensive clothes Liz bought him, along with other belongings, are still upstairs. Roger says Patterson checked around and no one saw McGuire leave. Blah, blah, where Jason was last seen, then Roger gets off a great one saying he wants McGuire's room fumigated. Liz decides to pack up Jason's things and give them to charity. Roger's all for it, because he knows McGuire would hate it.

Barnabas knocks and Vicki answers. Standing just outside the front door, he says something about Jeremiah building the house, then blathers about how beautiful the night is and how evil the sunlight. Crap, the dog howling is back. They finally step inside and babble some more in the foyer, with Barnabas setting it up so she can visit the Old House anytime. They then join Liz and Roger

84

in the drawing room, where Barnabas invites them all to his costume soirée, where they will all dress as Collins ancestors. Roger and Vicki love the idea. Why, Barnabas has even found clothes actually worn by said ancestors. Liz is hesitant, then says she won't come.

Liz is alone in the drawing room when Roger walks in, saying Barnabas is in the study, just crestfallen at her refusal. They argue about the party, with Liz incisively admitting something doesn't seem right about it. Roger makes an offer; she attends, but should she want to leave early, he'll make the excuse and bring her home. They ask Vicki and Barnabas back in and Liz accepts the invitation. Barnabas then assigns their 'roles.' He will be his 'namesake,' naturally. Roger is to be Joshua, the 'first' Barnabas' father, with Liz being Naomi, his mother. Vicki is to be Josette.

Episode #278 — Barnabas is bitching at Willie about something regarding clothing. Willie doesn't think Barney will be able to convince Liz and Vicki to come to the party. Haughty Barnabas informs him that the family *is* coming, so get the trunk and take it to Josette's room. Willie does as he's told and in the bedroom they open the trunk filled with perfectly preserved, two hundred year old clothing. Blah, blah, Vicki loved the idea. Willie tells Barnabas he should stay away from Miss Winters. He knows Vicki is to come as Josette and asks if Barnabas' next victim has to be her (his concern for people is rather endearing). He then anxiously requests Barnabas rethink the whole party, as people will think they can stop by anytime after that. Oh, they'll handle that later, dumbass Barnabas blithely replies. He tosses off another hollow threat, then leaves the room. Willie looks worried.

At Collinwood, Barnabas is asking Liz if Vicki can come to the Old House to help pick out the costumes. Liz inquires if dressing as ancestors is a good idea, as it seems wrong to get so close to the past. She confesses to being afraid in a way she can't explain (good instinct). Barnabas says he'll forego the costumes. Vicki laments and Liz relents, much to predator Barnabas' approval.

At the Old House, Sarah, sans cap, is sitting on the trunk, playing with her ball. She pulls a vanishing act hearing Barnabas and Vicki approaching. Upon entering, Barnabas senses someone was in the room and it seems to rattle him. They open the trunk and Vicki's all a-flutter over Josette's gown. Carolyn is to go as someone named Millicent and Barnabas gets his bloomers in a bunch when Vicki pulls Jeremiah's clothes from the trunk. Vicki then finds a little girl's dress that belonged to the 'first' Barnabas' sister, who died young. Vicki chatters about what she'd do if she knew her family and ancestors. He tells her she'll become Josette — for the *party*. Ass.

Vicki's back at Collinwood, showing Liz the Josette dress she'll be wearing. It's so delicious, she just *had* to bring it home. Blah, blah, Barnabas and the past.

Over in Josette's room, Barnabas is pining again and playing the music box. Our man Loomis comes in and receives instructions about taking the clothes to Collinwood in the morning. Willie sees the child's dress on the bed and says the little girl he saw was wearing one very similar. Barnabas insists Willie is wrong and cuts him off when he starts to describe the girl. Barnabas walks out and Willie, after a quick glance at the clothes, follows. Sarah is suddenly in the room and walks to the bed. Picking up the garment, she excitedly exclaims that she found her blue dress.

Episode #279 — Carolyn's in her room, looking over Millicent Collins' dress. Vicki comes in, dressed in Josette's gown and hair in an up-do; she just couldn't wait to play dress up! Vicki suddenly has a strange feeling of déjà vu. Carolyn says when she tried on her dress, she got a weird, negative vibe and that if it happens again, she's not wearing the gown. Vicki brushes off the strangeness and talks up the party, admitting she'll be proud to be a family member for the night. Carolyn says she should be one (why bother dredging all this up? The mystery of Vicki's parentage evaporated as quickly as Frank's resolve to find B. Hanscombe).

At the Old House, Barnabas heads to the parlor and asks furniture cleaning Willie how things are coming along. He then waxes ecstatic that Vicki must have tried on Josette's dress by now. Willie just keeps working, giving staccato, non-committal answers. Barnabas then earnestly tells Loomis that "that night… must go…nothing wrong." Willie flatly assures him the evening will be grand.

NewBurke arrives at Collinwood — and why is he dressing like a hybrid of Joe and Willie? Answer: NewBurke. He asks Carolyn how she's doing, no more Buzz? (Kind of miss the hippie cyclist and a scene ending that relationship could have been interesting. I imagine Buzz saying, "okay — who needs it?") Vicki comes along and Carolyn goes up to alter her dress. In the drawing room, NewBurke sucks at flirting, just like original Burke (at least something's consistent) as he asks Vicki to dinner the next evening. She explains she already has plans and simply *can't* cancel; it's an ancestor masquerade! Burke doesn't like the idea of her going as Josette; it disturbs him because of the séance when she channeled her spirit (man, I forgot about that, but wasn't Vicki seeing Frank at the time?). Vicki then hits on the bright idea of Burke attending as well, she'll talk Barnabas into it. She insists he drive her to the Old House and I wonder why they don't walk.

Willie's still hard at work, about to polish the silver candelabras, when Vicki shows up. She's effusive in her praise of his restoration work and our man seems almost painfully modest about it. She asks if he'll be at the party, in costume. He says he'll be around, but doesn't want to dress up. He then makes a very profound statement regarding his lot in life, just as Barnabas enters the room. In a stunning display of almost human behavior, rather than beat, choke or deride him, Barney suggests Willie take a break, as he's earned it. Willie slowly walks off, his face speaking volumes (another master class). Vicki and Barnabas talk party and she makes her request. Barnabas trots out the 'it's just for the family' excuse and Vicki points out *she's* invited and she's not family. Barnabas isn't too happy to hear how important Burke's attendance is to her, but then, with an evil glint in his dead eyes, says, why, yes, he can be Jeremiah, Josette's husband and builder of Collinwood! Vicki is delighted and thanks him. He calls her Josette as she's leaving and she plays along. Once she's gone, Barnabas calls to Willie and tells him that Burke is coming as Jeremiah, a man he despised and would have destroyed; tomorrow, he may get his chance.

Episode #280 — Up in Josette's room, Barnabas is wearing the old Barnabas portrait clothes as he sits looking at ancestor portraits in a family album. Sporting his vest and a necktie, Willie enters and the two rehash who's coming to the party as who and what the relation is to Barnabas for the benefit of anyone who missed the last three episodes. Coming across Jeremiah's portrait, Barnabas self-indulgently whines about how much he hated him, as he kept him from his precious. Then, like a twelve year old girl, he rips the page from the album and crumples it up.

In the Collinwood drawing room, Carolyn and Roger are attired for the shindig. She's nervous and feels weird. Blah, blah party. Liz ambles in wearing about eighty yards of fabric, diamond necklace, those giant emerald earrings and a freaking tiara and announces she doesn't want to go. Vicki comes along and jovial Roger is full of compliments for the ladies, (he's pretty loose, as he's already been drinking). The Collinses leave, while Vicki stays to wait for Burke.

In Josette's room, Barnabas is pleading with her to accept him and starts playing the music box. Willie apprises him that his guests, save for Vicki and Burke, have arrived. Our man Loomis then asks if Barnabas intends to give Vicki the music box, stating he thinks it's a bad idea. He then throws the 'free will' argument into the discussion, intimating that the music box is a cheat and says others will prevent her from coming to him — Burke, for instance. Savvy Willie knows Barnabas is planning something and looks worried. Barnabas goes to greet his guests.

In the parlor, Roger is commenting on the restoration and Liz looks like Queen Elizabeth II sitting in that chair. Barnabas comes in and takes all the credit for the restoration, even though we know he didn't lift a goddamn finger to pick up so much as a nail. While complimenting Liz, he almost refers to her as his mother. He covers by talking about playing ancestors while handing out booze. The talk turns to Jeremiah and Josette and when Carolyn mentions how much they were said to be in love, Barnabas snaps that it's a lie, then says the legends are numerous and contradictory. Vicki and Burke arrive and Barnabas makes a toast to the past. Vicki starts yammering about how much she feels like Josette. A bell begins to toll in the distance, which Liz comments on. Roger notes it's eleven o'clock and says it's a splendid time to be visited by a ghost. Liz is not amused. Carolyn points out the candles flickering (it's an old house, it's drafty) and Barnabas says it's an old house, it's drafty. Liz feels a chill and — damn, she is showing quite a bit of matronly cleavage — then swears she felt a hand on her shoulder. Most of the assemblage say it was her imagination, but, to our surprise, Roger thinks it may well have been a ghost and suggests a séance. Barnabas looks grim and protests. Roger won't let up and questions if big, bad Barnabas is afraid (I'm guessing yes). Liz says they might as well go ahead, as Roger won't give in. The others reluctantly agree and set up for some spirit raising (remember when Roger scoffed at Guthrie's séance suggestion? How times change). Roger begins, asking who's trying to reach them (where the hell is Willie during all this? I imagine him out back, having a smoke, a bourbon and listening to the ball game on a transistor radio). Everyone wants to call it quits, until Liz and Carolyn feel a chill. The candles gutter out and the front doors blow open. Vicki starts to moan and Barnabas looks on with constipated concern.

Episode #281 — Carolyn starts asking questions of whoever Vicki is channeling. Vicki doesn't answer, but says she has to run. 'Kay. I'll save a lot of time and just say that she's channeling Josette and recounting the night she died, just like Barnabas told in episode #233. Liz figures out it's Josette (why is Josette suddenly speaking English, when at the previous séance she only spoke French?). Barnabas shouts "no!" and Vicki collapses, trance broken. A short while later, Vicki's recovered and is told what happened and all speculate and comment. Vicki mentions that the last time Josette made contact, David was in danger, who could be this time? (Why is Burke standing in the background with his back turned? It seems so odd) Vicki mentions Maggie and that her killer may still be lurking around (honey, you don't know the half of it — look three feet to your right). Burke finally speaks, but it's nothing of consequence. Vicki decides to step outside for some air and sees Sarah standing on the up-stairs landing. When the girl walks away, Vicki calls to her. Burke comes over and asks what's up. Barnabas and the others join them and Vicki insists she saw a little girl wearing the dress that was in the trunk.

Back at Collinwood, the family and Vicki discuss the party, especially the séance. Vicki pouts that they should have stayed. After making some jovially mordant comments about chicks committing suicide, Roger goes up to bed (I think he's pretty well lit and feelin' fine). Liz also decides to hit the sack. Vicki feels sorry for Barney because he looked so sad (boo-hoo; he's a cold-blooded bastard). Carolyn asks Vicki if she really saw a little girl.

In Josette's room, Sarah's dress is on the bed and she's smoothing out the wrin-kles or something. Hearing Barnabas coming, she leaves. Barnabas picks up the dress and returns it to the trunk. Looking at Josette's portrait, he tells her that he had to make her go away, as she belongs in the past (then why try to turn someone into her?).

In the drawing room, Carolyn tells Vicki she doesn't give a crap that she's dat-ing Burke, she's over him. Miss Winters seems preoccupied, so Carolyn goes up to bed. Barnabas arrives and schmoozes Vicki. Blah, blah, little girl, ghosts, whatever, there's a whole lot of words to work up to the point; Barnabas gifts her the music box. Well, Vicki is just *entranced*.

Episode #282 — At Windcliffe, Maggie is having a session with Hoffman and seems more like herself. She says she just feels cold and angry, then mentions music, a far-away, tinkling sound.

Vicki's in the drawing room, playing that goddamn music box. Liz comes in, quite chipper. Vicki shows her the music box and explains it was a gift from Barnabas. Liz points out how attached/involved she is with Josette. The talk turns to the Sarah sighting, which Vicki now chalks up to her imagination. Liz walks out and the music box tortures us again (where's Willie with that poi-soned milk?).

Julia's asking questions about the music. Maggie says it frightens her and be-comes agitated. Hoffman tells her it's important she remember — what else can she recall? Maggie remembers a sweet scent, that's also frightening (why didn't Josette ever help Maggie? Bitch). Maggie starts remembering the cemetery.

Vicki, borrowed gown in hand, is escorted to Josette's room by Willie. She asks after Barnabas and is told he is not to home. Vicki blames herself for ruining the party, but Willie says, nah, Barney just gets moody sometimes. She tells him that Barnabas gave her the music box and how she's already listened to it for *hours*. Willie snaps that she shouldn't — uh, it's old and could break. He appears both angry and concerned (for good reason). He then says that the next day is Josette's birthday and Barnabas thought maybe the party should have been held then. Well, Vicki just feels that much closer to her.

Back at Collinwood, Vicki asks Liz if she can take some time during the next day to visit Josette's grave — it's her birthday! Liz thinks she's certifiable (does Vicki even teach anymore?). Vicki promises she won't go alone, she'll have Burke drag her there.

Psychiatric session over, Julia tells Maggie they've made progress. Maggie's frightened, but Julia's all 'courage!' The doctor suggests a trip to the cemetery for a dual purpose; for Maggie to face her fears and to hopefully jog her memory. The distressed patient pleads against going.

If At First You Don't Succeed

Episode # 283 — Windcliffe. Julia is teed off at the visiting Woodard, believing he's questioning her treatment of Maggie. He's frustrated that she's not forthcoming with info. Julia thinks he's accusing her of malpractice. Arguing ensues, with Woodard saying Sam and Joe are having a hard time keeping up the pretense of Maggie being dead. Julia suggests finding another doctor. They calm down and Julia reveals she was thinking of taking Maggie to Eagle Hill. Woodard pitches a fit (so, he's just always at odds with her, no matter what she says and does. Ass.). Julia backs off, saying it was just an idea and promises not to go. She then kicks him out, politely, as she has patients to see. He leaves and she has Maggie brought in. Miss Evans is dressed and ready to go on a day trip (gotta love that Julia; her way or the highway, baby!).

In the drawing room, Vicki's listening to that fucking music box. Burke shows up and proposes dinner in Bangor. Vicki says sure and oh, can we stop at the cemetery on the way? She wants to leave flowers on a grave. Burke thinks she means Maggie's, but Vicki somewhat sheepishly admits it's Josette's grave. Burke thinks it's a bad idea and Vicki keeps arguing. She once thought she was her descendant! She shows him the music box — a gift from Barnabas! Burke doesn't like that much, or the effect it has on her. NewBurke talks a lot of sense and Vicki acts like a teenager. He refuses to take her to the cemetery. Well, she'll just go alone, then, it's her birthday and *someone* has to remember! (She's been dead for over a century, give me a break). Burke gives up and says he'll take her, but he's still deeply concerned.

At Eagle Hill, Maggie and Julia walk the tombstones and Maggie gets panicky. Julia pushes her to try to remember *something*. Maggie isn't really trying and seems to be in denial. She turns around and they just happen to be standing in front of Josette's grave (1800-1822), but the Magster claims she doesn't recall having seen it before. They hear Burke and Vicki coming and scurry off to hide. Vicki and Burke are searching for the grave and Vicki notices two women in the distance. She and Burke find Josette's resting place. Burke comments that it's a pretty ignoble location for a Collins, and Vicki tells him that her husband, Jeremiah, buried her there out of revenge; her suicide was a betrayal (first we've heard of it and how the hell would Vicki know that?). Vicki espies the women again and insists to Burke that one of them was Maggie. He thinks she's losing it and convinces her to leave.

Julia and Maggie end up outside the Collins mausoleum (convenient, no?). Noticing the patient's reaction, Dr. Hoffman starts asking if she recognizes the place. Julia wants to check out the crypt and convinces Maggie to step inside. They find Sarah's tomb and Maggie grows more and more agitated, saying she has to leave, he'll kill her, she'll die! Julia comforts her and they depart.

Episode #284 — Back at Windcliffe, Julia's got her hypno-penlight out again and is asking Maggie who Sarah Collins is. She brings up the crypt and asks Miss Evans if anyone wanted to hurt her there. The name Collins seems to make Maggie edgy.

Julia's paying a visit to Woodard's house and he bitches at her about bringing Maggie along. She wants him to introduce her to the Collins family, as a historian/genealogist; ah, Hoffman's going undercover. Julia plays cagey and won't give him answers. He eventually agrees to introduce her to the family. They talk a bit more and, without saying the word, agree that Maggie's case involves the supernatural.

Julia's at Collinwood, where Vicki is apologizing for Liz's absence and gushing at the 'historian's' visit — you should talk to Barnabas! David comes in (for some reason, he looks younger) and is introduced to Julia and tells her that the house is full of books about the family. Vicki sends him up to do schoolwork. David's a bit bummed, because while he was out playing, he couldn't find Sarah. Julia asks if he means Sarah Collins and Vicki says no, just some neighborhood girl (they live on hundreds of acres of wooded estate on a freaking cliff — there is no neighborhood). David says he doesn't know the girl's last name and exits. Julia is very intrigued. Vicki suggests maybe Sarah is imaginary, then veers back to Barnabas and Old House talk. What, now Vicki says it's not good getting too close to the past? Oh, back to normal now, she mentions Josette's super-swanky bedroom. Julia asks if she can drop by the Old House that afternoon. Vicki oozes compliments for Barnabas (gag, but I think

Julia is suspicious of 'ole Barney).

Vicki has taken Julia to the Old House and they enter Josette's room (where the hell is Wil — oh, our man Loomis is mentioned and did his due diligence in trying to bar entrance). Blah, blah, party. Julia suddenly feels a chill; vapid Vicki doesn't. Uh-oh, Vicki notices that the sun went down. She says they should probably get a move on — then they sit down and discuss why Vicki felt she could show Josette's room, but not the rest of the house. Julia's ready to cut out, but Vicki *insists* she see the room by candlelight. The candle goes out and Julia again feels a chill. Vicki thinks Hoffman is afraid and Julia assures her that she's not afraid of anything (I'll buy that). Julia then cagily states she's looking forward to coming again and seeing Barnabas.

Julia is back at Woodard's. He wants to know if she suspects anyone at Collinwood. Nah. She asks if she can see Maggie before they head back to Windcliffe. Maggie comes in with the doll and Julia uses it to try to get info, under the guise of trying to find out the doll's name. She rattles off the names of Collins family members (clever). Poor Maggie has regressed again. When Julia mentions Barnabas, Maggie loses it completely, begging not to be hurt (Julia's a sly one and knows Barnabas is responsible).

Episode #285 — Guess who's listening to that goddamn music box? Carolyn knocks on Vicki's bedroom door and Miss Winters is so enraptured by the tune, she doesn't hear. Vicki tells Carolyn that she was thinking about Maggie and how she saw her. Miss Stoddard reminds her that Miss Evans is dead. Blah, blah, cemetery/Josette's birthday. Carolyn says the séance is still having an effect on her and Vicki becomes perturbed at the mention of how strange she's been acting lately. Carolyn then says Burke's been downstairs for a half an hour. Why, Vicki just clean forgot that their date had been fixed in advance for some time. Now, she doesn't want to go. Carolyn asks about the ~~torture device~~ music box and gets the (unnecessary) scoop. Torment briefly ensues. Carolyn heads back downstairs after extracting a promise from Vicki to stop listening to the damn thing. As soon as she's gone, guess what happens?

In the drawing room, Burke and Barnabas are talking party when Carolyn strolls in. Barnabas has brought a rare, old book for Vicki. Burke isn't happy and he and Carolyn tell Barnabas that Vicki is too involved in the past, even visiting Josette's grave. Barney is pleased as punch to hear it. Much like me, however, Burke thinks it's irritating and retarded. NewBurke starts complaining about the party and the costumes, telling Barnabas that Vicki's starting to see things — the little girl and Maggie. Mr. Collins gets a little nervous upon hearing the latter's name. Vicki is now magically in the drawing room (commercial break!) and mentions Julia to Barnabas. He's not crazy about sharing the family history with an outsider. Vicki notices the book and asks to look at it; Barnabas reluctantly hands it over. When she notices it's inscribed to her, Burke confesses that he talked Barnabas out of giving it to her and she gets pissy (I'm really starting to hate her). Barnabas apologizes for stirring up discord and leaves. Burke announces he needs a drink. Petulant Vicki doesn't want to go out now. They argue and I'm wholly on NewBurke's side; Vicki can stuff it. Burke leaves the bitch clutching her precious new gift.

A storm is rolling in fast and Vicki deemed it imperative to go to the Old House to apologize for Carolyn, Burke and her own behavior about the book (right, that's just an excuse to see him). Blah, blah, history/Hoffman. Vicki's about to leave, but — gosh! — that storm is too close. Barnabas offers to send Willie to Collinwood to tell them Vicki's at the Old House (oh, so *she* can't go out in the storm, but you can risk Willie getting struck by lightening while walking through the woods). Retaining some sensibility, Vicki says not to send Willie out, she'll just have to stay the night. Barnabas starts waxing Gothically poetic about the house during storms. Oh, she can stay in Josette's room, evil Barnabas suggests.

Episode #286 — Redo of stay the night talk, with predator-creeper Barnabas looking ready to pounce. Vicki's thrilled to sleep in Josette's room and Barney fuels her obsession with flattery. Lots of boring Josette talk. Dumbass Vicki asks who was chasing Josette in the story he told, because her memory sucks. He says it was her lover, Jeremiah. Vicki's confused (join the club, the writers play fast and oh-so-loose with continuity). Barnabas babbles in third person about loving Josette and the forlorn, sympathetic thing isn't working for me. As Vicki is about to head upstairs, Barnabas says the storm seems to be letting up, she can go back to Collinwood. Looking out the window proves otherwise. Barnabas seems conflicted, but I don't care.

Vicki goes to the bedroom and lights a candle. She lights another one, sniffs Josette's perfume bottle, then blows out both candles a minute later (filler) and settles onto the bed.

Willie comes into the parlor and asks if anyone was in the house, as he found something out of place. He produces a very old ball, but says the homestead was locked all day. Oh, yeah, he found it in the basement, near the coffin. Barnabas threatens Willie if he let David in. Loomis mentions Sarah and how Maggie had said she'd seen a little girl, though he didn't believe her at the time.

Barnabas decides to go check the basement himself and as he's leaving, Willie tells him he feels like someone else is in the house with them.

Upstairs, sleeping Vicki is woken to the sound of Sarah singing her favorite tune, but there's no sign of the petite chanteuse. Vicki goes downstairs, surprising Willie, who inquires what the hell she's doing there. She explains and says she'll be bunking in Josette's room. Our Willie doesn't think that's a good idea and offers to escort her back to Collinwood, no trouble at all. No, she wants to stay. Willie tells her she's making a mistake, just as Barnabas comes along and wants to know of what Willie speaks. Our man Loomis says if Vicki stays the night, people will talk. The two pooh-pooh the idea and Barnabas threatens to 'reward' Willie for his offer to take Vicki home. Miss Winters then explains about the singing, Barnabas says she imagined it and Willie observes all from the stairs. Vicki decides to go back to bed and gives Loomis the snottiest, bitchiest look as she passes. Willie asks Barnabas who the little girl is and is told no one. Barnabas then asks if Willie was trying to warn Vicki. Our Mr. Loomis says, yeah, kill me, I don't give a damn. Barnabas threatens, Willie asks if he's going to be killed and the pussy backs down because he's an ineffectual villain. Barnabas says he won't punish him and asks Willie to stick around and talk to him. Barnabas is worked up about something and becomes more so when Willie pegs him with the truth; he likes Vicki and doesn't really want to hurt her (Willie is starting to come across as the smartest person on the estate). Barnabas tells him to go to bed, then quickly mounts the stairs.

Barnabas enters Josette's room and approaches the sleeping Vicki, gazing down at her with longing.

Episode #287 — It's a vampire creep-up redo. After casting a quick glance at Josette's portrait, Barnabas goes in for a bite, but stops. Looking pained, he backs out of the room, foregoing his sanguinary repast.

The next morning, Vicki comes downstairs, and meets Willie who, among his other talents is also a five star chef, offers her breakfast. Good heavens, no, she's got to get back to Collinwood. Worried Willie asks her how she slept. Splendidly, she replies, then mentions at one point she thought someone was in the room with her — but, oh, it was just a dream. Taking a concerned glance up the stairs, Willie offers a "sure, a dream" response and Vicki immediately accuses him. Our man Loomis rightfully gets upset (because he's not the faux five skeeve version of Willie) and points out that he even offered to take her home. He adds that he would never hurt her and doesn't want anyone else to. She says she believes him (but doesn't seem sincere), then says she felt super safe in Josette's room (this dolt).

Julia's at Collinwood, talking to Liz in the drawing room. Liz is upset, thinking the maniac got Vicki — who just happens to walk in and offers an explanation for her absence (shacking up with two guys). Julia listens with great interest. A bit later, Liz tells Julia she's too busy to help her with her research. Julia says the public is fascinated by the family (are they Maine's supernatural version of the Kennedys?), so allow her to write her book. Vicki advocates for Hoffman and Julia assures Liz the current family isn't the subject of her book. Vicki relays that Barnabas isn't interested in helping either. Liz says her decision is final and leaves the room. Julia appeals to Vicki to convince Liz and, a bit later, Vicki is doing just that and man, I am sick of her slavering about the past. So is Liz, who tells her that she's too romantic about yesteryear and that some cold objectivity may show her the opposite is true. Liz gives the okay for Miss Hoffman to do her research.

Julia's at the Old House, annoying Willie who's trying to kick her out. She pays him no mind and asks about the restoration; what were Barnabas' references? (oh, she's on to him). Taking a seat, she decides to wait for the master of the house. Willie, nervous as a cat, paces; Julia's cool as a cucumber. Barnabas then is just sort of there and tells her he hopes Willie wasn't rude. He let's Willie leave the room and Julia starts talking about her project. He's not interested in helping and won't give a reason (he has no idea who he's dealing with). Julia says she may have some *very* interesting info on the family. He thinks she's fishing, or knows something minor. Sly Julia gives a great, knowing reply and ambles out, leaving Barnabas looking worried.

Episode #288 — Music box torture, courtesy of Vicki's mind. Vicki's spacing out, looking out the drawing room window, when David comes in. He finally gets her attention and tells her she's been flaking out a lot lately and seems like she's somebody else, which scares him. She tries telling him it's his imagination. Julia wanders in and Vicki tells David she'll be staying at the house to research the family (is she really staying, or is this like Guthrie? And who the hell is treating Maggie, or is she just being pumped full of diazepam?). Vicki goes off to get some privately printed histories and David pulls out the portrait album and starts naming ancestors. Julia mentions Sarah, who David's never heard of. Seeing the portrait, he says she looks just like the kid he plays with at the Old House and, get this, *her* name is Sarah, too. Crazy, ain't it? David then reminds us he's a bright kid by asking Julia if she thinks Sarah is a ghost. Vicki comes back in and gives David some recess time. Julia shows Vicki the picture of Sarah and the governess says she looks like the sketch of a girl the police were showing around after Maggie disappeared. Julia then switches gears to restoration talk. She says she saw a drawing of the Old House and the place was filled with gilt mirrors; funny how there aren't any there now. Vicki says the only mirror is in Josette's bedroom. Julia would like to show the portrait album to Barnabas (doesn't he already have one that he defaced?).

At the Blue Whale, Vicki is telling Burke about Julia and her research. Burke doesn't like and it's too involved in the past rehash. She tells him about the little girl singing and gets around to mentioning that she stayed the night in Josette's room. Burke is *far* from happy and wants her to promise to never go there again. Of course, she refuses and he wants to know what the fuck is the attraction to that house? She says she feels safe and secure, like she belongs there and she won't stop going (just dump her, Burke).

Another storm is rolling in and Julia shows up at the Old House, lugging that family album. Barnabas tries to give her the brush-off, but she's persistent. He finally lets her in. She shows him a picture or two (which he's already fucking seen!) and chatters about whoever. Barnabas takes the book and looks through it, his back to her. Julia, continuing the conversation, fishes her compact from her handbag. Gasp! Barnabas casts no reflection in the mirror. He finally turns around and asks what she's doing. Oh, nothing, just a little feminine vanity, checking the make-up is all. He hands the book back and she departs. Barnabas looks both angry and concerned.

Julia arrives back at Collinwood and meets Vicki in the foyer and tells our little governess that she thinks she's found out everything she needs to know.

Episode #289 — Night. As a storm rolls in, Vicki's looking out her bedroom window. Unable to sleep, she starts playing the music box. Carolyn, also awake, stops by to chat. Vicki's back at the window, saying someone's lurking behind a tree (guess who?). The ladies decide to hit the hay and Carolyn goes back to her room. Vicki gets in bed and tortures us for a spell with that fucking music box. For a moment, she nervously glances at the window. Some time passes and Barnabas, bone-dry despite the storm, is in her room. He creeps up, about to strike, then stops. Rather than attack her (and because I'm convinced by now the writers hate us), he opens the magical music box that *never* needs winding and backs away. Vicki wakes and the interloper is gone, naturally. Alarmed, she closes the box, sparing us any further torment. She tries turning on the bedside lamp, but it doesn't work. Carolyn shows up, bearing a candle, and announces a power failure. Blah, blah, music box was playing/Vicki's confused. Miss Winters says she thinks 'something' was in the room.

The two gals head downstairs for some java, with Vicki toting that damn music box like a four year old with a security blanket. They find Julia reading in the drawing room, who tells them that Mrs. Johnson is already brewing up the joe. Carolyn goes to check on its progress. Julia asks Vicki her impression of Josette. She liked parties — and fine clothing! Blah, blah, Barnabas/history and Vicki shows off the music box and, you guessed it, plays it. Vicki inadvertently proves useful by saying she likes the tinkling quality, which interests Miss Hoffman. Vicki just *loves* the melody — she plays it over and over again. She goes on to say that Barnabas let her wear some of Josette's jasmine perfume for the party. Julia's piecing things together and asks Vicki if it doesn't seem like 'ole Barney is trying to re-create Josette. No, our governess snaps, that's just *absurd*. Supremely butthurt, she dashes out, just as Carolyn brings in the coffee. Carolyn explains about Vicki waking up to the music box playing and being convinced someone was in the room (I'm surprised she didn't try blaming Willie again). The power is restored and Carolyn decides to turn off any lights before going to bed. Julia grabs her coat and heads out of the house, storm be damned.

Willie enters the parlor and Barnabas, staring out the window, whines about the coming dawn. He instructs Willie to return as quickly as possible from tomorrow's errand in Bangor, as he wants him to watch the house; he doesn't want that Hoffman woman around. Julia conveniently eavesdrops through the front door (which is apparently constructed of materials as inferior as the windows). Barnabas sends Willie off on the errand and heads to the basement. Outside, from behind a clump of trees, Julia (also not wet from the rain) watches Loomis depart. The sun rises and Julia, unable to get in through the locked door, climbs in through the parlor window (and that ended *so well* for Jason). Julia goes down to the basement and finds the coffin. She approaches and, as casually as opening a linen closet, lifts the lid to find the slumbering Barnabas. (I wonder how Julia and Guthrie would of gotten along?)

Episode #290 — Coffin opening re-do (is Barnabas wearing a different suit?). What I presume is later in the day, Woodard is in the Collinwood drawing room bitching at Julia over the usual. He announces that he's removing Maggie from her care as she's not treating her. Blah, blah, they argue about the same stuff and Woodard's a real pain in the ass. Julia tells him she's making no progress, perhaps she was wrong (she's lying). Woodard finally gets suspicous and Julia says she's bored with it all. He agrees to let Maggie stay where she is. They hear someone knocking on the front door and agree not to meet at the house anymore. Walking into the foyer, they meet up with Vicki who opens the door to allow Barnabas entrance. He's introduced to Julia's old college friend,

Dave Woodard, who takes his leave. Barnabas wants to talk to Julia and she heads toward the kitchen to get her notebook. While waiting, Barnabas asks Vicki how she likes Julia's work so far. Vicki complains of sometimes losing her grasp of the present and fears she may get stuck in the past! (now she cares?). She wants to return the music box, it's screwing with her head. Oh, no, she *must* keep it, he insists (where the hell did Julia leave her notebook? Did she stop to use the bathroom, make a sandwich?). Barnabas tries to convince Vicki to keep the music box (and Jonathan Frid is understandably thrown off his game by some offscreen noise that's either hammering or a fire extinguisher).

A little later, Barnabas and Julia are alone in the drawing room. He apologizes for his gruff manner before. She wants info on ancestor Barnabas and Sarah. He doesn't want to discuss. Julia employs some slychology. She plays games and puts Barnabas on defense (this is great). He suggests they meet at the Old House tomorrow to discuss things further. Julia suggests a morning meeting, but he can't make it. Afternoon? No, inconvenient. She assures him she understands *completely*. Walking into the foyer, she comments on the first Barnabas portrait and more entertaining cat-and-mouse ensues.

That night, Julia is readying for bed when Vicki comes by (guess Julia really is staying at Collinwood). The governess is confused! Blah, blah, if she keeps working with Julia, she'll get lost in the past! A dog starts howling and Vicki gets antsy, as she heard one the night Maggie disappeared. Julia sends Vicki off to bed because she doesn't really give a crap about whatever's bugging her. A little over an hour later, Barnabas is in Julia's room. He stealthily approaches the bed, hands outstretched, prepared to strangle — when Julia, from a chair in another part of the bedroom, greets him, saying she's been waiting for him for a very long time. Color Barnabas surprised.

Episode #291 — Redo, then Julia tells Barnabas she knows what he is; the original Barnabas Collins (wouldn't that be *who* he is?) and that she saw him in his coffin. He retorts that's bad news for her and she replies, yes, that's why she put a dummy in the bed (she carries one around, just in case?). He advances, corners her and threatens — to kill her! She tells him she's a doctor. He must not think much of the medical profession, because he starts throttling her. She manages to croak out that she can help him and he releases her, though he's skeptical. Julia massages her throat while they talk. She's always been fascinated in the threshold between life and death (oh, like Chillingworth in *Varney*, if I recall). She prattles scientific medical stuff and Barnabas admits to being intrigued.

Julia and Barnabas have gone to the Old House to continue their conversation. He asks her who at Collinwood knows she's a doctor; no one. He asks who else and she cops to Woodard knowing, but that's it (hey, Sam and Joe do). Willie comes in (when the hell does this man sleep?) and Barnabas tells him about Dr. Hoffman and that she'll be spending a lot of time there as she's going to try to cure him. He instructs Willie to take her to the basement so she can chose a room for a lab.

Sam's at the hospital with Joe, waiting for Woodard (what time is it?). Woodard comes along and Sam wants the skinny on Julia; she's at Collinwood, what gives? A lot of talk to say nothing, although logical Joe asks logical questions. At least Woodard says the answer to Maggie's issues could be hours — or years — away. Sam issues a threat to expose everything and storms off, with Joe following.

Barnabas is in the parlor, wringing his hands. He's joined by Willie, who tells him Julia's picked out a room, then asks if she can be trusted. Barnabas doesn't know and decides — to kill her! Willie steers the conversation to her talk of a cure. Barnabas asks Willie if he thinks things will change for him if she's successful; well, he'll never be free of him! (Willie has defied Barnabas, so take that declaration with a grain of salt). Barnabas tries to be evil villain, but is steered, *yet again*, by our man Loomis into the opposite direction and man, 'ole Barney flip-flops like a pandering politician. Nah, he decides to kill her. Julia joins them, with a list of medical supplies she needs from Bangor. Barnabas hands it off to Willie and Julia says the room needs to be sanitized (right, cause a musty, moldy, mildewy basement is the *ideal* place to do medical experiments). Barnabas tells Willie to get scrubbin' and as Willie passes her, he makes some serious eye contact, that does not go unnoticed by her. Once Willie's gone, Julia comments on the strange look and Barnabas just chalks it up to Loomis being a strange man. Julia grabs her coat, intending to head out, but Barnabas won't let her leave, as he can't trust her. Julia fast talks, saying that if she dies, the truth will come out about him. He starts throttling her again, asking who will tell, and she manages to say Maggie Evans. He loosens his grasp and she goes on to say that Maggie is hidden away, but suffering from amnesia. If she (Julia) stays alive, she can protect him by making sure the amnesia is permanent (that's a mark against her character, as it shows her to be ambitious and self-serving. What happened to the hippocratic oath; first do no harm?)

Episode #292 — Day and Woodard shows up at Collinwood. Julia answers and he wants to know what the hell she's doing there? He threatens to take

100

Maggie out of Windcliffe, unless Julia spills to his satisfaction. Blah, blah, Maggie/treatment, bicker and bitch, Sam and Joe are fed up. Julia admits that she thinks Maggie came into contact with the supernatural, which traumatized her. Woodard is incredulous. Julia appeals to his old med school desire to make some great medical discovery, but she won't give him details of her plans (it's all pretty dry and boring).

Out in the woods, Sarah's crying as David comes along. She says she's lost something and he offers to help her look for it. She tells him she lost her friend, Maggie. David breaks it to her that she's dead. Sarah just giggles, saying she's not dead, she's just lost. She knows she's gone away somewhere and *almost* knows where, but it slips away. David invites her to come play at Collinwood. They go back to Maggie talk, with Sarah emphatically saying she knows who's dead and who's not.

Julia answers the door at Collinwood and meets Burke and a lot of boring conversation ensues about her researching the family. Milquetoast NewBurke tries grilling her, but it doesn't come off, as he's not the bellowing, blustering Burke of days gone by. He tells her she doesn't seem the genealogy type. Vicki comes dashing into the house, bursting with excitement; she's found a house that she's absolutely fallen in love with. Retiring to the drawing room, Vicki explains the house is very old and isolated, right by the sea. She's enamored and Burke expresses interest in seeing it. Vicki states that she belongs there. Meanwhile, David and Sarah enter the house, with the lad intending to invite his new playmate to dinner. Vicki hears him in the foyer and the adults join him. Sarah, however, is nowhere to be found. David explains having found her in the woods and bringing her home. He also mentions her 'Maggie isn't dead' comment, of which Julia is very interested. Vicki and Burke tell David that Sarah is imaginary. The boy stands, with arms crossed, not buying a word of it (what do grown-ups know?), then dashes upstairs (stick to your guns, Davey, I'm with you!). Hoffman tells Vicki not to encourage David's imagination. Burke then announces he's feeling peckish and offers to take Vicki out for a knosh. As she goes to get her coat, Vicki finds Sarah's bonnet on the floor.

Episode #293 — Barnabas has just woken up. Willie comes down to the basement and informs him that Julia was there earlier, setting up, and will be back later to talk to him. Oh, what a shame, as Master Collins is going up to the main house. Willie wants to know why. Barnabas insults and (hollowly) threatens him, then walks out. Upstairs in the hall, Willie, like a tenacious terrier, accuses Barnabas of going to see Vicki. Oh, Barnabas enjoys her charming company. Willie tells him to leave her the fuck alone. Barnabas insults him.

Shrewd Loomis knows Barnabas is up to no good and says so. The undead predator tries to talk all gentleman-like. Willie thinks he's full of excrement. The talk turns to alive Maggie and Willie wonders if Julia can deliver. Barney gives him orders to keep an eye on her. The topic swerves back to Vicki and Barnabas insults Willie, yet again (keep it up, asshole, it looks like our man Loomis is keeping a mental tally). Walking out the door, Barnabas waxes poetic on eternal youth and life and Willie tosses off a great truth about the loneliness it entails. Barnabas' response is to close the door and run away.

Burke and Vicki are in the drawing room, with vapid Vicki staring out at nothing. They talk her dream house and we learn she trespassed (there's that moral relativism again). She starts babbling filler that's too boring to repeat. Burke suggests they check out the house that evening. Vicki doesn't want to, as she'd be leaving David alone. Barnabas arrives and Burke tells him that they're on their way out, too bad. More blah, blah, house/filler (apart from Willie, this episode is dull as dirt. Burke's okay, too). Barnabas horns in on the plans and Burke tosses off a great sarcastic comment. Vicki suggests they visit the house the next day, with David, and have a picnic. The nightwalker is, of course, full of excuses. Vicki decides they'll go that night, the hell with leaving David alone (my guess is at least Mrs. Johnson is there). Vicki wants to check in on her charge and change into something warmer and goes upstairs. The men wait in the drawing room and, quite frankly, boring conversation ensues. Barnabas tries to be all smooth gentleman and NewBurke is doing well with the sarcasm. Barney says that no one seems to know Burke (really? Talk to Sam and Roger) or where he traveled to become a success (again, writer fail bullshit; the original Burke episodes have this information; in one episode, Burke talked about washing glasses in some dive in Mexico or South America). Anyway, Barney is trying to get the upper hand, but Burke throws the same lines right back at him — no one knows *him* (yep, I'm pulling for NewBurke in this round. Lately, Barnabas seems to be picking the wrong people to try and screw with). Burke manages to get out of an uncomfortable Barnabas that he lived in London with a cousin, but nothing more. Vicki comes in, finally, and Barnabas oozes compliments in that sickeningly affected way.

Episode #294 — Windcliffe and normal sounding Maggie is at the barred window of her room, saying she wants to go home. Sarah is suddenly in the room and apologizes that it took her so long to find her, but, now that she has, she's going to help her get home. After receiving info from Maggie about the nurse having the key to the room, Sarah hatches the escape plan. The patient has second thoughts about leaving, as she's safe there. Pshaw — Sarah assures she'll keep her safe. She picks up her doll and hands it to Maggie, then tells her to call for the nurse. The nurse, Miss Jackson, unlocks the door to find Sarah sitting on the bed, singing her favorite tune. Maggie sneaks out and closes the automatically locking door. Miss Jackson tries the door and, turning around, finds Sarah's gone, too.

Burke, Barnabas and Vicki are outside the dream house. They break in and look around, having conveniently brought some candles (the room looks suspiciously like Roger's office, which we never see anymore — and where is Roger?). Burke thinks they should come back the next day. Oh, no, Barney protests, this house is meant to be seen at night (oh, brother). Lots of boring filler, then Barnabas decides to go to the attic to look for something from the past 'cause, ya know, mind rape.

Maggie and Sarah are walking in the woods. Maggie's afraid, but Sarah again tells her she'll take care of her and get her home. Maggie asks how she got into the hospital room and Sarah gives a vague answer that makes Maggie laugh. They continue on their way, singing *London Bridge*.

At the house, Burke thinks it's time to leave. They call for Barnabas, but get no answer. More filler, they argue about Barnabas and Burke suggests ditching him. I laugh, but Vicki's not amused. Barney finally rejoins them and hands Vicki a pristine, monogramed, lace handkerchief he found upstairs (in reality that thing would be musty, moldy and mildewy as hell).

The trio enter the Blue Whale. Barnabas heads to the bar to order, while Burke and Vicki take a table. They talk house, then Vicki starts in about sharing an interest in the past with Barnabas. Bob finally delivers the drinks and Barnabas joins them and starts with the charm crap again. They drink to the house. Vicki glances at the door as Maggie, doll in hand, walks in, looking confused. Everyone stops and stares, amazed, except for Barnabas, who keeps turning his face from her. As Maggie walks past him, she faints.

Houses, Hypnosis and Hubris

Episode #295 — Ready for this? The first color episode! (and it's a bit jarring). It's a redo of Maggie's return at the Blue Whale. Burke has, presumably, picked Maggie up and is propping her unconscious self on a chair, while Vicki tries talking to her. Barnabas, butthurt, declares that a hoax has been perpetrated on them. Maggie comes to, unsure if she remembers Vicki. She vaguely recognizes her surroundings and asks where the little girl is. Barnabas offers to look outside (anything to get away, right?). Blah, blah, hospital/little girl. Barnabas comes back in, looking nervous. *Lots* of boring rehash as Maggie tries to remember. Burke finally gets the bright idea to take the woman to the doctor and Barnabas offers to tell Sam his daughter has returned. Glancing at him, Maggie vaguely recalls her captor.

Vicki, Maggie and Burke are at Woodard's office and he pushes a sedative (I think). Blah, blah, memory issues, but it's starting to return. Woodard is very optimistic. Burke wants a word alone, so he and Woodard go into the hall and Burke lays into him for knowing Maggie wasn't dead. Hash is reheated, with Woodard hoping the kidnapper doesn't get to her again before she can identify him. Meanwhile, Maggie and Vicki talk memory, with Vicki being very supportive. Maggie recalls a room with music and a scent.

At Collinwood, Julia answers the door to find Barnabas, who wants to talk. He accuses her of betrayal and informs her that Maggie's back and with Woodard. Julia asks about her memory. Barnabas says it's returning and threatens to kill both of them, starting with her, and Julia is literally saved by the bell as the phone rings. It's Woodard, who reports about Maggie. Julia gives instructions that no one should question her and she's on her way. Hanging up, Hoffman arrogantly proclaims that when she's done with her, Maggie will *never* remember.

Woodard tells Maggie that Dr. Hoffman's coming. She starts remembering her house, Sam and the Old House. Woodard wants to give her another sedative. It's non-suspenseful suspense as Maggie recalls fragments, but not Barnabas as her kidnapper proper and it's all so freaking tedious. Julia walks in just as she starts shouting she knows the face of the man who held her captive! Blah, blah (isn't this episode over yet? The repetition is numbing). Julia boots Woodard from his own office and asks Maggie what she remembers. Turns out, all of it and she names Barnabas Collins as the psycho perv who kidnapped her and that he's not human. Instead of a penlight, Julia is wearing a hypno-medallion, which she immediately puts to use. A little later, Julia has Woodard step in. The patient is just great, she remembers everything — except for the last sixty-eight episodes.

Episode #296 — From color to b&w kinescope. Woodard's confused that Maggie doesn't remember anything and tells her she's lost weeks. Maggie doesn't even recognize Julia (huh, seems Hoffman's better at memory wiping than 'ole Barney). The two doctors tell her she'd been kidnapped and put in a sanitarium once found because her mind was slightly scrambled and they let people think she was dead (how is any of this good for her already fragile mental health?). Sam rushes in, elated to see her. More bullshit memory talk. The doctors step out to the hall and Woodard tells Julia he's confused! Crafty Julia looks crafty and her colleague's growing suspicious.

Meanwhile, smoking Sam is asking his daughter to remember (at this point, *I'd* like to forget). She remembers having a dream and someone in her room, then announces she's tired and just wants to go home. Sam opens the office door and asks Woodard if they can bail. Woodard says, sure, and advises having the sheriff post men around the house (really?). Julia then says she'll make arrangements for Maggie to head back to the nuthouse in the morning. All the others argue against it. Julia finally backs down, but impresses upon the patient that no one must know she's a doctor; around others, she's just a writer. Sam and Maggie finally leave and Julia says something cryptic.

Maggie's back at home in her room. Upon opening the French doors, she panics, seeing a man outside. Sam assures her it's just a cop standing guard. Someone knocks on the front door; it's Joe. Maggie recognizes him and they have a tender reunion. Unfortunately, memory/kidnap/crazy house talk ruins the moment.

At the Old House, a worried looking Barnabas is pacing the parlor. Julia shows up and haughtily strolls in. She tells him that she's hypnotized Maggie; she remembers nothing because she got to her before she could talk. Julia then warns him not to hurt the girl. He asks, fairly, I think, what happens if the hypnosis wears off or fails. Lighting a cigarette off a candle, Julia insists it won't fail. She also says she'll expose him if he harms Maggie, so he has to cooperate. She leaves. The cock crows and Barnabas pronounces he'll be snuffing Maggie out tomorrow night.

A howling dog wakes Maggie, who finds Sarah's doll on the bedside table, which wasn't there before (that I recall). Comforted, she goes back to sleep.

Episode #297 — Joe wakes from a doze on the Evans' living room sofa. Sam comes in with coffee and blah, blah, Maggie/kidnapper. Sam thinks maybe they should move, an idea that Joe doesn't care for much, but understands. Cheery Maggie comes in and seems totally back to normal, in fact, she wants her job back at the coffee shop (we haven't seen that set since she passed out there and I doubt we ever will again). Sam says that's a no-go (and Joe has very nice blue eyes) and it's the usual kidnapper talk (boring).

Later, dressed Maggie is in her room, French doors open. She settles down with a book and Sarah appears just inside the threshold of the open doors. Maggie notices her and invites her in (hey, Maggie's phone is back, only now it's on the right side of the bed). Maggie doesn't remember Sarah, but agrees to play ball with her and sing *London Bridge* (kill me!). Sarah fills in that she used to come and visit Maggie, but is hurt that Maggie has forgotten her, like everyone else. She takes her doll back and, crying, leaves via the French doors (without being told, we know Sarah is the ghost of Barnabas' sister by now and I like how the writers try to explain the confusion a ghost-child might face).

That evening, Maggie's in the living room, looking at the sketch of Sarah. Sam asks her for a critique of a landscape (my verdict: it's nice, I like it). She asks him about the girl in the sketch and Sam says he doesn't have a clue. Maggie would very much like to find her, then goes to her room. Barnabas shows up, asking after Maggie and fishes as to whether she remembers anything. Nope, but we already freaking know that. He asks to see her and happy, cheerful, polite Maggie joins them. Sam needs to deliver a painting and leaves his only daughter in the care of a predator. Blah, blah, rehash, with Barnabas looking sinister, but sounding refined. This tedium is killing me. Barney fishes some more. Maggie relays the visit of the strange little girl. She describes her, tells how she claimed to visit her when she was missing and when she reveals the girl's name, Barnabas looks like he has a sudden case of acid reflux.

Later that night, Barnabas enters Maggie's bedroom through the unlocked French doors (the hell? And where's the deputy that's supposed to be guarding the house?). He approaches the sleeping Maggie and picks up a throw pillow from a chair, intent on smothering her. He's halted in his plan by the sound of Sarah singing. He backs out of the room, asking the ceiling, in a stage whisper, what she wants of him (there is some fantastic Grand Guignol style lighting in this scene. I hope we see more of it in future).

Episode #298 — Morning at Collinwood. Carolyn drifts downstairs to the drawing room, seemingly bothered by something. Liz comes in, looking for Vicki, who's gone into town to visit Maggie (and Liz looks lovely in color, although maybe being free of rat-fink McGuire has something to do with it; she looks less stern and her youthful hair bow is color coordinated to her outfit). Blah, blah, good news about Maggie (first time seeing the drawing room in color; the sofa is a mossy green velvet). Carolyn says she has a feeling something bad is going to happen soon. Burke shows up, wanting to talk to Liz about ~~Barbie's~~ Vicki's dream house, which is called Seaview. Liz goes to get the keys and the deed, while Carolyn invites him into the drawing room. Blah, blah, house. Liz comes back and says the deed has been marked 'not for sale,' but doesn't understand why. Oh, well, they'll sort it out.

The three go to the house (yep, it's Roger's/Frank's old office sets). Carolyn gets a positive vibe off the place and goes to look upstairs. Burke wants to know the price, like yesterday. Liz says he doesn't seem the house-buying kind, but she knows the reason (as does her daughter; Burke's thinking marriage). Carolyn rejoins them, saying the upstairs is just as nice as down. Liz admits to not liking the house much, as there's a coldness to it.

Over at the Evans cottage, warmed over hash is on the menu and it's awful. Vicki tells Maggie that she saw her at the cemetery with someone when everyone thought she was dead. She mentions Josette Collins and Maggie comes over funny, as if the name's familiar; she knows it means something! Maggie then remembers seeing a coffin and — someone knocks on the door. Vicki answers; it's Julia come to see Sam for research on her book (so she says). Don't mind her, Ms. Hoffman says, she'll just browse the paintings while she waits. Vicki resumes her attempt to help Maggie remember by saying Josette was a super special lady and Barnabas restored her bedroom (because he's a psycho who can't let go). Maggie's on the recall train and Julia whips out her handy hypno-medallion and interrupts. Look at the heirloom her grandmother handed down, ain't it grand? Hey, can she have a cup of tea? Vicki offers to make the tea, allowing Julia to conveniently hypnotize Maggie and reinforce the amnesia. Mesmerism over in record time, Vicki returns with two cups of requested beverage (also brewed in record time). Vicki asks Maggie what she was remembering and Maggie doesn't remember (the writers need to wrap this up, it's long since worn out its welcome).

Episode #299 — Night. Vicki's on the terrace, wearing an ugly, shapeless and sleeveless orange dress that does nothing for her. Barnabas creeps up and touches her neck (like pervy faux five Willie) and startles her. Blah, blah, it's a beautiful night, night and moonlight are beautiful (boring). Barnabas says he's found more family histories in a trunk and invites her to the Old House. Gee, sorry, she's got a date. Tomorrow? Sorry, her calendar's full and Barnabas is crushed that she's so interested in Burke. Julia steps out for a bit of air and Miss Winters excuses herself and thanks Barnabas for the invite. Once she's gone, Julia reminds him that he promised to leave Vicki alone (did he? Like Maggie, I don't recall). Blah, blah, experiment/agreement. Barnabas insists he and Vicki are just friends (oh, come on). Julia tells him that Vicki is in love with Burke. Impossible, aggrieved Barnabas sputters, such a delicate flower couldn't possibly care for a vulgarian like Burke Devlin. He leaves and Julia thoughtfully lights a cigarette.

In her room, Vicki can't decide between a pink print or powder blue dress for her date. Julia comes along and Vicki asks her thoughts. Julia likes the blue (me, too), so blue it is. Julia then brings up the Barnabas invitation and advises Vicki against going. As Vicki is a bit dense, Julia has to explain that Barney has the hots for her. No, that can't be! Julia says since he's such a sensitive type (spare me), he's easily hurt (I'm gagging), so it would be best if she stayed away from him.

Later, in her powder blue dress, Vicki and Burke are in the garden off the terrace, next to a rather noisy water fountain. Devlin tells some story about his dad that breaks with canon (he abandoned the family; but OldBurke said it was just him and his dad against the world). Vicki tells an orphanage story (at least that's consistent with the character). Burke asks Vicki if she knows how he feels about her and she gets all coy and virginally blushing ingenue. Why, yes, she does. He asks how she feels about him. She stammers, he says she doesn't have to say anything (why can't they say 'I love you?' It's not a crime or censorable words for Christ's sake). Anyway, they kiss, rather awkwardly, and milquetoast NewBurke says he's wanted to do that for a long time (uh, but you did, when you were OldBurke, episode #114. In fact, Vicki used to visit your tacky motel room quite often — another set long gone. Why have the writers watered down these characters?) Ewww, peeper-creeper Barnabas is spying on them from nearby. Freak.

Now Burke and Vicki are making out in the foyer, right in front of the old Barnabas portrait, which I find highly amusing. Julia, attired in nightgown and robe walks in, interrupting them. Vicki goes up to bed and Burke wants to talk to Julia about her book. The two head to the drawing room and he bitches at her about Vicki helping with the research. Vicki has an active imagination, she's 'seeing' things. To his surprise, Julia agrees with him that Vicki should stop assisting her and will make sure she stays out of it. Happy Burke leaves at one a.m.

Two hours later, freak Barnabas skulks down the hall and into Vicki's room (how did he get into the house? He didn't just 'appear' — he walked down the hall and went in via the door). He wusses out on biting her and — *NOOOO!* — opens that damn music box, which we've been spared the last ten episodes.

Episode #300 — B&W kinescope. Vicki's in the drawing room, waiting for Burke. Julia joins her, just as the sun is setting. Vicki tells her she's bothered by a dream she had the night before; someone was in her room, but she wasn't afraid. She then says she thinks someone actually *was* in her room because the music box was playing when she woke up that morning. Julia's suspicious and Vicki's frightened. Blah, blah, Julia convinces her she opened the box while she was half-asleep. Liz strolls in and asks about the book progress. Julia says she's off to see Barnabas and departs. Liz informs Vicki that Burke made an offer on Seaview.

At the Old House, Barnabas is up and in the parlor. He calls for Willie and asks him for an update — geez, he's got Willie staking out Collinwood to watch the comings and goings of Burke and Vicki. Pathetic. The stalker then tells Willie — get this — to follow the couple on their date and report back everything they say and do. Willie's like, the fuck? He can't get close enough to do that. Just do it, Barney barks. Astute Willie then accuses Barnabas of being afraid of losing Vicki to Burke. Nuh-uh, he's not afraid. Savvy Loomis tells him to wise the fuck up — she's in love with Devlin. Barnabas' response? A strangling, one-handed choke hold and issuance of a nasty-sounding, but ultimately hollow, threat about (ho-hum) killing Mr. Loomis. He then sends Willie out on his ridiculous task.

A bit later, Julia's at the Old House and tells Barnabas he's responding to the treatments. She checks his heart rate (he's dead, there shouldn't be one), which is normal (there shouldn't be one, he's dead). Blah, blah, Barnabas wonders what it would be like to be normal, no more loneliness, whatever. Julia then calls him out on going to Vicki's room. He lies at first, naturally, then says he was just there to look at her (nah, that's not perverted *at all*). Julia doesn't buy it, so they bicker and bitch. Julia lays down the law about leaving Vicki alone and 'ole Barney has to swallow his pride and agree. Obviously, neither trusts the other.

Burke and Vicki are on the terrace after their date, kissing and sweet-talking. Moving next to the too-loud, trickling water fountain, Burke tells her about his bid on the house and that he wants it to be *their* home. Surprisingly, she seems a bit put off. He finally says those three little words and proposes. She looks at him like he's the substitute postman, although she says she feels the same. She finally admits she loves him, but isn't sure about marrying because — David! The family! She needs time to think. Burke says okay, but he'll keep pestering her every day until she says yes. Oh, please — Vicki says she's searched all her life for her identity (a search that was promptly dropped after episode #95) and if she marries him, then she'll have one! More kissing and we discover that poor Willie has had to eavesdrop on all of this from nearby.

Barnabas is in the drawing room with Liz, asking if she's sold the house to Burke yet. The liar expresses interest in the house. Liz intimates that Burke is buying it with the intention of marrying Vicki. Affronted Barnabas says surely Miss Winters won't marry that troglodyte and Liz is like, why not? She doesn't object and Barnabas looks like a teenager after his prom invite has been rejected.

Willie returns to the Old House, looking for Barnabas, and obviously none-too-thrilled with the news he has to impart (this episode seems really long for some reason). Barnabas comes home and asks for the low down. Willie lays it on him and tells him to suck it up, she's marrying Burke. The arrogant a-hole says there'll be no wedding because…Burke Devlin must die!

Episode #301 — Old House and Willie and Barnabas are continuing their conversation and — wait, what? Now Loomis is saying Vicki might turn down the proposal and Barnabas is saying, no she'll marry him. I'm confused. Willie asks so what if she does? Since narcissist Barnabas always gets his way, Devlin has to die (btw, Willie looks good in both color and b&w). Willie applies his street-wise, common sense skills to talk Barnabas out of killing Burke. The dumbass Barnabas thinks offing Burke will be as easy as McGuire. Loomis reminds him that McGuire was different because nobody liked him, whereas Burke has roots in the town; his disappearance will garner more attention than Maggie's. When that happens, the law will come around and there's stuff in that basement he doesn't want found. In a moment that is worthy of celebrating with a libation, Willie has rendered Barnabas speechless (once again proving that Willie is perhaps the wisest goddamn person in town). Loomis advises patience. Barnabas finds his tongue and says okay, but when the time comes, Willie will have to help kill Devlin. Barnabas walks out and Willie breathes a sigh of relief (and ain't it somethin'? He saves *another* life and will get no credit for it. *Ever*).

Outside the front doors of Collinwood, Vicki and Burke make-out and Vicki promises to give him an answer soon. They go inside and meet Liz in the foyer. Vicki bids goodnight and goes upstairs, while Burke stays to talk with Liz in the drawing room. She tells him she's selling him the house. He's so thrilled, he pronounces their fighting days are over (oh, that happened when you replaced OldBurke). They have a drink and Liz toasts his happiness (remember when Liz was ready to fight to the death with OldBurke? Makes me nostalgic). Later on, after Burke's left, Vicki comes downstairs. Liz tells her about selling the house and decrees Burke is a changed man (no kidding, and unintentionally hilarious). Blah, blah, Liz knows Burke's in love with Vicki and Miss Winters eventually gets around to mentioning the proposal. But, she's confused! Help her decide! Liz points out she can't do that, marriage is an important decision (unless it's to a blackmailing, Irish piece of shit). All this is needless filler.

Burke's at the Blue Whale, yukking it up with Bob and an aged barfly. Barney steps in and Burke buys him a drink. Sitting at a table, they talk in circles, which is supposed to be clever, but in reality is just annoying. Ha, Burke then says that they always intimate, but never say what they really mean (didn't I just say that?). He then equates their acquaintance to a card game. Barnabas says, no, it's more like a duel. Burke says duels are pretty desperate life-and-death stuff, then turns the conversation to Barnabas and asks for the name of his cousin in London. Barnabas remembers the name, then, since Bob is closing for the night, scurries out like the ferret he is. Burke hits the payphone and asks for the overseas operator; he wants to make a call to London (and yes, that's how you used to make transatlantic calls back in the day).

In Search Of…

Episode #302 — Broody Barnabas, wearing a smashing silver and green dressing gown, is sitting in the parlor, looking through a family album. Julia comes
in from the lab and tells him his next treatment will be in twenty minutes. He
threatens her and she mentions that he's been looking through that album a lot.
He says he's been fascinated lately with the portrait of Jeremiah; Devlin looks
so much like him and he wants him as dead as Jeremiah (which album is he
looking at, because he tore out the picture before the party, in episode #280).
Julia reminds him no killing and he retorts that giving orders is unattractive in
a woman (this ass). Julia lets it roll off her back (I'm sure she's heard worse
from psychotic patients), calls him sensitive and says she thinks he's looking
through the book because of his sister. Poppycock! Julia believes his incessant
sturm und drang could jeopardize the experiment. Barnabas admits that spec-
tral Sarah has come back, as he heard her. Wily Julia asks where might he have
been when that occurred and badgers him until she gets the answer; Maggie's
(I'm a bit confused though; she mentions him going there to kill her, but he
never said that's why he was there. I guess Hoffman just surmised). Julia wants
to know why Sarah has such an effect on him. Barnabas wangsts about her innocence and purity and he loved her so much, ugh. Lots of blah, blah, about
why Sarah's come back and he wants to talk to her *so bad*. Yeah, well, time for
your injection, Julia announces.

At Collinwood, Liz comes into the drawing room, attired in deep blue velvet
loungewear that always looked black in b&w (I think the matching, youth-
making hair bows will be a constant). Vicki's there, waiting for Burke. Julia
comes home and Vicki goes off to meet Burke on the terrace. Julia asks Liz
what she knows about Sarah Collins, which is basically nothing. Liz asks for
more info on Julia's work. It's obvious by her questions that Dame Stoddard

has become a tad suspicious. Julia tries flattery in an attempt to change the subject. Liz, however, is hip to the jive and calls her out.

Burke meets Vicki on the terrace. He's late because he had business with — my God, Blair! (Remember cultured, soft-spoken James Blair? Good times.) The two start talking married life and Burke starts rattling off some of his personality traits as if he and Vicki are complete strangers. She asks what his business was with Blair and he doesn't really answer. She then says she knows nothing about Burke (same crap Barnabas spewed a while back, which is total bullshit). Devlin, thinking she's stalling, pops off at her. She takes a moment, reconsiders, then accepts his proposal.

Barnabas is in the drawing room with Liz and Julia, seeping with phony charm. The happy couple walk in and Vicki announces their engagement. The ladies immediately offer congratulations, but piqued Barnabas turns his back on everyone and pouts "Jeremiah!" which is heard by Burke. Vicki approaches him and the insolent one can barely make a positive comment. He then makes an excuse to leave with Julia and Liz comments on the change in his demeanor.

Out in the garden, Barnabas is whining about Vicki marrying Burke. Julia points out that she's in love. Since it's not with *him,* Barnabas doesn't believe it (as a shrink, Julia must be having a field day with this). He wants her to get moving on those experiments, because when they're finished, Vicki won't be marrying Burke (man, what a petulant, undead brat).

Episode #303 — Burke's at Woodard's and makes a call to Blair. Through the one-sided conversation, we find out that Barnabas' London cousin lived a hundred and thirty years ago. Hmm. Woodard joins Burke and Devlin wants to go over every aspect of Maggie's case. The doctor shoots down his request to read the files, patient confidentiality and all that. Burke says he has a hunch and asks about the neck wounds and I ask why are they rehashing stuff from two or three months ago? Woodard, without knowing what it is, urges Burke to go to the sheriff with his hunch, no matter how strange (need it be said that Devlin suspects Barnabas?). Already this episode is as painful as an abscessed tooth.

At the Evans cottage, Maggie mouths off to Joe; she's stir-crazy, I guess. God, now *they're* rehashing two to three month old stuff (Bob — a Stinger, stat!). Maggie wants to go back to work on the day shift, but Joe tells her both doctors say she's not well enough yet. Maggie calms down and they play cards. She asks how Hoffman got involved in her case and says she comes across as cold. Burke shows up a little later, wanting to talk to Maggie. He finds it strange that she remembers less now than when she first resurfaced (tell the kitchen to heat up that old hash). Burke tries to refresh her memory, to no avail. He seems puzzled upon hearing that Barnabas stopped by to visit her. As he readies to leave, Maggie mentions having a vague bit of music in the back of her mind, but she shrugs it off.

In the Collinwood drawing room, we are assaulted, both visually and aurally, by the hideous orange dress and that goddamn music box. Thankfully, Burke arrives and spares us the music. The two talk filler (this is obviously a dud of an episode). Vicki grabs the box to take it upstairs and tells him how it has a tendency to open on its own during the night. Burke asks to hear it and makes a connection. Vicki thinks Burke's jealous of Barnabas. We're tortured by the music box tune again.

Episode #304 — Morning and Burke goes to the Old House. Willie (wearing that ugly check shirt that looks worse in color) pauses before answering. Burke demands to see Barnabas, but, he's outta luck, as he's 'not home.' Milquetoast NewBurke tries to talk tough guy and claims Willie is lying, as he espied Mr. Collins enter the house just before sun up. Willie wants to know why he's spying on them. Burke's reason? Barnabas is weird and so is he. Willie politely tells him to buzz off, they never did anything to him (to *this* Burke, technically true; OldBurke — Willie wanted to kill him. Hey, NewBurke? Willie saved your worthless life the other day). Burke pushes his way into the house; he *knows* Barnabas is there; he'll wait, Willie can't stop him! Loomis again tells him Barney's not there. Burke yells for the master of the house and Willie says knock yourself out, asshole, he probably left through the back door. Burke asks where Barnabas works. Willie says all over, but he doesn't know specifics, he's just an employee. Willie asks why so curious and suggests he leave them alone. Dumbfuck Burke takes it as a threat (hmm, Burke *can* die now; you don't mess with our Mr. Loomis) and storms out.

At Collinwood, Vicki comes downstairs and joins Julia in the drawing room, where the doctor is puzzling over Sarah's bonnet. Vicki says it looks very old, with intricate hand sewn needlework. David strolls in and complains that his breakfast included burnt toast (Mrs. Johnson strikes again!). He's ready for his promised walk with Vicki. Julia offers to go instead, as she wants to get better acquainted with him. Miss Winters thinks it's swell, as she has other things to do. Julia suggests looking for Sarah. David admits to being mad at her for her disappearing act the other evening. The two head out on their walk.

David takes Julia to the spot in the woods where he usually finds Sarah. Julia says she'd like to meet her and asks about her. David describes her and there's some time killing filler involving her bonnet that has no relevance to the plot, so I'll skip it.

Returning to Collinwood, David rushes upstairs to get his stamp collection to show Julia. Vicki comes into the foyer and is pleased Julia and David are getting along. Why, it's so easy and breezy, Julia says (yes, because he's outgrown his homicidal phase). Vicki looks different this episode and it's her false eyelashes; she looks sexier. Anyway, Burke shows up, wanting to talk to Vicki pronto — but not at Collinwood, said with a bit of a side-eye to Julia. Vicki goes to get a sweater and in the drawing room, Burke tries to grill Julia about her book and Barnabas. He asks if she's ever seen Mr. Collins during the day; no one else has. She lies. Burke says he didn't like Willie's answers to his questions earlier. Blah, blah, boring — oh, geez, Julia says if Barnabas is 'odd' it's because he's a gentleman, a true rarity nowadays (gag) and that she's fond of him. She's obviously worried. Walking into the foyer, Burke comments on the uncanny resemblance Barnabas has to his ancestor. Vicki, who may have actually knitted the sweater for as long as it took, finally comes down and the couple leaves. Julia is perturbed.

Julia heads to the Old House and gets the skinny from Willie. She complains that he couldn't come up with a better answer to Burke's 'where does Barnabas work' question (screw you, that gentleman comment was lamer than anything Willie said). Burke could ruin everything!

At the Blue Whale — hey, that's not Bob! Vicki and Burke enter and have coffee, because the coffee shop has ceased to exist now that Maggie doesn't work there anymore. Burke eventually spits out that he wants Vicki to promise to stay away from Barnabas and the Old House, but won't explain why.

Episode #305 — Hmm, I believe we've seen our first color chromakey effect. David's in the woods and is found by Sarah. He asks where she lives and she says she'd tell him, but it's hard to explain (the spirit world and Davey would understand, trust me). She has to keep it secret, but will tell him other things. She seems pleased and amused to hear that people ask questions about her. As it's getting dark, David says he's got to boogie. She asks him to stay, with the promise of showing him a great secret place to play out at Eagle Hill. He agrees and they head off (isn't Eagle Hill five miles away?)

Barnabas shambles into the parlor, seemingly under the weather, if that's possible. He asks the dusting Willie where Julia is. As he's feeling poorly, Barney has to decide about continuing with the experiments. Willie's all for it (no surprise), but Barnabas isn't and — gah, starts musing over Sarah's presence. Julia shows up. Barnabas complains about his malaise, but Dr. Hoffman is pleased with the change. Willie observes. Julia heads down to the lab and Barnabas snivels that he doesn't trust her. He then tells Willie that if he discovers Julia's doing something untoward, he should kill her (you can't outsource your murder to Willie, moron).

At Eagle Hill, David seems to have temporarily lost his playmate. She shows up, with a laugh, then leads him to the secret place; the Collins mausoleum. David doesn't want to go in, but she convinces him.

Lab coated Julia walks into the parlor and tells Barnabas the test results are dandy. Barnabas argues, complains and issues a hollow death threat — oh, man, Julia asks if he has to continually threaten her! (Hilarious) Experiment, blah, blah. Barnabas needs his strength to deal with Burke; he's suspicious. The doctor agrees Burke needs to leave them alone, but violence isn't an option.

In the crypt, David's all, it's nifty enough, but kinda dull, too. Uh, oh, Sarah shows him the ring on the lion's head and tells him to pull it. The secret room is revealed. She takes him inside, where they find the coffin. David asks who's in it. Sarah says open it and find out. David would rather not, thanks, but she persuades him.

Episode #306 — Night and secret room opening redo, with some eerie Grand Guignol lighting and alternate camera blocking. The coffin is empty, but Sarah says someone used to be there, but he went away. David deems the place a little too cold and creepy and wants to leave. He'd rather come back and play during the day. He promises not to tell anyone about the room and they leave.

At the Old House, Barnabas is preparing to go see Vicki at Collinwood. Julia wants to know why. Barnabas bitches, calls her domineering, and proves he's a raging sexist/male chauvinist. He goes on to say he's going to show her how to handle a crisis. How about some warmed up Maggie returns hash? (No, thanks, I'll have a White Russian). Barnabas is going to handle Burke and off he goes.

David sneaks into Collinwood, but on the way upstairs is caught by Vicki, who scolds him for being out so late (it's nine o'clock). Roger will be angry when he hears about it (where the hell *is* Roger?). David explains he was playing with Sarah, you know, the girl she said he made up. Blah, blah, Sarah; she's strange, but nice. David promises to always be back on time. Vicki says she'd like to meet her. David mentions Barnabas' costume party and says Sarah always dresses as if she's going to it. Vicki then recalls the little girl she saw on the stairs.

A bit later, Vicki's still in the foyer, lost in thought, when Barnabas arrives, wanting a brief chat. So much for Vicki avoiding him. He starts by apologizing for his uncivil behavior upon news of her engagement; it was because he's so fond of her. He then starts discussing Burke and smoothly intones that, my dear, I do believe he's having me investigated. Dirty pool, no? It's vexing, as I'm such a paragon of virtue. Miss Winters is dismayed at the news. Barnabas is sorry for upsetting her; what should he do? Oh, Vicki will handle it (this manipulative asshat). Barnabas then drops the old Laura Collins "I'll be eternally grateful" line (that proves, without a doubt, he's a piece of crap). Vicki promises to talk to Burke that night. Julia arrives and asks if David ever made it home. Yep, he was out playing with Sarah. Upon hearing that, the vole scampers off. Julia heads upstairs where she meets pj'd David, who tells Vicki that he's hungry. Vicki heads to the kitchen. Julia and David, blah, blah, secret place/Sarah.

Barnabas, amid some appropriately ghoulish lighting, is strolling the cemetery and hears Sarah playing her flute. She's sitting on her grave, in the crypt. She stops playing and he calls to her, then goes inside the mausoleum, but she's gone. Barnabas keens (no, really, he's about to cry) for her to come back — he loves her, he needs her! (he fails to emotionally move me!)

Episode #307 — Still night. Sam's painting and stir-crazy Maggie harps about wanting to go out and even tries to, but Sam stops her and the two sling weeks, nay *months* old hash. Joe shows up and Maggie's bitchy to him, too, and states she's going out — then goes to her room (uh, she has French doors, she can stroll on out whenever she wants). Sam tells Joe maybe it would be okay if she went out with them (well, duh) and sends Joe to the Blue Whale to save them a table (crowds have not been a problem there in ages).

Joe goes to the bar, where he finds Vicki drinking alone while waiting for Burke. He joins her and orders a beer (I'll have a Sidecar). Lighting a cigarette (that is rare, he must be really stressed) they talk Maggie, then blah, blah, music, little girl, hash, hash, hash (had the ratings significantly gone up at this point? Was this done for the benefit of new viewers? It's the only logical explanation). Sam and Maggie come in and have a large helping of hash. Why, yes, Joe Haskell is a handsome man, but why is the shot lingering on him so damn long *when he's not speaking*? The men decide to search for Sarah. Burke comes in and brrr…Vicki's icy as he tries to give her a peck on the cheek. Joe and the Evanses leave and Vicki starts chiding Burke for investigating Barnabas. The dumbass thinks her affianced is jealous. Burke says if Barney is clean, then no harm, no foul — but he's odd, so he must be hiding something. He then tells of the long dead cousin Collins claims to have lived with. The dolt makes an excuse for Barnabas — he was just tired of your questions and said the first name that came to him! (is she for real?) Burke mentions the Jeremiah comment when they announced their engagement and Vicki avoids by changing the subject, asking if their whole marriage is going to be like this (you mean Burke talking sense and you talking nonsense? Looks like). Burke points out how when Maggie resurfaced there at the bar, she didn't recognize either of them, but seemed to recall Barnabas. Oh, no! Vicki protests, Barnabas is wonderful. Stop it, or I won't marry you!

Episode #308 — Maggie's dusting while Sam paints. Joe arrives and tells them the ineffectual Sheriff Patterson can't find Sarah (funny how people seem to be locking their doors now). Sam thinks Sarah isn't the girl's real name, a theory which comes way out of left field. Blah, blah, the men decide to go see David and ask him for help. Huh, the police can afford a twenty-four hour guard? (Where was he when Barnabas returned to kill Maggie or when Sarah visited her in broad daylight?)

At Collinwood, David's on the stairs, yelling to Carolyn to get the lead out, as they'll miss the bus to Bangor. Carolyn joins him and says they can always drive (I was wondering), but apparently she promised a bus trip. Sam and Joe arrive and no amount of alcohol can numb the pain of all this damn repetition. David mentions that Miss Hoffman is also looking for Sarah. Sam and Joe want him to help search today (sure, go ahead and disrupt the kid's plans). Sam, being sensible, says nah, take your trip, but tell us where to look. David obliges and the men set off for the woods while the cousins head for the bus.

In the woods, Sam and Joe come across an old swing moving back and forth and make the absurd leap that Sarah was just there (like it couldn't be the wind, a raccoon or bear cub?). Logical Joe finally says it may have just been the wind (they're reading my mind!). Haskell then suggests they hit the Old House and ask Barnabas if he's seen the elusive child. Once at the homestead, they knock and Julia answers. Sam wonders why she's there and she says it's part of her cover. Sam doesn't see how that helps Maggie and admits he doesn't believe her, then mentions Sarah (Bob – refill!). Julia says Barnabas knows nothing about the girl. Sam insults her and storms off. Joe apologizes and follows.

Evening and Carolyn and David return home. Despite having eaten enough for six people throughout the day, Davey's hungry and heads to the kitchen to make a sandwich. Julia, on her way out, is questioned by Carolyn about Sarah (long past time for a new drinking game. When anybody asks about, or looks for, Sarah, take a drink. Standard marathon/binge watching warning from episode #62 still applies). Anyway, Julia leaves and Carolyn looks pensive.

Sam and Joe return to the cottage. They wake the sleeping Maggie, who rushes out of her room with Sarah's doll, exclaiming, "she was here, she left it while I was sleeping!"

Episode #309 — Julia's in the Old House parlor, fiddling with a syringe and Barnabas asks why is she so nervous, what's she hiding? He grabs her throat and demands an answer (how can she talk when you're choking her, genius?). He lets her go and she relays that Sam and Joe were there, wanting to ask him about Sarah. Barnabas wallows — she knows all about me, why has she come back? Wait, now he says she never knew what he became, so how could she know all about him? (This inconsistency is frustrating) He goes on to state that she's come back, to his enemies, which makes *her* one (yeah, it's always all about you, right? Suck it up.).

Burke goes to Collinwood and Vicki's still an uptight, imbecilic bitch. Burke caves and apologizes, but she's still a frigid cunt with a stick up her ass. Blah, blah, Barnabas and Vicki's a freaking hypocrite (OldBurke would have never folded like this, no matter the woman, though he came close with Laura). Anyway, they kiss and make-up, then Vicki asks NewBurke to apologize to Barney because he was so hurt! Fortunately, Barnabas arrives with a book for Vicki and in the drawing room, Burke girds his loins for the unpleasant task at hand. Alone with his adversary in the drawing room, Burke 'apologizes.' Barney smugly thinks he's won, but I think Devlin was snowing him.

In the Old House parlor, Julia gets the feeling she's not alone, that Sarah is there (and Barnabas needs to open the purse strings for better, non-drip candles, as the floor candelabra is loaded with wax).

Vicki, attired like a co-ed at a Catholic university, anxiously sits in the foyer. The men emerge and everything's great! Best buds! Burke then says he's hitting the road and Vicki walks him to the door.

Julia, meanwhile, is out in the woods, calling to Sarah (does she hear the flute music that we do?).

Vicki joins Barnabas in the drawing room and he asks if she ever believed any of Burke's spurious claims about him. Why, no (because she's stupid).

Julia's back in the Old House. Barnabas comes home and she tells him that Sarah had been there. Butthurt ensues; why would she appear to her? Julia then notices that the album of portraits she had been perusing earlier is open to the picture of Sarah (they had photographs that long ago?). Barnabas then says he knows Sarah will come to him.

Episode #310 — Willie's dusting the chandelier when he notices someone outside. He dashes out, calling after them. Barnabas joins him to see what the ruckus is about. Willie says it was Sarah — and she just sort of vanished. 'Ole Barney is perplexed. Going back inside, he asks Willie if he talked to Julia and made the whole thing up. Willie, resident genius, asks why would he — or anyone else who saw her — lie about it? He then wisely expounds that Mr. Collins is afraid Sarah will tell someone the truth about him. If she loves him so much, why does she bolt whenever he's around? (Point, Loomis) He goes on to say that Barnabas better find her quick, then exits the room. Barnabas wangsts as to why Sarah won't come to him (because you're a psychotic, mind-raping thug?).

David's in the drawing room peering into his crystal ball. Carolyn comes along and tells him it's nearly dinner time. He's busy, trying to divine where Sarah is. Carolyn threatens to have missing-in-action Roger take the ball away if David doesn't obey her. He sees his answer and knows where to go. Joe shows up, looking for David. He wants to know the super-secret-special place he and Sarah go to to play. The lad can't reveal that, but offers to go get her and bring her back. Carolyn nixes that plan and sends him off to dinner. While she and Joe murmur in the drawing room, David grabs his coat and sneaks out of the house.

Sarah's sitting outside the family crypt, cradling her doll, which Maggie had two episodes ago.

In the parlor, Willie's lighting candles and Barnabas is all woe betide before announcing that they have to go to Sarah's grave in order to find her (can we please get Willie out of that hideous shirt?).

David makes the five mile trek to Eagle Hill and finds Sarah. She wants to play, but he says they have to go to Collinwood and talk to Maggie's friend, Joe. Sarah convinces him to play catch. As David searches for the ball after a bad throw, Sarah disappears.

Carolyn rushes into the drawing room to tell Joe that David is missing (did you offer Joe something to eat? I'm just curious.). Worry-filled filler. At Eagle Hill, David checks the mausoleum, but no playmate. He opens the secret room, but still no dice. As he's about to close the panel, he hears Barnabas and Willie coming and rushes back into the secret room. The two men enter the crypt and how the hell did David close that stone door from the inside? Somehow, the boy manages to hear the conversation through that thick wall and is relieved to hear Willie say she's not here, let's book. Barnabas then demands Willie open the secret panel. David scrambles into the empty coffin (any port in a storm, right?).

Episode #311 — Redo/replay of the Sarah crypt search. Willie wants to go, but Barnabas tells him to close the panel. David's hiding in the coffin. Willie wants to leave, as the place gives him the creeps. Barnabas asks why he doesn't like the place (I'm guessing because you attacked, beat and forced him to bury his friend there, asshole), smugly calls him a coward (pot, meet kettle) and Willie rightfully points out that the Big Bad is afraid of a little girl. Nuh-uh, Barnabas replies and Willie takes the opportunity to rub a smidgen of salt in the wound. Barney gets all melancholic again about how pure she was (and I'm not buying his angst). Also, how convenient that in this scene, neither calls Sarah by name. Anyway, Barnabas decides it's time to leave. Willie pauses, believing he heard something and is insulted by Barney, because the undead one is a jag-off. Willie opens the panel by the lever/button or whatever under a stone step. They exit, close the panel from the main crypt and leave the premises. David emerges from the coffin and discovers he's locked in.

It's nearly eleven o'clock and at Collinwood, Carolyn's worried. Joe comes into the drawing room having searched the East Wing and finding nothing (did you search the West Wing?). Carolyn blames herself, but self-aware Joe says it's his fault David is missing. Talk then turns to Vicki's engagement and Carolyn tells Joe she made an ass of herself over Burke before and is happy for Vicki. She then worries some more about David, who is futilely yelling and pounding on the crypt door. Vicki comes home and gets the low-down. Carolyn and Joe decide to go check the woods. Meanwhile, David pulls out a pocketknife and tries to jimmy the door. Seeing it's useless, he sits down and laments.

Carolyn and Joe search the woods and mention Sarah (drink!) Miss Pessimistic says disaster looms because her nightmares told her so. David starts calling to Sarah and I'm again confused about that flute music. He cries some more. In the woods, Joe and Carolyn hear someone coming — it's Willie. Joe asks him why he's prowling the woods (Joe, I like you, but don't be an asshole. He lives on the property and it's none of your damn business). Loomis explains that he's gathering firewood, then asks Joe what the hell *he's* doing out there. They tell him about the missing David and want to search the Old House. Nervous Willie brusquely says they can't, he's not there, and rushes away. Joe thinks Loomis is hiding something, because Willie is everyone's favorite scapegoat (which only endears him to the audience). In the crypt, David again starts searching for a way out.

Though she's supposed to be manning the phone, Vicki's in the garden (she was wearing a coat when she came home from her date; now she's outside in a sleeveless dress. I have no idea what season it is; Barnabas skulks around in his Inverness coat all the damn time, while others don't wear a coat at all). She's joined by Barnabas and blah, blah David. She's so distraught! He offers to stay with her. He starts jabbering about children, Vicki starts weeping, he gets handsy, embraces her and moves to take a bite.

Episode #312 — It's a comfort Vicki redo, then Carolyn and Joe arrive, interrupting the nosferatu before he can attack. Barnabas offers assistance; blah, blah, Sarah/Maggie goulash, warmed over. Joe mentions David said something about a secret place and Barney gets concerned. Joe goes in to call the sheriff. As Carolyn tells Vicki they should alert Liz and Roger down in Boston (one mystery solved), Barnabas slinks away.

At the Old House, Barnabas starts shouting for Willie, who says he hasn't seen the mischievous young scamp in days. Blah, blah Sarah/David and Barnabas frets. Willie asks what happens if David knows too much and is basically told he already knows the answer to that question. Our man Loomis is appalled; he's a *kid*, he's a *Collins*.

At Collinwood, Joe's smoking again when Patterson shows up. During the conversation, the sheriff floats the idea that David's been kidnapped. Carolyn breaks out quavery voiced distress at the thought. Joe's back on his Old House kick (filler, with a side of drinking game) and convinces Patterson to go there with him.

At the Old House, Barnabas wants to go search for David again, but Willie points out that it's nearly dawn. Joe and Patterson arrive, wanting to search the house. Blah, blah, no need to say about what — enjoy your cocktail! Barnabas allows them to split up and search the domicile. Frantic Willie's worried that they'll search the basement. Barnabas tells him to shut up. Willie says, sure, but don't lie to him about not being scared. The cock crows and Willie worries some more. Patterson comes back to the parlor, as does Joe. As the resident Mensa member stated, they want to search the basement and are *very* insistent. Mr. Collins claims the room has been locked since he moved in and there's nothing down there anyway (how would you know if it was locked, huh?). And wouldn't you know, he lost the key. Willie's hanging back, listening to this exchange with an 'I can lie better than this' expression. Joe says they'll just break down the door, which is problematic for me, because A) it's not his house, B) *he's* not a cop and C) there's something called the Fourth Amendment. Barney agrees with me and says you can't destroy property, then gets more flustered as the mantel clock chimes. Fortunately for him, Carolyn comes rushing in with news that David might be found. Patterson asks if Barnabas wants to come along. No thanks. Once the others leave, Barnabas tells Willie to search all day for David and bring him to the Old House if found. Barnabas then goes to the basement. (When the hell does Willie sleep? He's doing stuff during the day, up all night; is he on amphetamines? And can he *please* change out of that shirt?)

Episode #313 — Collinwood, six thirty a.m. and — glory be! — Roger walks in, suitcase in hand. Going to the drawing room, he finds Vicki dozing on the sofa. He asks why he just saw the sheriff leaving and is upset to hear that his son has been missing all night. Meanwhile, David's still trying to yell for help through the stone wall of the crypt. Roger's irked to hear that the governess was out when David disappeared and what the hell does Joe Haskell have to do with this? Blah, blah, rehash. Joe and Carolyn walk in and we learn Liz is still in Boston. Joe takes responsibility, which Roger seems to appreciate and more filler/hash ensues. Roger agrees to go out with Joe to hunt for the littlest Collins. In the crypt, David calls for help some more, then collapses in despair (guess that's karma, baby, for locking Vicki in the abandoned East Wing).

In the drawing room, Carolyn is spacing out while looking out the window. Get this, she tells Vicki that the person who might have seen David last night was an old woman and unreliable (is she from Phoenix? Remember this same shit in the Laura story arc?). This whole conversation is pretty much filler. Quavery Carolyn thinks David is in danger.

Joe and Roger are in the woods, against a chromakey landscape. Blah, blah police/search. As they're near Eagle Hill, Joe suggests they check it out, you know Maggie/Eagle Hill rehash (even Roger looks fed up with this and he just got back). In the crypt, a now dirty-faced David struggles to stay awake and —

oh, dear mother of God, no— Bob, a Stinger! Crazy Pants Old Man Coot is outside the mausoleum and mumbles that the gate was closed last night (bullshit! This crazy bastard wasn't around). He goes into the crypt, asks if anyone's there and David starts shouting for help (how anything is heard though that thick stone panel is beyond me). Crazy Old Coot backs out, scared, and says there's no help (kill this hoary trope already!). From a short distance away, Joe sees the caretaker. Roger wonders why bother, but tags along. Tedious bullshit ensues asking about David and Crazy Old Man talks about some other dead kid and I sure wish Roger was toting his shotgun. Crazy Old Man says he heard a call for help in the crypt. Roger's as annoyed as I am and the character from hell shuffles off (don't come back). Joe persuades Roger to check the mausoleum and we see that David has, conveniently, fallen asleep so they can drag this tiresome storyline out a little longer. Anyway, Roger snarks at Joe a little bit and then, something wonderful happens. As Joe is about to leave, Roger says, hold up, several of his incestors — his *ancestors* are buried there (this is a classic gaffe and Louis Edmonds' immediate catch/correction adds to the fun). Roger takes a look around, commenting on Naomi being a beauty and Joshua being a tyrant. Then, because there is no God, Crazy Pants Old Man Coot shows up and urges them to leave. They all depart and gosh, darn, David wakes up *just* after they're gone and starts shouting for help again. (This episode was mostly a bore, except for Roger; I'm glad he's back — *incestors*!)

Episode #314 — Morning at the Evans cottage and Maggie looks worried. A scruffy bearded and exhausted Joe shows up and is told Sam has gone out with another group to search for David. Joe thinks the supernatural could be in play, what with all the strange occurrences lately. Maggie insists David is all right and Joe is not responsible. Woodard then shows up, having been asked to come by Joe. The two complain to the doctor that Julia doesn't do anything when she comes to see Maggie, just a cursory check. Woodard's incredulous and Joe bitches about Julia being at the Old House all the time — she's hiding something and shouldn't see Maggie anymore. Woodard agrees to talk to his colleague, then Sarah talk begins (choose your beverage!). Maggie mentions the doll being left and shows it to Woodard (but Sarah had it again after that, the hell?). Woodard borrows the doll, as it could provide a clue!

Our man Loomis (wearing a sweater instead of that awful shirt) is strolling the woods and hears flute music. Turning around, he finds Sarah standing right behind him. He tells her people are looking for her, especially Barnabas, and she says she's looking for him (more writer bullshit to drag an arc out). Willie offers to take her to him, but she says she can't at that moment, as she has to look for David. Willie starts questioning her about her friend and their secrets, which makes for a cute scene. He gets worried when she says she told David the biggest secret she knows. Willie asks to be let in on that, insisting that she can trust him as he's her friend. She's thrilled at having a grown-up for a friend, but gets angry with his queries; she has to look for David before all else. Of course, when Willie turns away for a second to point out the Old House, she disappears.

Willie goes to Collinwood and needs to talk to Julia, pronto. He explains to her that he saw Sarah, who was looking for David. He also reveals that if Barnabas discovers she revealed secrets to the lad, he's a dead boy walking. Willie worries about Davey's well-being and Julia worries about her fucking experiment. She tells him not to say anything about the turn of events. Woodard arrives and Willie takes his leave. Woodard starts in on Julia spending time at the Old House and not treating Maggie and I suddenly have a taste for a Lime Rickey. He goes on to say that he concurs that something supernatural is going on in regards to Sarah. Woodard hands Julia the doll and informs her that the local librarian, who's an expert in toys, deems that, though the doll appears brand new, it's over one hundred and fifty years old (never mind that for the longest time, the magic number for Collins ancestor talk was one hundred thirty years).

Episode #315 — Night and Julia is in the Old House parlor. Barnabas strides in looking for Willie, as he wants a report on the missing David. Young Collins is trying to figure out the egress from the secret room. Julia attempts to keep Barnabas from going out — his injection time is coming up soon. Since Barney is in a hurry, Julia accuses him of holding the lad prisoner as a means to find Sarah. Oh, no, you foolish woman and there's a veiled inference about killing the kid. Upon leaving, the bastard says it would be a pity to off him, but, oh, well, *he's* more important. Barnabas and Julia trade barbs and he threatens both her and Willie with death (yawn).

Barnabas goes to Collinwood, where Vicki tells him David is still missing. She's worried that the boy had an accident, or is in the clutches of the maniac who kidnapped Maggie. She mentions Joe and Roger searching Eagle Hill and how the caretaker claimed to have heard a voice in the mausoleum. Barnabas is relieved the crypt search yielded nothing, then goes out to join the effort.

David, meanwhile, starts calling to Sarah to help him, then curls up in the fetal position (where the hell is Josette, who supposedly helps the family when in trouble?). Oh, crap — Crazy Pants is at the cemetery. Barnabas comes along and Crazy Old Man blathers about Barnabas being dead in England. The senile old codger irritates Barnabas, who's just looking for David info. Hash, hash,

hash. Barnabas gets testy, then worried, when told a voice was calling for help from behind the wall in the mausoleum (not enough liquor to counteract this tedium and this obnoxious character makes episodes grind to a halt).

David's still pleading for someone to help him when Sarah shows up. He asks how she got there (David used to be more perceptive; why hasn't he figured out she's a ghost?). Blah, blah, she ran away and left him there, he had to hide — now, how the hell does he get out? He promises not to tell anyone about the room and she shows him the lever/knob/switch or whatever. Sarah pulls the vanishing act when he turns his back for a second. He leaves the room, closes the panel, exits the mausoleum — and literally runs straight into Barnabas.

Episode #316 — David escapes redo. Barnabas asks the lad why he was in the mausoleum. David lies and though the kid is a very good prevaricator, Barney doesn't believe him. Barnabas won't let David go, even blocking his way with his cane, and asks why the boy is afraid of him. The elder Collins lies then, saying David can't go to Collinwood because everyone is out looking for him, best come to the Old House (this whole scene is quite irksome). Blah, blah Sarah. Barnabas tries grilling the kid and takes a firm hold of the lad when Burke is suddenly heard calling for David. When Burke arrives on the scene, he gets a huge hug from the relieved kid and man, does David give Barnabas the side eye. Barnabas lies to Burke and Burke knows it. He's caught in another lie when David asks Burke if anyone's at Collinwood; yes, Vicki and Roger, Burke informs.

Vicki's in the drawing room when Roger walks in. He pours a drink and gives her the update; no sign of David and the search will be called off in the morning (the search for the missing kid of the wealthiest family in town? Yeah, right.) The trio arrives and — gasp! — David hugs Roger. Blah, blah mausoleum. While leaving the room with dad, young Collins pauses to give cousin Barnabas the side eye again. Vicki, Burke and Barnabas rehash a bit and I kind of wish OldBurke was around for this. Barnabas departs.

In his room, David's in his pajamas and munching on a sammich. Roger's desirous of a man-to-man talk, but his son would prefer to wait until morning. Roger prevails and David tells about looking for Sarah and getting lost in the woods. Roger doesn't buy the latter. David muses aloud why Barnabas was at the mausoleum, then says they know nothing about him — he just showed up one night. Roger tells David to go to bed, they'll resume the conversation in the morning. David hits the sack.

Barnabas is back in the Old House and sits down for a bit of a think. Willie comes downstairs and is promptly bitched at and insulted. He lies to Barney, who informs him that David was found at the crypt, so he has to know about the secret room. Blah, blah, our man Loomis advocates for David, reminding the Big Bad that he's just a little boy.

David, restless, gets out of bed and goes to look out the window. Vicki comes in and comments he looks a little pale. David admits to being scared; he's not safe and someone evil is watching him. Evil Barnabas stares out the Old House window, sarcastically wishing David goodnight, via voice-over.

Episode #317 — The next evening, after taking a moment to collect his cruel thoughts, Barnabas prepares to go out. Julia arrives and tries to convince him to leave David alone. Oh, he's just going to see what the boy knows, then kill him if he *has* to (this bastard). Blah, blah (for the most part, these recent episodes have been unbearable). Barnabas leaves and Julia follows a second later.

At the Evans cottage, Sam opens a desk drawer and checks the gun inside. Woodard shows up, maniac/Maggie/mausoleum/Sarah talk (remember when Sam was a big-time boozer? Good times — let's have a vodka martini in his honor). Sam wants to go to the cemetery. *Now.* He convinces Woodard and grabs the semi-automatic from the drawer.

Walking through the woods, Barnabas suspects he's being followed and he is — by Julia. At the cemetery, Woodard seems jumpy, but Sam says no reason to be, he's got his gat. A storm is moving in, lots of lightning and thunder, and Woodard keeps pronouncing mausoleum as mausolayum, which annoys me. Barnabas goes into the crypt and Julia strolls in just as he's about to open the secret panel. Hollow death threat is issued and he almost slips and mentions McGuire is buried there. Barnabas then admits to having a bit of buyer's remorse for not killing Julia when he initially planned (you snooze, you lose, Barney).

NOOO!! Woodard and Sam run across Crazy Pants Old Man Coot (this show hates us). Old Man says the mausoleum has ghosts and that the crypt is cursed, per Joshua Collins, who wrote as much the day before he died (new and interesting). In the mausoleum, Barnabas is wrapping up a story, saying chains were wrapped around the coffin and he thought he was imprisoned forever (more interesting stuff, let's run with it). Julia asks where the coffin is and he opens the panel. Hmm, once in the secret room, Barnabas just pushes that big, stone door closed, maybe it's vampire super-strength. Anyway, Barnabas says he was trapped for over one hundred years in the coffin and still would be if it weren't for Willie (so treat him like a god instead of dirt, asshole). Barnabas looks for evidence that David was in there and finds his broken pocketknife. He then leaps to the conclusion that David knows everything about him and has to die. As the duo starts to exit the room, they hear Sam and Woodard approaching and scurry back inside (like we didn't see that coming). Barnabas and Julia listen though the thick stone door with their extraordinary hearing. Woodard finds Sarah's nameplate and states what the viewing audience has known for ages — maybe little Sarah is a ghost!

Episode #318 — Redo of Woodard and Sam looking around tomb and the ghost comment. Barnabas and Julia look at each other with alarm. Sam laughs at the phantom theory, as there's no such thing as ghosts. Woodard mentions talking to Julia and her supernatural comment. Infuriated Barnabas starts to choke the lady doctor, who manages to let out a brief bark. Sam hears the yelp coming from behind the wall, but Woodard says nah, it's solid rock! (Which is it, writers? You cannot have it both ways, damn it!). Blah, blah, Maggie in greater danger, need to protect her. Woodard decides to head to Collinwood and confront Julia. The men leave. Barnabas, having released his death grip on Julia's throat, bitches at her over Woodard. Angry Barney decrees that David must expire. Julia argues and the selfish troll threatens to confine her in the coffin. She warns that there will be one hell of an investigation if David dies. Blah, blah, Sarah and oh, poor Barnabas angsts that David, Vicki and Willie have all talked to the dead urchin (don't forget Sam) — why not him? (You're a jerk?) Julia rather lamely advises he find little sis and tell her to stop sharing secrets with David.

Woodard's in the Collinwood drawing room and when David comes in (roused from bed, it seems) he asks him about Sarah. David doesn't want to break the Children's Clandestine Code, so he says he knows nothing. Mausolayum talk. David mentions that Julia's interested in Sarah, too — just a split second before Hoffman walks in. Woodard asks how to contact Sarah and it's all so painfully dull. He warns David — something (I stopped paying attention) and Julia takes the boy up to bed. Once she's returned, there's bitching and bickering between the two physicians. Julia becomes distracted by the howling of a dog that sounds as if it's dying a slow, painful death from cyanide poisoning. Pissed off Woodard announces Maggie is no longer her patient and departs. Despite the storm, Julia rushes out as well.

At the Old House, Barnabas is about to go out when Julia, magically dry, dashes in and says she's there to stop him killing the boy. Nothing can stop him!

Barnabas declares, but then, the door suddenly blows open, candles flicker, chandelier swings and a somber flute rendition of *London Bridge* fills the room. Julia points out to melancholic Barnabas that a little girl *can* stop him.

The Great Frame-Up

Episode #319 — Maggie comes home from a brief walk to find a worried Sam, who tells her she's still in danger. She insists she's not, but he shows her the newspaper; another woman was attacked. Woodard shows up and says he treated the victim, who lost some blood, but is otherwise okay. The men then hustle Maggie off to make coffee so they can talk maniac. Woodard proposes a risky plan; let people think Maggie's memory is returning. The psycho will try to get at her again, but he'll be nabbed by the police when he walks into their trap. Sam's against using his daughter as bait. Dogs start a-howlin'.

Barnabas, wearing his full length, full skirted dressing gown, throws the newspaper with the attack headline into the fire. Willie rushes into the house and asks him why the hell he attacked the girl, as people were starting to forget the previous assaults. Barnabas doesn't owe any explanations. Willie inquires if he's going to stop the experimental treatments. Loomis posits that Barney is scared of losing his power and living as a normal man. He says the cops will catch up to him and find out everything; he can't take chances. Willie, a greater mind than anyone realizes, drops a hydrogen truth bomb on Barnabas; that he's scared of a lot of things, like David, Maggie and losing Vicki. Rankled Barney tells him to shut up and Willie retorts that he hopes Barnabas is as safe as he thinks. Barnabas wants Willie to go into town and see what the scuttlebutt is. Willie says that shows he *is* scared. Barnabas barks at him to leave and Willie departs.

Maggie can't remember, but Woodard's optimistic. She asks him what he and Sam were talking about. Blah, blah, plan. Maggie wants to try it and says she'll convince her old man to go along. Woodard leaves and Maggie heads to the phone. A little bit later, Sheriff Patterson arrives. Sam walks in (guess he was taking a nap or something) and blah, blah, plan. Sam forbids it, which is stupid, because Maggie is a goddamn adult and he doesn't control her. Patterson says there's a flaw in the plan; if Sam talked in public about her memory returning, everyone would know it was a set-up, it's too obvious. Sam happens to pour a drink (I thought he was dry?). Maggie says, hey, Pop, pretend you're drunk and let it 'slip out.' Patterson jumps on board. Sam's still against it and argues with Maggie. Dogs howl and Maggie gets a bit shrill in her fright. Sam relucantly agrees to the plan.

At the Blue Whale, Willie's sitting at the bar, nursing a beer and crunching on a pretzel. A two hundred and eighty year old barfly sits nearby, talking to Bob. Sam stumbles in, with Patterson right behind, offering to drive the 'drunk' Sam home. Sam, who we've seen drunk in the past, now plays the worst fake drunk ever. Evans orders a "double martooney" from "Bob-a-Rooney." Bob asks the sheriff about the recent attack. Our man Loomis listens with interest. Sam drops the first bit of verbal chum and the patrons crowd around. Patterson tries to ignore the drunken rambling, but Bob asks if they're close to catching someone. Concerned Willie continues to listen. Patterson sends Sam to a table and the patrons disperse. George then tells Bob to forget everything Sam said, he's talking out of his ass. In the background, we notice an empty space where Willie used to be. Patterson joins Sam, convinced enough people heard to spread the rumor.

At the Old House, Willie's reporting back to Barnabas what just transpired. Barnabas wants Julia to make Maggie forget. Instead, Willie suggests that Barnabas go on the lam — tonight. Never! The undead one responds.

Episode #320 — Sleeping David is *very* restless. He has a nightmare that he's in a cemetery. Barnabas, standing near the family crypt, advances toward him and grows gigantic (remember this crazy shit with Laura's ginormo head?), then bares his fangs. David starts screaming (only it's pre-recorded and I don't believe it's actually David). The lad wakes up, calling out for help and crying. Burke and Vicki rush in and calm him down. He says he can't remember the dream, but isn't keen on going back to sleep. He asks Burke to leave the light on. In the hall, Burke and Vicki talk David for a minute, before the boy opens the door and asks to speak to Devlin. Back in his room, David tells Burke he lied about the dream, because it was about Barnabas and Vicki likes him. He explains most of the nightmare and Burke asks if David has a reason to be afraid of Barnabas. Davey says that sometimes his cousin looks at him in a way that freaks him out and requests that Burke keep Barnabas the hell away from him.

Down in the drawing room, Burke and Vicki discuss Barnabas/David/dream. Burke says maybe the boy's child instinct is right. Vicki cheerleads for the wrong person, then cancels her date because of David. Barnabas knocks on the front door. He's looking for Julia and leaves an urgent message with Vicki, then leaves. Burke comments on Barnabas' strange demeanor, then blah, blah, Julia/Barnabas/Old House/book crap. Vicki goes to check on David. Julia comes home and meets Burke in the foyer. He delivers the message and asks her boring questions about her book, trying to catch her out, and doesn't believe her answers. Julia heads out to the Old House.

Anxious Barnabas is bitching to Willie — where's Julia? Loomis advises he keep his shorts on. Julia shows up and Barnabas starts in on her about Maggie's memory returning. Willie relays the Blue Whale events. Julia tells Barnabas he's getting worked up over nothing, while Willie watches with worry. Bicker and bitch and Barnabas commands Julia to go see Maggie. She tells him she can't, as she's been pulled off the case. Hollow man threatens, advancing on her while watchful Willie watches. Arguing continues and Willie finally weighs in on Julia's side. Pussy Barnabas decides not to kill Hoffman — but he still plans to kill Maggie. He lies, badly, that he'll wait to see if the Maggie memory rumor is true. Barnabas then asks about his injection. Julia goes off to prepare the treatment. Wise Willie waits a minute or so before confronting Barnabas about lying to her and his plan to kill the Magster. He asks when the murder is taking place. Turns out, that night. Need I say Willie looks concerned?

Episode #321 — Willie calling out Barnabas redo. Mensa member Willie points out the problems with killing Maggie and that Julia may narc. Bah, she'd ruin her experiment, Barnabas scoffs. Julia comes back with the injection. As she administers the treatment, she blithely chatters about trust and Maggie and Willie looks concerned.

Maggie's in her room, looking out the French doors. Sam comes in and assures her the place is crawling with well-hidden flatfoots. They discuss the plan to catch the maniac. Maggie decides to stay up and read and sends Sam to bed. Outside, Sarah's by the gate, presumably looking at the house. Maggie dozes off while reading and drops her book. Sarah, now in the room, wakes her and hands her the tome. Maggie's glad to see her, but asks how she got in through a locked door and without being seen. Oh, Sarah has her ways. Maggie asks her to wait there while she gets some milk, but Sarah knows she wants to get Sam. She says she won't stay, as she only came to see her. She then asks where her doll is, as it's important that she (Maggie) have it (this doll hopscotches more than a kindergartener). The Magster opens her bedroom door and calls to

Sam and Sarah, of course, vanishes. Sam comes in the room, blah, blah, Sarah. Maggie believes the girl is trying to warn her.

Julia steps out into the Collinwood garden. Willie, who issued the summons, meets her and rats out Barnabas about his plan to kill Maggie. Loomis urges her to stop him — she's the only one who can. Julia's incredulous, Julia ponders, and Willie's like, get the hell on with it! She tells him to wait there while she goes to have a chat with Mr. Collins.

After checking with the cops, Sam tells Maggie they didn't see Sarah (guess that ghost theory was promptly forgotten) and that Joe is going to get the doll from Woodard. Dogs howl and Maggie's scared (and shrill).

Barnabas, at the Old House, is looking out the window, thinking it's time to get to killin'.

Episode #322 — Barnabas death thought replay/redo. As he's about to leave to commit homicide, Julia shows up. He tells her he was going for a walk. She says she knows about the murder plan. Oh, she talked to Willie, well, he's unreliable (that's right, lie and insult). Julia knows he's full of shit, but goddamn, these two talk about murder like they're brokering a business deal. Cold. Julia then says if he kills Maggie, he'll be exposed. Also, if he kills *her* he'll be exposed, as she left a letter, detailing all, with someone who will turn it over to the authorities. Barnabas isn't sure if she's bluffing or not. Hoffman leaves and he stares out the window some more.

Sleeping Maggie wakes with a start and calls for Sam. She tells him she felt like she was being watched. Sam checks outside; nothing.

Willie's pacing the garden and hides when he hears someone coming. It's only Julia, who informs that she talked Barnabas out of the killing, with the mention of a non-existent letter. Willie knows that Barnabas doesn't believe the overconfident Julia.

In the parlor, Barnabas wonders about the letter and watching the metaphoric hamster on the wheel is somewhat amusing. He decides that Julia is fibbing and that Maggie Evans must die! He's prevented from leaving yet again when he hears flute music and gets all whiney.

Joe's gone to the Evanses' with the doll. The three discuss Sarah/maniac. Joe says cops are everywhere, he had a hard time getting to the house. He's going to stay and keep watch with Sam. Maggie comes over with a weird feeling of being warm, which she keeps repeating, and unafraid . Sam says it's the drugs kicking in, go with it. She falls asleep.

Alone in the Collinwood garden, 'ole Willie voice-overs his inner turmoil. He knows Barnabas will kill Maggie, just like Jason, but he deserved it (brother, you just said a mouthful), then do the same to David and Burke. He's busted up that he's unable to help. He determines to warn Maggie to leave town, then laments that he's fooling himself.

Outside the cottage, Sam and Joe discuss sending Maggie up to Canada the next day and tell no one where she is (you're going to exile her for the rest of her life?). As it nears three a.m. the out-in-the-open cops notice someone lurking in the darkness. A large shadow looms outside the French doors. A gunshot sounds. Maggie wakes with a yelp. The cops are instructing someone to halt, Maggie screams, eight or nine shots are heard and Sam and Joe rush in. Sam comforts his daughter while Joe dashes outside. A deputy comes in and informs that they got the intruder. No, he's not dead, yet, but he should be, what with five bullets in his back (shot in the back? Really? There are no words.)

Episode #323 — Shooting the intruder replay. Maggie and Sam head to the living room. Joe rushes in and announces — wait for it — it was Willie Loomis! (Allow me to drown my sorrows in a sea of alcohol; first Bill Malloy, now Willie. What do they have against guys named William?) Sam says it's all right now, he's dead. Patterson happens to walk in at that moment and asks to use the phone because — miracle! — Willie has yet to shuffle off his mortal coil. Patterson tells a deputy to get on the radio and call for an ambulance, while he uses the phone to call Woodard and poor Willie bleeds out on the cold ground from multiple gunshot wounds. Maggie and Sam have a hard time believing quiet, timid Willie was the kidnapper. Joe tells the sheriff that Willie was trouble when he first came to town with Jason — he made a pass at Maggie! — because George Patterson has his own amnesia, forgetting that he harassed Mr. Loomis in episode #237 and tried again in #241. Blah, blah, but Willie's changed so much since then, Maggie states, asking Patterson if he made a mistake. Nope, George says, Willie was at the Blue Whale when we set the trap. A deputy apprises them that Woodard has arrived and a siren sound effect tells us the ambulance has made the scene. Patterson's off to the Old House and Maggie says Barnabas will be *so* upset, he's always been so kind to Willie (kind, cruel, what's the difference?).

At the Old House, Barnabas is looking at Sarah's portrait and whinging. Julia shows up, claiming since she can't sleep, she'll do a little work (it's got to be at least four in the morning!). Blah, blah, Maggie/trust and Barnabas admits Sarah stopped him from killing again. Patterson shows up and breaks the bad news. Barnabas seems genuinely shocked at first. When Patterson says Willie was Maggie's kidnapper, the heinous one sees an opportunity to cover his ass. The sheriff relays that Willie is in bad shape and will most likely die. Barnabas asks after Maggie and wants to apologize to her for Willie's actions. Patterson's heading back to the cottage and invites both to accompany him.

Outside the cottage, Patterson explains what happened and ghoulishly points out the spot where poor Willie was gunned down. They go to the house and Barney lies through his canines. Sam mentions that the trap worked and explains the memory rumor. According to Patterson, Woodard removed four of the five bullets from Willie (in about an hour's time). Loomis is in a coma now and on death's door. Even though he's going to die, he sure hopes he gets a chance to talk to him. Fuck you, George.

At the Old House, dressing gowned Barnabas frets alone because, well, you know, no more Willie. Julia shows up and says she couldn't get near Loomis, as Woodard was still operating. She did see his chart, however, and he's a goner for sure (I miss him already). What if he survives? Barnabas fusses, he'll talk! Nah, Julia replies, he dies and you're good (this callous bitch). Blah, blah, Maggie's memory. Oh, it's another Barnabas threat.

At the cottage, Sam and Joe have an early morning belt of scotch as Maggie sleeps. At the Old House, Barnabas thinks that Willie dying will be fantastic, but he has to figure out what to do with David.

Episode #324 — Morning and David tries going out to see Sarah, but is stopped by Liz. She asks him if anything's wrong. He says no, then takes a moment to stare at Barnabas' portrait before running upstairs (maybe he was frightened off by Aunt Liz's horrific green, yellow and pink print dress). Vicki comes home from visiting Maggie and gives a Willie update; still comatose and expected to die later that day (if he's really going to die, make it quick and merciful; he's suffered enough). Oh, and she can't believe that he's the guilty party. Liz responds that any friend of McGuire's is scum (uh, you were about to marry him, what does that say about *you*?). Vicki's still on Willie's side — until Liz convinces her not to be. Talk turns to David, who is acting frightened and weird. Liz tells Vicki to watch him closely until they figure out why and he's not to go out alone.

In the study, David's thinking instead of writing his assigned paper. As he tells Vicki that nothing is scaring him, Julia comes in. Vicki suggests taking a break and going for a walk with her to the Old House to see Barnabas — he did so much for Willie (like psychological torture, physical abuse, raping his soul and being responsible for him getting shot?). David passes on the invite and tells Vicki she shouldn't go, as it's not safe. Julia listens to the exchange with concern. David is adamant in his refusal to see his cousin and exiles himself to his room. Julia tells Vicki that Barnabas is away for the day and the governess jokes that he must really be sleeping, as he loves the night so much.

A bit later, Woodard and Julia are in the study. All bullets have been removed from our man Loomis and the outlook is pretty grim. Julia fishes; will he be able to talk? Will he be paralyzed? She hopes he survives and confesses, as it will prove her right; she suspected him all along! (Bitch) Woodard's surprised and Julia lies; Loomis has a severe personality disorder, he's a psychopath (this insufferable cow). Blah, blah, supernatural/ Sarah/Maggie all wrapped up in some very bad lying. Julia says the case is solved, but she'll stick around for a few days, so as not to blow her cover. She balks when Woodard suggests she come clean to Liz. Woodard then says he knows the real reason she's staying; she's hot for Barnabas, everyone knows it (oh, doctor, something for my nausea, please).

Pensive Vicki is alone in the drawing room. Julia strolls in (guess Woodard left) and they talk David and his newfound Barnabas/Old House fear. Julia offers to talk to him, which Liz is doing right now. Up in David's room, auntie is trying to get the boy to open up. She tells him he's safe, the kidnapper was shot and caught last night. David immediately states that it wasn't Willie, then tries to run out to find Sarah — she'll know for sure. Downstairs, Vicki and Julia hear David and Liz arguing in the foyer about going outside. David stops and freaks out while looking at the Barnabas portrait, the eyes of which are supposed to be glowing, I guess, but the effect didn't work very well.

Episode #325 — Night and robed David heads downstairs to look at the portrait and remembers what Barnabas said when he found him in the cemetery. David starts shouting about going back to Collinwood. Liz comes out of the drawing room and David dashes upstairs to his room. There, he ruminates on Barnabas, the secret room and Sarah. Vicki comes in and they talk filler. Coming back downstairs, Vicki finds Liz putting on her coat; she's heading to the Old House to talk to Barnabas. She opines that David needs help and Vicki suggests he talk to Burke, who'll be back in town tomorrow. Liz agrees and then asks if they've set a wedding date. Not yet. Liz says that given the current situation, David might not accept a new governess. Vicki agrees to stick around as long as she needs to. Barnabas then shows up and seeps greasy charm. In the drawing room, they engage in Willie talk and Barnabas can't help but back that bus over him a few times. Liz turns to the topic of David and — holy crap — mentions Laura (in passing). Barnabas decides a man-to-man talk with the lad is in order (no, only Roger gets to have those with his son). Liz asks him not to press the child. Oh, he'll be gentle (oh, yeah, as gentle as wielding that cane on Willie's face). Barnabas is escorted to David's room and acts a menacing dick to the frightened boy. He then badgers the poor kid about his secret. Blah, blah, secret room, then Barnabas confronts David with his broken pocketknife. David insists Sarah never told him about herself or her family, despite him asking. Vicki comes in, inadvertently saving the youngster from further browbeating.

Later, in bed, David tosses and turns and recalls his coffin conversation with Sarah, then Barnabas' interrogation. He has another nightmare. In a misty, subterranean passage, he calls for his friend and comes across no-face Julia dangling her hypno-medallion (truly creepy, with one of those black morph masks obscuring her face). He resists her and walks away. He finds Sarah and asks her to answer a few questions. She explains how she got sick and died when she was ten. Former ghost believer David asks why she's around now. She says she's looking for someone, then leads him to a coffin. It opens and Barnabas sits up and (off-camera) climbs out. David backs away, trying to warn his friend as Barnabas approaches her. Barnabas then turns his attention to David and advances, threatening him with his cane.

Episode #326 — A replay of the end of the dream. The previous episode was a kinescope and this sequence looked better in b&w; I can't image no-face Julia looking creepier in color. Anyway, distraught David is shouting in his sleep. Vicki rushes in and he babbles that he saw him come out of a coffin — cousin Barnabas is *dead*. Oh, no, Vicki soothes, you were just dreaming. He goes on to inform Miss Winters that Sarah is dead, too, and a ghost (finally!). Vicki again brushes it off as a dream (she hasn't heard of precognitive dreams?). David mentions the faceless woman with the shiny jewelry. Vicki suggests a glass of milk, but the boy's not interested. He says he'll find Sarah tomorrow and have her show him where the coffin is. Vicki says he can't go out and humors him, but doesn't believe the ghost explanation (this from the woman who saw Bill Malloy's specter and insisted Josette visited her when she was a captive of Matthew Morgan).

At the Old House, Julia is reading in the parlor when Barnabas comes home.

With much hand-wringing, he says he went to the hospital, hoping Willie was dead, but was dismayed to learn that he hadn't kicked off yet. He insults the man by inferring he's leech-like (this *asshole*) and asks Julia why he isn't dead yet. Hell if she knows, she's not his doctor, but he'll die. Barnabas wants to know *when.* Unable to wait, the Evil One wants to off him before he "miraculously recovers and writes his memoirs" (okay, that line was absolutely hilarious). Julia says if Willie is killed, the investigation will continue. Barnabas whinges about Maggie, David and Willie — boo-freaking-hoo. David knows too much, blah, blah. Also, evil Julia proposes hypnotizing David (like peas in a pod, these two).

The next day, Julia eavesdrops a bit as Vicki and Liz discuss David's latest dream. Julia walks into the drawing room and fakes interest and concern about the lad. Dumbass Hoffman says she's had experience with child psychology, which gets a do you now? raised eyebrow from Liz. Oh, *she's* not a child psychologist, but she's seen situations like this before, let her talk to him. Liz says sure and goes to check on him. Julia asks Vicki for dream details.

David's at his desk, drawing, when Liz comes in and tells him Miss Hoffman would like to speak with him. No thanks. Liz asks him to give it a try. She then asks to see his drawing. He reluctantly shows her; a picture of a coffin and a headstone with Barnabas' name on it. Needless to say, Liz is a bit surprised.

Alone in the drawing room, Julia admires her hypno-medallion for a moment before tucking it back into her handbag. David joins her and she asks him about his dream. She puts him at ease, then starts asking more questions. She eventually whips out the medallion. David fights off the hypnotism attempt and exclaims that *she* was the one in his dream, with that exact same medallion. He then jumps up, opens the drawing room doors, and calls for Vicki.

Episode #327 — Failed hypnotism redo. David runs out to the foyer, with Julia following. Liz and Vicki come along and Dame Stoddard, looking divine in turquoise, asks what the hell is going on, while David clings to his governess. Julia lies, saying she was just showing him some jewelry. David says otherwise and flees upstairs. In the drawing room, Julia lies some more about the incident and Vicki says he must still be freaked out from his dream. Vicki says that the medallion is the same one Julia showed Maggie, then goes upstairs to David.

In his room, the boy is peering into his crystal ball, looking for Sarah. Vicki tells him the medallion is a coincidence. Young master Collins would prefer if Miss Hoffman left the premises; she's scary. Checking his divination device once again, David gets excited, as he knows where to find Sarah. Vicki harshes his mood by telling him he can't go out. He promises he'll tell her what their secrets are if she allows him to leave. After a nanosecond, Vicki gives the okay.

Later, Burke and Vicki are in the drawing room, blathering about the usual dream/fear stuff. He observes that Julia spends a lot of time at the Old House; maybe she has a crush on Barnabas. Vicki tells him David is out of the house, blah, blah, and Burke sets out to find him.

David's in the woods and Sarah eventually shows up. She knew he consulted his crystal ball to find her. He asks her to explain his dream. Burke hears the two talking and calls to David; Sarah doesn't bother to stick around. Devlin joins David, blah, blah dream (boring). The talk turns to Sarah and David says she's a ghost. Burke is bemused.

Back at Collinwood, Burke suffers from a bad entrance cue on the landing, which makes for a what the hell? moment. He joins Vicki and Liz in the drawing room and engages in Sarah ghost talk (why is everyone so shocked at the idea all of a sudden? What about Laura, for God's sake?). Ah, Vicki believes the child *is* a specter and challenges Burke to prove otherwise by finding the flesh-and-blood girl and bringing her to Collinwood.

Later that night, sleeping David is woken by Sarah (who is unseen in a dark corner until bathed in an eerie, blue light which gives her a ghostly look). She tells him to stay away from the Old House cellar. He asks her if Willie kidnapped Maggie and Sarah, bless her dead little heart, says no, poor Willie went to warn her. She's got other places to be, so she fades away — we get to see it this time — as she repeatedly warns David not to go to the Old House.

Episode #328 — Night. Woodard is in Willie's hospital room and our man's head and upper chest are obscured by an oxygen tent, leading one to ask if that's really him under there.

Barnabas, meanwhile, paces the parlor. Julia comes in and says all is well — Willie's still in a coma and will most likely kick off soon. That's not imminent enough for Barnabas, who decides to hasten Willie into that inevitable meeting with his maker by decreeing that...Willie must die! Tonight! Julia tells him he's a dumbass and reminds him that Loomis is surrounded by all kinds of people. Determined Barney wants to go to the hospital anyway. She says he won't be allowed to see the patient and besides, the sheriff is coming to talk to him and search Willie's room for proof he's the kidnapper. The cow then sighs if only there was a way to prove Willie was the guilty party. Barnabas hits on a plan.

Hey, a new Patterson. The sheriff is hanging out in Willie's room and Woodard declares if Willie survives, it will be a miracle. Oh, *now* Patterson thinks he's innocent (I can't keep up with all this flip-flopping).

At the Old House, Barnabas is showing Julia Maggie's ring (remember, from episode #253?). Oh, they're in Willie's room (which is quite tidy). Gloating Barnabas plants the ring in the hollow base of a candlestick. Her henchman work done, Julia decides to go back to Collinwood. Barnabas commands her to go to the hospital and prevent Willie from recovering. She says he's crazy for ordering her to kill him and refuses, but Barnabas wants what Barnabas wants.

The vigil continues in the hospital room. Sam strolls in, casual as can be (I thought it was hard to get in to see him?) and now *he* admits to believing Willie is innocent. All three blah, blah Willie's not a psychopath. Woodard then brings up Sarah, which has absolutely no relevance to the conversation. Patterson announces he's going to the Old House to search Loomis' room. Sam asks to tag along. Why, sure, Patterson replies, then instructs Woodard not to let Willie talk to anyone if he wakes up (is he a doctor? A lawyer? No? Then fuck you).

At the Old House, Barnabas is damn near wetting himself in anticipation of the sheriff's visit. Patterson and Sam arrive. Barnabas feigns concern and allows them to search Willie's room (a civilian conducting a search? Really? That would be tainting the scene and anything found would be inadmissible. A slick defense attorney could try and argue that the owner of the property, Liz, never gave permission for a search. Barnabas is a familial freeloader). Patterson starts rummaging and as Barnabas lights some candles, Sam decides to play Ellery Queen by asking a question or two. After a soft room tossing, Barnabas tries to be ever-so-helpful by retrieving the key to Willie's suitcase (bullshit! When Willie — and that's faux five Willie — came to Collinwood, he had a *seabag*, not a suitcase) and knocks over the candlestick. Oh, my, butterfingers — look! — and he fishes the ring out. Patterson takes it and shows it to Sam, who positively identifies it as his daughter's and that she was wearing it when she disappeared (she was wearing a different one before the ring became a minor plot point and I'm not sure she was wearing one when she 'died' in the hospital). Well, that proves it, Willie's their man.

Julia's at the hospital in Willie's room and gets an update from Woodard. The patient suddenly moans and Woodard peeks under the tent. He's coming out of the coma! The attending physician rushes out to put a call in to the sheriff. Julia looks at the IV/transfusion and recalls Barnabas' words to off the poor son-of-a-bitch.

At the Old House, the men come downstairs and Patterson and Sam now proclaim Willie to be a drooling psycho. Barnabas just can't believe it. Oh, he blames himself (asshole), then offers any help he can give to the Evanses. A deputy shows up with the news about Willie. Barnabas looks worried.

Episode #329 — Well, the old Sheriff Patterson is back in the parlor redo and he invites Sam to come to the hospital. Evans would rather go home and check on Maggie. Barnabas asks if he can tag along and feigns belief in the patient's innocence.

Willie's out of the oxygen tent, but still unconscious. Woodard's amazed at his recuperative powers and Julia suggests maybe he wasn't as seriously injured as first they thought (five bullets, in the back? Please). Woodard believes the transfusions are responsible (really?), but wishes they hadn't sedated him. Julia, in a moment of decency, says that he had to be, as he was in a great deal of pain. But Woodard wants a confession! Julia fires up a cigarette (in an ICU patient's room no less) and Woodard doesn't even bat an eye (that's how it was; hell, if Willie came to and asked for a smoke, they'd probably give him one). Woodard tells her that Patterson no longer believes Willie is guilty and Julia is alarmed. He asks her to stay while he checks on another patient and make sure that needle of the fifty-seventh transfusion doesn't slip out of his arm. Woodard ducks out and Julia stands over the bed and thinks things over — so easy to kill him. She slowly reaches for the needle when Woodard comes back and asks what the hell she's doing. She lies, claiming Willie started moving, so she was checking the IV.

Out in the hall, Patterson and Barnabas have arrived. The sheriff tells Barney to wait there, he can't see Willie until after *he's* talked to him. Barnabas asks if he can be present during the questioning. No, Patterson prefers to be alone (hey, screw you, George, there's something called Miranda and Willie is in no condition to be making decisions whether to talk to you or not without representation. Go fuck yourself). Barnabas pathetically tries to persuade Patterson, but fails.

Patterson enters the room as Julia fiddles with the IV. Woodard tells him Willie is sedated and it could be three or four hours. The lawman will wait. George asks Julia what she's doing there, blah, blah, she's a doctor and has been helpful. Patterson is now convinced Loomis *is* guilty and shows them the ring. He mentions that Barnabas is out in the hall and Julia goes out to fill him in while Patterson waits for the patient's drugs to wear off.

In the hall, Barnabas commands Julia to kill Willie. She tells him she can't and even when she had the opportunity, she couldn't bring herself to do the deed. Barney bitches, then everyone plays the waiting game.

Willie starts writhing and moaning in pain, then opens his eyes. Woodard stops Patterson from talking and asks Willie how he's feeling, which is a pretty god-damn stupid question to ask a guy who's been shot five times and just came out of a coma. Willie moans that everything hurts and Woodard says, sure, he'll give him a sedative (no painkillers, a nice morphine drip, perhaps?) *after* he answers some questions (hey, screw you, too, Woodard; you should be hit with a malpractice suit and your license should be pulled for that stunt). Willie says he doesn't recognize either man and Woodard explains he's a doctor and Loomis is in the hospital. Willie whimpers in pain again, but since Woodard went to the Mengele school of medicine, he lets him suffer. Patterson asks him why he went to Maggie's. Willie repeats the name, then turns away and begs not to be hurt. Patterson asks again and Willie asks if it's dark, saying he's afraid of the dark and the night and don't hurt him. George shows him the ring and asks whose it is. Willie gets that look when he sees pretty, shiny things and, reaching for it, says it's his. Patterson says it's Maggie's and that Willie stole it. Willie freaks out again about being afraid.

In the hall, Barnabas bitches, as dawn is approaching. Julia tries to calm him down. Woodard and Patterson step out and Patterson, who does not hold a degree in psychiatry, abnormal or forensic, pronounces Willie to be "hopelessly insane," which isn't even a legitimate diagnosis. Woodard piles on, saying his mind has snapped, he was always deranged, but now he's just reduced to incoherent babbling about being afraid of a voice from the grave. Oh, he's guilty, George decrees, case closed. Woodard pipes in that poor Willie will be shipped off to an institution for the criminally insane (not on your say so, asshole; that's for the courts to decide). Barnabas and Julia show fake concern and are given permission to see the patient.

Willie is staring at nothing when Barnabas and Julia walk in. Barnabas says his name and Willie glances over at him (this is where I deviate from others) with what I perceive as a crafty look and a barely perceptible smile. In a very calm voice, he asks who he (Barnabas) is, a doctor? Barnabas says, yes, he's a doctor. I contend that our man Loomis is faking.

(I don't doubt that when Willie first came out of his coma, disoriented and in pain, he relived the traumatic event, or aftermath, of being attacked in the mausoleum by Barnabas, hence his fear of the dark and of being hurt. On top of that, he's groggy, in pain and the law is badgering him about Maggie, the ring, etc. I think that when left alone, Willie had a chance to sort things out and his old, street smart ways kicked in. To avoid prison for something he didn't do, he played crazy; he's in survival mode.

Another thing that chaps me about this episode, and the preceding, is the flagrant illegality of the search and subsequent questioning. It's ridiculous. The ring would be inadmissible for a number of reasons and too many people touched it; Maggie, Willie, David, Vicki, Barnabas, Patterson, the 'evidence' is loaded with smudged fingerprints. Willie could get himself a lawyer and absolutely ruin Patterson and Woodard's lives; and be totally justified in doing it. Sue the town, too, just for the hell of it. If this is how they write Willie off the show, it's a travesty.)

Hello? Child Protective Services…?

Episode #330 — Afternoon. David is staring at the old Barnabas portrait in the foyer and we get that shitty light effect again, although it looks better from a distance. Liz comes out of the drawing room and asks what the hell he's doing. Blah, blah, eyes, he's watching the kid. David's afraid of Barnabas because he wants him to die. Liz is shocked but David insists his cousin hates him and that he's hiding something in the Old House. He almost mentions Sarah's warning. Just after relating that Sarah is a ghost, Roger, paper in hand, steps out of the drawing room, fed up. David insists he's not imagining things. Arguing ensues, with Roger finally sending his son up to his room. Liz tells Roger punishment isn't the way to deal with the problem. David sneaks back downstairs and with a determined face, grabs his coat and heads out.

At the Old House, since the door is locked, David climbs in through the window. He steels his little self and heads for the door leading to the basement, just as the sun is setting. The door is locked and he's caught by Julia. He tells her he has a right to be there, his aunt owns the house. He asks why *she's* there. Working. Where's Barnabas? Out. Why is the door locked? She doesn't know, now go home, it's getting dark. She grabs his arm and hauls him out.

Liz comes downstairs to the drawing room, to find Roger at the piano, plunking out Beethoven's *Minuet in G*. David's missing! Julia delivers the errant boy just as Liz and Roger enter the foyer. Roger tries sending David to his room and Julia tells them Barnabas would appreciate it if they kept the boy away. She's alarmed when David claims Barnabas wants him to die. Rehash, filler. Julia impresses on the siblings not to tell Barnabas about David's recent adventure.

Up in his room, David muses on the locked basement door.

Later, Julia's at the Old House and has just given Barnabas another treatment. He asks why she's uneasy. She tells him Willie, whom she's fond of (not enough to save him, bitch), has been shipped off to a nuthouse for the criminally insane. Barnabas claims he's fond of Loomis, too (bull). Julia then shows how much she doesn't care about him by saying that at least everyone thinks Willie was the kidnapper — he's safe! Barnabas brings up David; did she hypnotize him? Nah, that didn't work. Blah, blah, secret mausoleum room and the Evil One comes up with some diabolical plan to deal with the boy.

Roger goes to David's room for a talk, not to punish him. The topics *du jour* are covered. Roger wants his son to stop disobeying him and promise to stay away from the Old House. David agrees, since the place scares him anyway. Roger leaves and a moment later, the window blows open and a rubber bat on a wire swoops in and chases a terrified David though the room.

Episode #331 — Rubber bat redo! Terrified David yells for help. Roger and Liz hear him and rush up to his room. They help him off the floor and he tells of the bat attack; but the bat is nowhere to be found. The lad explains what happened, but skeptical Roger points out that the window is closed and locked. Dejected David knows they don't believe him and starts crying. Liz sends Roger out to call Woodard. David tells her that Barnabas sent the bat because he wants him dead.

Meanwhile, evil Barnabas is staring out the parlor window. Jerk. Seeing Roger coming, he answers the knock and puts on a gag worthy act of politeness. Rog is there to talk bat attack. Barnabas wets his pants with glee at his prank, but fakes concern. Roger apologizes for David being there earlier, looking for something he believes is hidden in the basement. Roger thinks it's nonsense, then brings up the latest Sarah visit and her warning to avoid the Old House. Oh, Barnabas gets depressed. Roger then brings up David's Barnabas in coffin dream. Assmunch Barnabas asks if he ever considered sending David away (why, yes; yes he has, when the lad, in his callow youth, was an 'incipient psychopath'). Roger says he has, but Liz would protest. Barnabas thinks she can be convinced.

David's now in bed, insisting to Woodard that he's not lying — is it safe to give a sedative to a ten year old? Upon mentioning Sarah, the doctor gets interested. Blah, blah, Old House warning. Oh, and she also said Willie is innocent of everything. David goes on to say he liked Willie and doesn't think he could hurt anybody. The drugs kick in and David falls asleep.

In the drawing room, Liz strongly protests against sending David away to a 'special' school. Roger gives up without much of a fight. Woodard comes in and Roger asks him for a shrink referral and the doc says David might be telling the truth.

David's sleeping and from the dark corner of his room, eerily lit Sarah calls to him (that blue lighting really gives a nice ghostly vibe). She goes to his bed and sits on the edge, waking him. She scolds him for going to the Old House and again says to avoid, or he'll get in trouble. Blah, blah, repetition ad nauseum. She then gives him a gift, a very old toy soldier that will keep him safe, so he should keep it with him all the time. David wants to get Liz, but Sarah fades away.

Episode #332 — Barnabas is staring out the window (and it occurs to me that he does that with the frequency that Laura stared into fire). Julia comes into the parlor with another treatment. Barney's bloomers are in a bunch and he complains about loyalty, or a lack thereof, then starts choking her (well, since Willie's in Bedlam...). He bitches about how she failed to protect him during the day, that's when he's vulnerable! (Then I guess you shouldn't have tried to kill Maggie and fucked over Willie — it all comes back to you, loser) Julia says she is loyal, but he gets her to admit David was there earlier (how about a mini-drinking game, whenever 'danger' is mentioned — you'll be unconscious in the first five minutes of this episode). Barnabas says he took care of things, but he won't tell her what he did to the poor kid. Julia says if he harms her or the boy, everyone will know Willie is innocent. Barnabas gets all *sturm und drang* and goes on about how he has to find his bride, his Josette (what? Aren't the treatments supposed to *cure* him? Does that mean he'll just be a regular run-of-the-mill evil psycho? I'm confused).

The next day, Julia and Roger are having tea in the drawing room. She asks after David and he tells her about David's hallucinated or dreamt bat. She says it could be true, she's seen them around. Blah, blah, David/Barnabas and now *she* suggests sending the lad off to school. Roger says Barney said the same thing when he talked to him and told him everything about David's visit. The boy comes downstairs and hears the renewed talk of sending him away (remember that back in the early days?). David starts back upstairs, vowing to himself to prove something's in that basement, then hears Sarah's voice warning him. David has a bit of a think, then pulls the toy solider from his pocket, wondering if it will really protect him. He then heads through the door under the stairs and returns a short time later. Seems he has purloined a set of keys. Vicki comes downstairs, wearing that hideous pumpkin orange dress, and asks him what he was doing in the study and what did he just put in his pocket? He shows her the soldier and says he went to the study to show the toy to Liz. Vicki suggests he show it to Julia. Maybe later and he refuses to give it to her to show Julia.

Entering the drawing room, Vicki tells Roger and Julia about the toy. David sneaks outside. Julia claims to have seen a drawing in a family album of a little boy holding a toy soldier like she described (how convenient). Vicki says why not go up and talk to David and Ms. Hoffman does just that.

At the Old House, David uses the keys to unlock the front door. Julia rejoins Vicki (where did Roger go?) in the drawing room and says David's not in his room, maybe he went to the Old House. Blah, blah, almost dark. Julia offers to look and bring him back if found. Vicki blathers and Julia looks oh-so-worried as she leaves. David, meanwhile, tries unlocking the basement door as the sun sets. Barnabas rises from his nap. David finally finds the right key and heads down — hey, candles are lit, does Barney need a nightlight? David finds the coffin open and empty. Looking around the room, Barnabas comes from around a corner and noisily slams the lid, startling the boy.

Episode #333 — Basement visit redo/replay. Barnabas interrogates a frightened David and grabs him in order to mete out punishment. Julia calls for David from upstairs and Davey yells for help, then bolts upstairs, straight to Hoffman, who comforts him. Barnabas follows and claims he was just going to spank the boy. He inquires how David got in and then asks him to hand over the spare keys, which he'll keep for the time being (Liz might have something to say about that). Barnabas lets David go and Julia asks what the kid saw in the basement. The coffin, and Barney gets that evil glint and smiles with menace. Julia knows he has a plan.

At Collinwood, Burke and Woodard discuss David as Liz and Mrs. Johnson search for the boy. The doctor asks Devlin who he really suspected as the kidnapper; Barnabas, perchance? Yep. David runs in pell-mell and tells them there's a coffin in the Old House basement — because Barnabas is dead! Julia's also back and tells David to stop talking about his dream. Blah, blah, Old House incident/coffin/kill David, Julia says there's nothing in the basement (after the first interminable basement storyline, the writers need to wrap this one up fast). David pleads with Burke to go to the Old House. Roger strolls in and repetition abounds (these episodes are dull, but young Henesy is the bright spot). Fed up Roger sends David to his room. Rog then apologizes to Julia and with a bizarre lightness of tone, she says she understands, the boy is disturbed. Not so fast, Woodard interjects, let's go to the Old House. Bicker and bitch. Burke sides with Woodard and off they go. Julia's concerned.

At the Old House, the duo ask to see the basement. Barnabas fakes concern over poor cousin David's mental health, then says there's nothing but some trunks down there and gets offended — nay, *insulted* — at the request. He vehemently refuses to allow them access. Burke says, fine, they'll come back with a search warrant (on what planet? They're not cops and no judge would issue one based on their cockamamie hunch if they were. And *now* Barnabas is uncooperative, when it's *his* ass on the line, but he sure backed that bus over Willie multiple times. If he were in prison, he'd deserve to get shanked). Eventually, Barney agrees to take them downstairs. The coffin is gone, there's just some boxes and trunks in its place (but that cellar is cavernous, the coffin could be anywhere— or did the basement shrink after Maggie escaped and its capaciousness was of no further use?). Woodard and Burke apologize and Barnabas smugly smiles. (Good, effective lighting in this scene; they seem to be doing it more and more. I also have to laugh that since Willie is gone, Barnabas has to lower himself to do physical labor and heavy lifting.)

Episode #334 — David anxiously waits in his room with the still pumpkin dressed Vicki. He's sure he'll be vindicated. Vicki starts burbling about the story of Bluebeard as a time filler (that would have worked better during Maggie's captivity). Outside the front door, Burke and Woodard discuss Barnabas. Burke admits to never liking him and Woodard always found him strange. They then discuss how to break the news to David and what they should do for him. Entering the foyer, they encounter Roger and fill him in. Roger's in fine form and tells Woodard that David's not disturbed, but a child with an active imagination who's playing a game. He goes on to admit that when he was a boy, he was afraid of the house, shadows and ancestral portraits, but he grew out of it and his son will, too. He then sends the men upstairs and, walking into the drawing room, casts a concerned look at one of the family portraits.

Burke and Woodard go to David's room and hustle Vicki out. They tell the boy what occurred. Poor kid is upset; so much so that he breaks his promise to Sarah by telling them about the mausoleum's secret room. The window blows open and a strange rendition of *London Bridge* flute music is heard. David knows she's mad at him. He tells of hiding in the coffin there when Willie and Barnabas came in and offers to take them to the crypt. Woodard grudgingly agrees to go, if Roger says it's okay.

Vicki and Roger wait in the drawing room. When the trio joins them, Woodard makes the Eagle Hill request. Absolutely not and how dare he insinuate anything about Barnabas, Roger splutters. Roger slams another brandy as the doctor quietly pleads his case. Roger allows the trip, but if nothing is there, that's the end of all of it. Father and son then start arguing, but Vicki jumps in, taking David out of the room to get his jacket. Roger admits to Woodard that he's deeply concerned about his son and thinks it's time for professional help, a psychiatrist (hey, there's one living in your house). David and Vicki come back in and Roger acts gruff again. The trio leave. Roger then asks Miss Winters about her upcoming marriage. Vicki says she'll stay for David and Roger utters some profound words about David's fragile mental health.

David, Burke and Woodard arrive at Eagle Hill. Once inside the crypt, David explains how to open the panel, but when he tries, it won't budge (this is bullshit). David figures that Barnabas did something to prevent it opening. Both men say he imagined the secret room. Woodard goes on to tell the boy that he can only believe what can be seen — and David sees Sarah's flute sitting on her sarcophagus and picks it up. Woodard's intrigued, David remains distraught (another dull episode, except for David and Roger).

Episode # 335 — Kinescope. David's in his room, with the crystal ball. He calls to Sarah and she appears, telling him she wasn't going to show because he sang like a canary. She confirms that 'somebody' prevented him from opening the panel. David's mad because Aunt Elizabeth is fetching a shrink for him; he doesn't want people thinking he's crazy and be shipped off to a funny farm (like Willie?). Sarah wants her flute back, but Woodard still has it. Liz knocks and Sarah takes a powder. Liz comes in with a Dr. Fisher. Blah, blah, not crazy. The doc asks about the crystal ball, then wants to talk to David alone. Through a bit of a time jump, David is wrapping up recounting his dream about dead, mean, fanged Barnabas. No, he doesn't think about death, no, he's not afraid of dead Sarah, just Barnabas. Oh, God, Fisher asks for the dream details again, but, thankfully, they cut away just after David mentions the faceless woman.

In the drawing room, Burke is talking to some guy about David, etc. Why is Burke talking to a nebbishy looking accountant about Maggie and David? Rehash. The CPA asks who was responsible for Willie's wounds? (Who is this guy?) A bit later, Fisher comes downstairs and proclaims to Liz, Burke and ? and the Mysterians that David is very disturbed, then posits that perhaps David didn't accept his mother's death, hence the faceless woman in the dream is his mother, Laura (oh, great, a goddamn Freudian. Sorry, doc, David can barely remember that harridan bitch of a mother of his). Blah, blah, the boy's afraid of death (no, he's not and this is boring). They all go to the Barnabas portrait in the foyer and tax accountant recites some poem I've never heard of and I swear to God, whoever wrote this episode was familiar with an analyst's couch. When Fisher mentions dream Barnabas devouring David, the CPA looks concerned — oh, that's Woodard (the hell?). Woodard announces he's got to split and Fisher leaves as well. Liz has some bad news for Burke. The lawyers looked over the Seaview house deed; the last occupant, an eccentric, put a provision in his will that no one but a Collins could live in the house for one hundred years after his death — the provision still has five years left. Liz says she'll gift them the house when it's available, but Burke is still depressed.

With Sarah's flute in tow, the new Woodard has gone to the Collins crypt. Via voice-over, he's made the leap of faith and knows Barnabas is evil. He tries to open the panel, but his hand pulls away (unseen force?). He turns around to find Sarah standing behind him.

Episode #336 — Crypt redo, with Sarah startling NewWoodard by calling him by name as he reaches for the ring. He's glad to see her and she says she knew he would come. They talk David and Maggie for a bit. Woodard tells her David might get put away, like Maggie, so he needs some answers. She confirms that there is a secret room and that someone sealed it, but she's reversed the action. She opens the panel and the two walk into the secret room. He sees the coffin and talks aloud to himself a lot. He asks if anyone was ever buried there — how the hell did Woodard hit on the idea of a strange or shameful death occurring? He finds chains on the floor (oh, please, those haven't been there in ages) and babbles a lot more, asking Sarah who was buried there, but she's gone.

In the drawing room, Vicki and Burke are talking house. He says he's going off on a business trip, but when he gets back, he'd like them to set a wedding date and find another domicile. Vicki says, sure, *if* they marry. Burke's like the hell? Oh, for fuck's sake, Vicki says not getting the house is a sign that they shouldn't marry just now, but Burke finally gets her to admit it's because of David. She wants to wait for his sake and Burke agrees, but then says *he's* afraid of losing her. She assures him that won't happen. Later, after Burke has gone, Woodard shows up looking for him and is told by Vicki that he's out of town on business, but she doesn't know where (wouldn't you tell your fiancee where you were going or ask if they didn't?). Woodard inquires where Julia is; the Old House, naturally. He asks to look at some family histories, but won't say why, and heads to the study. Julia comes home and asks after David, blah, blah, psychiatrist. She hopes now everyone will leave Barnabas alone because *he's* the victim (retch) and he'll be furious to hear about the mausoleum visit.

Vicki tells her Woodard is there and Julia, stricken with consternation, hustles off to the study.

Woodard is pouring over books (that didn't end well for our man Loomis). He tells Julia he found out Sarah is Barnabas' sister and that she's real; he's seen and spoken to her that night, in the crypt. She tries to laugh it off, exclaiming that he's been working too hard, but he's not falling for it. He mentions Sam saw Sarah, too, but she writes that off; he's an artist, he was under a severe, emotional strain, he's a drunk (oh, keep spinning, Julia, just like a Rototiller). Woodard's determined to find out *why* Sarah has come back.

Episode #337 — The Stockbridge crypt and — oh, crap — Crazy Pants Old Man Coot is doddering around. Hmm, it's a different, younger actor, made up old. Woodard shows up and asks the caretaker why the Collins crypt is cursed, per Joshua's journal. Though Fake Old Man talks old fashioned by eschewing grammatical contractions, he is not irritating in the least — hallelujah. Woodard wants to look at the family records because of the attacks on women and the Magster kidnapping. Fake Old Man starts gathering the books.

Barnabas has just exited Collinwood and meets up with the returning Roger. Blah, blah, David. Roger has decided to ship his son off. Evil Barnabas thinks that's swell.

The caretaker finds mention of Sarah's death in one of the books and mentions that when he met Barnabas the (not) new, he thought he was the original. Woodard discovers that Barney the old had suffered a fever like Sarah, resulting in a personality change, shortly before he left for England. A day after his departure, his father ordered the mausoleum be built at Eagle Hill (but I thought Barnabas was around when Sarah died; did they move her?). Woodard finds it curious and says family histories don't always cover everything (a convenient method to explain the canonical inconsistencies). He goes on to say that he doesn't think the original Barnabas went to England (and damn it, it's *Collinsport*!).

In the drawing room, Liz and Roger quarrel about David going to military school. She defends Dr. Fisher and he asks her to at least visit the school. Roger reminds his sister that David is *his* son and he can pretty much do what he wants, without her approval. She intimates he better think twice about that and he says he'll hold off for the time being. Woodard arrives, wanting to see the boy. Liz goes off to get him and Roger and Woodard blah, blah old portrait. Roger pours a drink and more David talk. Liz delivers the lad, then retires to the study with Roger. Woodard tells the boy he believes him and that he met Sarah. However, he says he has to investigate some more before telling people. He concedes Barnabas might be dead and says he knows the secret room is/was for him. David suggests getting Burke to help, but Woodard says he can't wait for Burke to return, he has to act fast. David tells him to be careful.

Barnabas is lighting candles in the parlor (bet you're missing Willie, huh?). The doctor shows up, wanting to discuss David. He tells Barnabas that the kid isn't crazy. Barnabas acts a haughty prick. Woodard puts the screws to him a little bit (not as good as Guthrie did to Burke and Laura, but still fun to see). Oh, boo-hoo, Barnabas slaps down the victim card. Woodard calmly states that he saw his sister. Barnabas says he's obviously deluded, too, as he has no sibling. Woodard then says maybe he misheard and she didn't say *sister*, but *ancestor*. Barnabas, just having had his ass handed to him in Guthrie-like fashion, coldly bids Woodard goodnight. Woodard departs, like a boss.

Episode #338 — Victim card redo, followed by smack-down, Guthrie style. As Woodard steps outside, he meets Julia, who's suspicious of his being there. They cat-and-mouse a tad before he leaves. Julia enters the house and, after a moment, Woodard pulls a McGuire, listening through those cheap-ass parlor windows. Barnabas complains of Woodard knowing about him. Julia brushes it off. The two engage in a lot of words to get to the salient point; she's keeping notes on her experiments. Barnabas wants them destroyed, but she insists they're safe, locked in a strongbox in her room. Blah, blah, Woodard saw Sarah and poor Barney had to deny his own sister — boo-freaking-hoo. Julia actually says "poor Barnabas" and lays a comforting hand on his shoulder.

Burke arrives at Collinwood and tells Vicki, looking pretty in lavender, that he's got to go away on business again; South America this time. She still holds back on setting a wedding date. As they discuss, Liz pauses outside the room to listen a moment, then interrupts. She apologizes for holding up their plans and offers them the closed off West Wing of the house; Vicki will still be near David, but the couple will have their privacy. Burke thanks her and says he'll think it over. Once Liz walks out, Vicki bitches at him for not accepting right away (OldBurke would never acquiesce). Vicki gets petulant and asks if they should move to South America. Burke explains why he doesn't like the idea; he feels that the weirdness that affects the family will latch onto them if they live there. Vicki laughs at him and they kiss and make-up.

Barnabas and Julia are still talking Woodard. He wants her to find out what Woodard knows about Sarah. As she's leaving, Barnabas slathers on some obvious flattery, pronouncing that Julia, not Woodard, was the smartest student in their med school class (vomit-inducing). She smiles at the ego stroking.

Julia arrives at Woodard's office and immediately starts talking Sarah, explaining that she was startled at his declaration. He knows she's full of excrement. She asks what's the connection to Barnabas? Woodard says let's drop Sarah and talk about your buddy, Barney. He confronts her with the list of medical supplies she bought and wants to know about a particular, troubling item. She says he could have just asked her instead of investigating. She feigns embarrassment at admitting that he was right; she's emotionally attached to Mr. Collins. Woodard is all hmm-mmm, fine — now, what about this list? You're doing some doctoring down at that house. Julia stutters and stumbles, then tells him not to ask, for his own good, and warns him to let it go.

Episode #339 — Barnabas is pacing the parlor — don't think too hard! Julia comes in and tells him that Woodard knows she's conducting experiments on him. She told her colleague that Barnabas has a rare blood disease and he's all why the fuck did you tell him that? She's scared Woodard is onto something. Barnabas bitches and moans; she has to burn her notes. Julia says no way, they're locked up tight. The two then have some warmed over goulash. Julia then tells him that Woodard once thought she had a thing for him (Barnabas). Preposterous! he exclaims. No, it's not, hurt Julia rejoins. He asks what that means and she says nothing. Barnabas pushes that nonsense aside and reverts back to note destruction.

At Collinwood — hey, Mrs. Johnson and she looks different; younger. Must be the light pink lipstick. Anyway, Woodard arrives, there to see David, but he slyly finds out the location of Julia's room. He then hustles upstairs. Later, in the foyer, Roger and Liz are having a screaming match about Burke living in the West Wing. Mrs. Johnson shuffles in to tell Liz that Woodard's there, then heads upstairs, while Liz and Roger go to the drawing room. Woodard goes to Julia's room and starts searching (did she switch rooms? The door is in a completely different location, as is the furniture).

Barnabas and Julia continue to argue over those damn notes. He insists they go to Collinwood and burn them. She finds it amusing that he's afraid (big deal, Willie knew Barnabas was afraid of a lot of things).

Hey, what's Carolyn's green sweater and blue skirt doing in Julia's dresser drawer? Mrs. Johnson, dusting out in the hall, hears when Woodard knocks something off the dresser. He does the old hide behind the door trick when she steps in to check things out. Once she's gone, more searching.

In the drawing room, Roger's on a tear about Burke. Barnabas and Julia come in and she offers a lame excuse about showing him some West Wing architecture. Fired up Roger asks his cousin's opinion on Burke living at Collinwood and a possibly drunk cameraman focuses on who knows what. Liz explains how the West Wing offer is really to keep Vicki around. Well, Barnabas intones, he'd *hate* to see her go. Is Julia's expression one of jealousy?

Woodard rummages and rifles and eventually finds the strongbox on top of the armoire. He breaks it open and pockets the locked, red diary/notebook and its key. He puts the box back and beats a hasty retreat.

In the drawing room, the West Wing debate continues. Woodard pokes his head in and says he saw David, gave him a sedative, gotta run, bye. Julia and Barnabas head upstairs and astute Roger comments to Liz that Cousin seemed nervous and wonders why. Once in Julia's room, the diabolical duo discover the notebook is missing.

Death by Windex

Episode #340 — Missing notebook redo. Barnabas then states the obvious; Dr. Woodard knows what he is and has to go. Oh, and Julia has to help him in the dispatching. Julia's not keen on committing murder. Barnabas tells her she has to use her medical knowledge to devise an 'accidental' death (by drowning? Still miss ya, Bill!). He blackmails her and though what he says is true, he's still an asshole. Now he tortures her by saying Woodard's death will be slow and painful. Julia suggests administering a drug that will mimic a heart attack, but kill instantaneously, then immediately regrets it. Barnabas snarks and she has a moment of self-awareness, looking depressed and resigned. The Big Bad then commands that they get crackin' and they head off to the Old House.

Woodard scurries into his office and gets to reading. Sam shows up, asking if he forgot his appointment to stop and see Maggie. Seems she's out of sleeping pills, can Dave scribble out an Rx? Woodard hurriedly writes out the prescription and Sam asks what he's so worked up about. Woodard gives Sam the bum's rush and gets back to the notebook.

At the Old House, Julia fills a large syringe with what looks like Windex. She tries passing it off to Barnabas, but he tells her *she* has to give the injection. More back-and-forth bullshit ensues (don't you miss victim's advocate, Willie Loomis? I do.). Julia says maybe she can convince Woodard to cooperate with the experiment. Barnabas thinks she's gullible for believing that one (he's right and I hate to admit it). He does, however, tell her to go talk to him, but tells her to take the hypodermic with her.

Woodard's finished reading and places an urgent call to the sheriff's office, telling them that he'll be there in fifteen minutes. Julia walks in just as he's about to leave. He knows why she's there and makes the fatal mistake of admitting that he knows all. Blah, blah, experiment and how Julia was willing to sacrifice people, like Maggie and poor, lunatic Willie (hey, at least he remembers him). Julia tells him he can't leave, Barnabas is lying in wait somewhere out there. Woodard tries calling the sheriff again (goddamn it, it's *Collinsport!*) and she tries to stop him. He's distracted by the squeaky bat shadow outside the window. Barnabas fades in via chromakey, bounces once, then basically tells Woodard his time's up.

Episode #341 — Redo and that bat sure can hover. Julia pleads with Barnabas to allow her to convince Woodard, but Woodard says no, thanks, and Barney says too late. Woodard prefers death over being the undead, like Collins, and regrets that he can't destroy him. Barnabas threatens to vamp him and Woodard says he'd find a way to off himself, as a shred of human decency would remain. Barnabas acts all evil villain, replete with speechifying, then orders Julia to kill her friend. Woodard lays a guilt trip on her as she readies the Syringe of Death ™ and she cracks, saying she can't do it. Barnabas takes the hypo and grabs hold of his victim, who pulls a fake-out, saying Sarah's there. With Barnabas distracted, Woodard makes a run for the door, but is caught and injected with the drug, then Barnabas wangsts Shakespearean-like about his pain and I laugh. Julia is overwrought. Thanks to a brief time jump, Barnabas has plopped and propped Woodard in his desk chair and says he was a good man (what?) and then torments Julia. Acting all Big Bad, he forces her to fish her notebook from her dead friend's coat pocket. The phone starts ringing and they gape at it. A cop (Patterson?) is on the other end. As the two leave the office, Julia hears the accusatory voice of Woodard.

At the Blue Whale, Sam's at the bar (off the wagon, I see), when a mustachioed FakePatterson comes in and asks if he's seen Woodard. *A lot* of filler ensues. NotReallyPatterson says Willie's too 'sick' to stand trial, gosh darn it (screw you, fake cop). Sam says when he saw Woodard earlier, he seemed excited about something. A woman screams outside and FakePatterson runs out to check it out; nothing, just some dame scared of a bat. Back to Woodard, blah, blah. Sam, who's more cop-like than the fake he's talking to, decides to go to Woodard's office. NotPatterson tags along. Just as they're leaving, they see HoverBat outside the window (have I mentioned this episode is a real dog already? Mr. Rooney, a Stinger, if you please).

At Woodard's office, after receiving no answer to their knock, NotPatterson has Sam break the door in. They find Woodard slumped in his chair. The dumbass sheriff gets on the phone to call the hospital but Sam ~~Spade~~ says forget it, he's dead; killed. FakePatterson says there's no evidence of foul play — but agrees it was murder (honestly, this is some shit writing and I'm sparing the details).

At the Old House, Julia is obsessing over the Syringe of Death before throwing it into the fire. Barnabas walks in and pokes at her with his sarcasm, while Julia clutches her red notebook and tells him to fuck off and leave her alone. Soulless Barnabas plays head games and when she tries to throw her notebook in the fire, he stops her (now he *doesn't* want the notes destroyed?). She says she'll just stop conducting the experiment and Barnabas replies that she won't, as he's her only friend (what the hell does that have to do with it?) Julia then hears Woodard's voice again, saying she has no friends.

Episode #342 — A pensive Sam returns to the cottage and sits down for a smoke. Maggie comes out of her room wearing a crazy, floor length quilt skirt containing every color of the rainbow. She offers him some coffee, because waitressing habits die hard. After talking in jumbled half sentences for a spell, Sam gets around to telling her Woodard is dead. Maggie responds by rubbing her temple as if she has a sudden migraine, which is an odd reaction. We're then treated to a long, laborious rehash of the last two episodes and oh, look at that, Maggie immediately suspects murder, too, believing Woodard knew something about her kidnapping. Sam says no, as they caught Willie. She hears someone outside and he reassuringly tells her it's just a deputy. Doesn't that mean the psycho is still out there? she inquires. Nah. Sam then remembers he saw Woodard reading a red notebook and decides to go back and look for it, though he doubts he'll find it.

At Woodard's office, Sam (who acts more like a cop than the supposed cop) meets up with NotPatterson. Burke crashes the party and blah, blah, dead Woodard and Devlin also thinks it was murder most foul. He is then force fed some lukewarm hash. Burke brings up Woodard's thoughts on the supernatural being part of Maggie's case. NotPatterson is consistent with the old, saying it couldn't be where Willie is concerned — *subnatural*, maybe (say it with me; fuck you, George, why the hard-on?). Blah, blah, supernatural, evil thing. The conversation continues and squeaky HoverBat appears outside the window, but no one notices.

At Collinwood (what time is it?) Burke is in the drawing room with Vicki (who looks fabulous in a turquoise dress and matching hair ribbon) with some bad news. She thinks it's about his upcoming business trip. Yeah, that, but mainly, Dr. Woodard's dead. He says the autopsy results should be in later that afternoon (guess it's morning, then). Julia happens by and asks who's dead. Vicki tells her. Julia plays shocked and asks for details. Burke says it might have been a heart attack. Oh, yes, the guilty one babbles, he was working too hard. Burke brings up murder and Julia gets worked up. He then asks the women if either of them saw Woodard with a red notebook. Why, no (this episode still sucks, but Grayson Hall's overwrought acting is a scream). A bit later, Vicki pushes a brandy on Hoffman and talks Woodard, which eats Julia up (hmm, Burke must have left).

Sam's back home with Maggie and blah, blah. She's scared and uptight. The phone rings and Sam has a one-sided conversation with NotPatterson. Hanging up, he tells the Magster that Woodard died of a heart attack. Maggie smiles — she's safe! He died of natural causes! Yeah, natural causes, skeptical Sam repeats.

Episode #343 — In the Old House basement, lab coated Julia checks over what looks like an elaborate moonshine still and drops dry ice into a cauldron. Switching off the machine, Barnabas comes down and tells her not to stop (apparently this is some new phase of the experiment). She tells him the autopsy findings and he adds more dry ice to the nasty looking witch's brew (what part of the basement is this? We've never seen it before). Oh, please, Barnabas says he knows what it's like to have a conscience (doubt it), then proves the opposite by tormenting her about Woodard. She wants to quit the experiment; he wants to proceed, then monologues about hope and being human again. Since Willie is gone, Julia has to smack talk him about being human and how he couldn't hack it. Oh, he's looking for love (in all the wrong places). He announces the first treatment will begin at midnight.

Vicki and Burke are in the garden arguing about David and the West Wing. She says David stays holed up in his room and that they haven't told him about Woodard. Barnabas is on the terrace, eavesdropping, before he interrupts. Burke goes inside to make a phone call. Barnabas smooth talks Vicki while Dr. Hoffman eavesdrops from behind the gate and I believe she's a bit green-eyed. Barnabas and Vicki, blah, blah, restore the West Wing and he'll help. Julia is jealous and pissed. Vicki says Burke isn't interested in the West Wing, so, nah. Barnabas keeps yapping about Collinwood, family and the past and Vicki tells him she's not interested in the past anymore.

Julia is in the foyer as Burke finishes up a call confirming some meetings. Once he hangs up, she enters and asks him if it's a good idea to leave town at the moment; Vicki's upset about David and Woodard. Vicki comes in and blah, blah, postpone trip talk. Vicki asks Julia if she'll attend the funeral with them the next day. Upset Julia will let them know and hurries out. Having gone to the garden, Dr. Hoffman tries to collect herself when an apparition (Woodard, I guess) appears behind her. It disappears *before* she turns around and screams. Vicki and Burke hear her and rush out to find Julia babbling and over-emoting.

Later, in the Old House basement, Julia has gotten her shit together and still seems to be brewing up some absinthe or maybe crème de menthe (how about a Grasshopper?). Barnabas comes in and she tells him she doesn't want to do the experiment. They quibble over whether she has the fortitude to kill him or not. Barnabas takes a seat in a sort of reclining medical chair. Julia tells him that if the treatment is a success, he'll no longer want Josette. Oh, there could be someone else, he replies. She asks if it's Vicki. He changes the subject. Julia tries to tell him there might be a woman out in the world (a foot away from him) who can love and accept him as is. Either Barnabas is dense or he's toying with her and she drops it. He tells her to begin with the experiment.

Episode #344 — Somber David is in his room with Sarah, who is apologizing for telling him about Woodard, but he needed to know. She says she thinks she knows how he died and it wasn't pretty. David asks if it was murder. She doesn't want to confirm, then disappears. Liz walks in, in appropriate funeral attire of black and a strand of pearls. She attempts to tell him about Woodard, but he beats her to the punch. Liz tries to tell him Woodard was well liked, lots of people attended the funeral. As she's leaving, David says he liked him, because he believed him; maybe that's why he's dead.

In the drawing room, Liz is relaying the David conversation to Carolyn and Vicki. Carolyn offers to try talking to him and heads off on the task. Vicki asks Liz if they should maybe call Fisher again. Liz rather hopes someone in the family can get through to her dejected nephew.

Carolyn has taken despondent David his lunch and tries talking to him. She pretends to believe him about Sarah, but he knows she's faking. She then confides that when she was a child, she had a friend that she played with, but still doesn't know if he was real, imagined or, as David suggests, a ghost. David says Sarah is real, though a ghost. She has a change of heart and does believe him and they both hear plaintive, *London Bridge* flute music. David says it's his friend and starts interpreting the music. It's a warning that something terrible will happen soon, far away, but there's nothing they can do to prevent it. Needless to say, Carolyn gets a tad freaked out by the prophesying.

In the drawing room, Burke is declining the West Wing offer. Vicki and Liz explain David's reaction to Woodard's death and Burke says he'll reconsider. Walking into the foyer, Liz wishes him a good trip. On the landing, David overhears. He comes down and solemnly thanks Burke for everything, he'll miss him, goodbye. Everyone tries to convince him that Devlin will be back and Burke offers to bring some stamps for Davey's collection. Sure, the boy replies, as a remembrance. David apologizes for scaring them and starts upstairs. Burke calls to him that when he comes back, they'll go out fishing. David says goodbye with finality and heads to his room. The three adults look worried and a drunk cameraman is badly out of focus on Liz.

Vicki and Burke go to the garden and he's done a one-eighty on the West Wing, not realizing how messed up David was. Blah, blah, David and suddenly spooked Vicki doesn't want Burke to go on his trip. She insists they go inside and the widows are briefly heard on the wind. She grows even more anxious and Burke tells her it's nothing, just a zephyr. Sure, she repeats, not believing it, as the widows sound again.

Amazonian Aviation and The Perils of Home Chemistry Sets

Episode #345 — Liz is sitting at the desk in the drawing room when Mrs. J comes rushing in, distraught. She just heard on the radio that Burke's plane has crashed in the Amazon. Liz tries to keep a cool head, saying they don't know that for sure, then heads for the phone and instructs the housekeeper to keep mum. On the phone, Liz gets nada from the airline; they have to wait for the manifest.

In the Old House parlor, Julia is making notes. Barnabas mocks her, then complains about how dreary the night is and starts yammering about how delightful his life will be when Vicki becomes Josette. Julia tries to tell him he's an idiot and burns him good by asking if his precious ever came to him willingly. Cat got your tongue, Barney? Julia manages to get out another snarky comment before Barnabas tries to act villainy and says she's acting like Josette is her rival. He then tells Julia to grab her coat, he'll take her to where Josette died and explain all.

Liz is pacing the drawing room when Vicki stops by, about to head out on a walk. She sees the floor plans for the West Wing on the desk and starts looking them over, happily chirping about Burke. Mrs. Johnson and Liz exchange knowing glances. Vicki mentions some sailor saying about ships out on crappy nights like that one. Blah, blah, Liz and Mrs. Johnson exchange more anxious looks. The phone rings and Liz takes the call. After hanging up, she delivers the unpleasant news. Looks like Burke is jaguar food. Vicki doesn't believe it, then nearly faints. Liz sends Mrs. Johnson to fetch some sedatives while she helps Vicki upstairs. A little later, Mrs. J joins Liz in the drawing room, where they discuss Vicki and the Burke tragedy. Vicki appears in the doorway, intent on going on her walk and exhibiting major denial by claiming Burke will come back! before dashing outside.

Emo alert! On Widows' Hill, Barnabas is waxing Byronic to Julia about when he first met Josette, the bride to his middle-aged uncle. Oh, he fell in love with her and determined to have her, but she loved her husband. He claims that as the years passed, young Josie saw that her husband was an old man and she began to fear time and he alone could remedy that (this will test your gag reflex). Vicki comes along and tells the news about Burke. Naturally, soul-challenged Barnabas sees an opening and gets rid of third wheel Julia. Vicki is still on her Burke will come back kick and Barnabas is sickening in his comforting. Blah, blah bullshit about the West Wing. Hmm, a bit of widow wailing is heard. Miss Winters walks to the edge of the cliff and says if she knew Burke wasn't coming back, she'd take the jump. Barnabas stops her, of course, and assures her that she'll be a bride. The widows' wailing seems to negate that sentiment.

Episode #346 — Now in that pumpkin orange dress, Vicki is sleeping on the drawing room sofa and has a dream. She's in Josette's room and puts on a bridal veil. Barnabas and Julia walk in and everybody talks in a weird, robotic monotone fashion. Barnabas sends Julia out. Vicki asks about Burke and he tells her to look at the bed. They walk over and find Devlin's shrouded body and Barnabas pronounces him dead. She runs out of the room. Dream over. Carolyn is coming down the stairs and hears Vicki calling out in her sleep. She goes in and Vicki wakes. Blah, blah, still in denial about DeadBurke (is it really the end of Devlin? We'll have to wait and see). The phone rings and Vicki answers. She informs Carolyn that the Amazon search has yielded nothing (I told you, jaguar food).

Julia goes up to Josette's room (the portrait looks great in color). She voiceovers about Barnabas' weird obsession for a chick dead over a century. She hears a rattling noise and is startled. She believes she's being watched. Josette? Maybe Woodard? Someone comes in downstairs. It's Vicki and Julia calls her up. Blah, blah, Vicki's decided to restore the West Wing and wanted to talk to Barnabas. Jealous Julia brusquely tells her he's too busy to help, she should leave him alone.

Back in Collinwood, Vicki paces the drawing room. Barnabas arrives, asking for news about Burke. Vicki rats out Julia; he does a slow burn, but slathers some flattery on Miss Winters. Vicki worries that Julia's working too hard. Ms. Hoffman then walks in with a cheerful disposition, an apology, and flowers for Vicki, who goes off to get a vase. Angry Barnabas slams the bouquet on the desk and gets to bitching, telling Julia to knock off the jealousy, they're just doctor and patient, nothing more. And be nice to Vicki! Vicki comes back in and all are surprised to see the flowers are dead (but why, because he touched them, or is it a sign from someone else?)

Later, in the Old House laboratory, Julia checks the tubing on the crème de menthe still. As she fills a syringe with blue curacao, she pokes herself with the needle. Barnabas glares at her and she snaps at him to stop staring. Blah, blah, Woodard. Barney wants the treatments fast tracked. She refuses, saying she's got a schedule devised for maximum safety. Barnabas blathers that if Burke is alive, he's only got a short window to ~~steal~~ win Vicki. Hey, he's sitting in a different chair, one that looks suspiciously like Old Sparky. Julia comes with the hypo and he roughly grabs her arm and bitches. He torments with Woodard talk, then threatens her if she sabotages the experiment. And oh, she was mean to Vicki, too, who's more saintly than Mother Teresa and the Virgin Mary combined. *She* may forgive, but *he* doesn't; so there.

Episode #347 — Barnabas and Julia talk about speeding up the treatments. She then straps Barney into Old Sparky (for real, it's an electric chair, if only she could throw the switch). She turns on the equipment and adds dry ice to the pot (how does all this work? Nothing's connected to him — and nothing is explained). Fluids bubble, knobs are turned, electricity sizzles on Strickfaden type gizmos. Julia switches off and unstraps Barnabas. She asks how he is and he says he feels a difference coursing through his body. Oh he's just ecstatic. Julia is clinically skeptical and wants to run some tests, but Barney wants to go outside — no, he'll go up and watch a sunrise! (I can't help but laugh at this exuberance, because I hate him). Julia is wisely cautious. Ah, yes, Barnabas exalts, I'll *share* a sunrise — with Vicki! (What happened to him not wanting to deprive himself of every syllable of her name?) Of course, Julia is none-too-pleased at that.

In the Collinwood drawing room, Carolyn and Vicki blah, blah. Julia comes in and blah, blah, West Wing. Carolyn decides to go make some coffee. Julia tells Vicki that she found a crystal in an old trunk that may match the chandelier in the West Wing. Isn't it pretty? she asks, holding it up. Let's look at it in the light, she suggests, walking over to the lamp. Needless to say, Julia hypnotizes Vicki and we get a funky kind of kaleidoscope effect. That Hoffman is up to something. She takes Vicki for a little walk — over to the Old House basement, where the coffin is. She tells Miss Winters that what she'll see she will never remember and never forget (that's neat). Vicki at first resists opening the coffin, but is finally convinced — and finds Barnabas napping and looking a bit green and ghastly. They head back to Collinwood, with Vicki back to normal as Carolyn comes in with a tray (she may have harvested the damn beans in Colombia for as long as it took — watch out! Boom mic!). Carolyn doesn't join them and gets a bit pissy before walking out to do — something. Julia asks Vicki if she wants to compare the crystal to the chandelier and Vicki gets weird when she mentions Barnabas. Julia smiles like the proverbial cat that ate the canary.

Later, Barnabas pays a call and Vicki is uncomfortable. She mentions the chandelier crystal and avoids making eye contact. He asks her to watch the sunrise with him from Widows' Hill; oh, never mind, it's silly. She agrees, then notices something off about his left hand. Quickly hiding it from view, he claims he injured it earlier in the day, then rushes out, postponing their sunrise watch.

Julia's in the lab, jotting down notes. Barnabas charges in, plays games for a minute, then shows her his rapidly aged left hand.

Episode #348 — Carolyn's sleeping in her room. David steals in and wakes her, which provokes a scream. He earnestly tells her he just wanted to make sure she wasn't dead (no, but those harvest gold sheets and burnt orange bedspread can kill). He doesn't know why he was compelled to check on her; no, it wasn't a dream, he just doesn't know. He then gives her the toy solider for protection. Liz knocks, having heard Carolyn scream, and upon entering, wonders what the hell David's doing there. Carolyn covers for her young cousin, gives him a kiss and sends him back to his room. She then explains to Liz what happened. Lost as to the root cause of his behavior, she tells her mother she has to send him away. Dame Stoddard protests. Blah, blah, Barnabas fear rehash and Carolyn wishes she could protect the youngster somehow.

In the Old House laboratory, we discover that both of Barnabas' hands are withered with age now. Julia comes in, announcing it's almost dawn. Oh, he'll hit the casket in a minute. He then launches into poetic *sturm und drang* about time. Julia says the aging may be temporary and that they shouldn't have sped up the procedure. He grabs her throat and issues a warning. Hoffman proposes counter measures, but they'll have to wait to see what happens from this overdose. Nope, he's only interested in another accelerated treatment — or else! (this makes no freaking sense).

The next day, Carolyn's in her room, tidying up, when she hears a cheerful flute rendition of *London Bridge* — and sees Sarah in her mirror. She and the waif wraith have a confab, with Sarah saying Carolyn has to believe in her or she wouldn't have shown up. She goes on to say that they shouldn't send David away and maybe he's acting the way he is because no one believes him. Miss Stoddard is arguing politely with the ghostly girl when Liz knocks. Sarah disappears. Liz is looking for Vicki, as she wants to apprise her about shipping David off. Carolyn tells her to hold off on that (overnight they both change position? Really?), but doesn't explain the reason for her change of heart. (Isn't Carolyn a little old to have a stuffed animal tiger on her bed? I bet it was a gift from Uncle Roger to his 'Kitten.') Carolyn again hears flute music, but Liz doesn't.

Carolyn goes to David's room, to return the soldier. He wants her to keep it. She tells him she saw Sarah and now he's upset she did. Reason? Woodard saw her and died. Now, he doesn't want anyone to believe him — he lied about everything. He breaks down crying. She gives him a comforting hug and says she can help him now.

Down in the lab, Barnabas is in a hurry, damn it! Julia tells him that whatever happens, she only wanted the best for him. He mouths off that he doubts that (this asshole). The treatment starts. Switches are switched, knobs turned, oscilloscope lights up, electricity snaps and crème de menthe bubbles. Julia switches off the machinery, looks over and squawks (she never really screams) in horror. Barnabas (who we see from the back) is slumped in the chair and his hair is — blond? (So it was all a dye job gone horribly wrong?)

Episode #349 — Julia has hustled on up to the parlor, followed by hunch shouldered, white haired, aged Barnabas. She haltingly tells him that the ramped up treatment was too much. He's, well, ancient. He blames her, naturally. Julia tries to logically argue that his insistence of a massive dosage is the cause. Hmm, he never considered that the cure would make him appear his real age. Since *she* didn't consider it either, he says he's making all decisions from now on. He has to save himself in the only way he knows how. He tells her to go break his engagement with Vicki and she snarks. He tells her to spare the sarcasm (hilarious). He also tells her to relay to Vicki that he's going out of town — oops, Vicki's there and overheard. Julia buys some time at the front door while Barnabas turns a chair around and slumps low. He and Julia tell Vicki that he's not feeling well and she shouldn't come any closer, it could be catching. They finally get rid of the governess. Julia assures him that if anyone saw him, they wouldn't recognize him. Oh, he'll never forgive her for doing this to him (you did it to yourself, fool). Sly Julia says he should use Vicki to revert, he'll have her then, isn't that what he wants? Oh, no, she must come to him willingly, as his Josette. Julia screws with him some more, which I enjoy immensely.

Vicki's back in her room. Carolyn comes in and tells her she's going to meet Joe at the bar. Vicki inquires if any calls about Burke came in. He's alive, she knows it! Carolyn asks where Barnabas is. Vicki explains the West Wing activities have been canceled, as he's not feeling well and he's going away. She'll miss him, she relies on him! (Shouldn't she be freaking out; you know, the hypnosis?)

At the Old House, Julia is still delighting in tormenting Barnabas by urging him to attack Vicki.

At the Blue Whale, Carolyn tells Joe that she saw Sarah; she really exists! She goes on to suggest that maybe everything else David said is true, too. Blah, blah, coffin/Barnabas/bat (who thought Joe's straightened, slicked hair was a good idea?). She wants him to go with her to Eagle Hill to look for the secret room. He refuses. Squabble, squabble, Joe says to give it up and Carolyn is visibly disappointed.

Carolyn's back home and stops by Vicki's room. Carolyn admits she has doubts about Barnabas. No, that can't be! dim Vicki protests.

Hoary Barnabas paces the parlor, glances at his portrait, then recalls Julia's words about snacking on Vicki.

Squeaky HoverBat appears outside the window of sleeping Vicki's room. The aged Barnabas is then in the room and creeps up to the bed. He gazes at her wistfully and thinks to himself that he can't do it. Out of nowhere, and for no reason, Carolyn suddenly calls and comes into the room, waking Vicki. Barney is gone, of course. Carolyn claims she heard something (there's still some questionable writing going on). The women then see and hear the bat outside the window.

Episode #350 — The following day, David meets up with Carolyn in the drawing room. He once again gives her the toy soldier for protection and she agrees to keep it. David gasps as he sees dehydrated Barnabas outside the window (guess it's the following night, then). When Carolyn turns around, nothing is there. Liz comes in, asking what's wrong (that godawful green and pink print dress, that's what). David knows they don't believe him about seeing an old man outside (didn't he say last episode that he *doesn't* want anyone believing him anymore?) and goes to his room. Liz and Carolyn blah, blah (why won't the blonde mention having seen Sarah?) send David away talk. Carolyn finally tells Liz about having seen, and talked to, Sarah. Liz thinks she's nuts. Blah,

blah, Barnabas/coffin talk (it is nice that Carolyn is trying to champion for David, the poor kid has no one else in his corner). It turns out, David is eavesdropping out in the foyer and hears Aunt Elizabeth rather bitchily state that her nephew is disturbed and must be sent away (has she cleared this with Roger?).

Julia is waiting at the Old House when Barnabas comes in from a stroll. He's made up his mind to attack someone that night, most likely a stranger. Julia suggests an alternative; herself. Barnabas is surprised that she'd do so willingly and, much to the lady doctor's pleasure, he calls her by her first name for the first time. He ultimately refuses, saying he appreciates the offer, but he needs her as a doctor. Rebuffed, Julia heads down to the lab.

Carolyn is in the drawing room with the soldier. David comes in and asks her if she thinks he's crazy, like Aunt Liz does. He then says everything he said about Barnabas isn't true. Carolyn muses aloud about going to the Old House and David very animatedly tells her not to. She promises she won't and sends him up to bed. Carolyn thinks things over a bit more, then leaves the house.

Carolyn goes to the Old House and sneaks in (you would think that the doors would be locked, given the current situation, no?). Finding no one in the parlor, she figures Barnabas is asleep. She stealthily heads down into the cellar and finds the coffin (Barnabas should really relocate that thing to a more out of the way spot — it's practically right at the bottom of the stairs). She opens the casket and finds it empty. Where is Julia? Is she deep in the bowels of the magically expanding basement? — oh, there she is, slamming the lid of the coffin shut. Julia impresses on Carolyn to get the hell out, but, too late, desiccated Barnabas ambles in. Miss Stoddard is stunned at his appearance and screams when he grabs her. Barnabas then strokes her hair (just like faux five Willie), creepily tells her he won't harm her, then lunges with fangs bared for his somewhat incest tainted repast. Carolyn lets loose with a piercing scream.

Episode #351 — Carolyn attacked in the basement replay. Afterwards, the blonde is unconscious, lying down in Josette's room with attentive Julia tying a scarf around her neck. Carolyn comes to. Hoffman asks if she knows where she is and what happened. Why, yes, she does. Julia asks how she feels about it. Enthralled Carolyn somewhat dreamily replies that she's cool with it. Julia explains why Barnabas did it — to stop the rapid aging. Carolyn wants to see him, he may need her. Footsteps sound on the stairs and the two women wait with anticipation through the non-suspenseful build-up. Barnabas enters — he's fine.

At Collinwood, robed Roger is having a nightcap in the drawing room. Liz comes down, worried about where her daughter is. Roger says no need to, she's probably on a late date. Liz is all worked up; Carolyn's started believing David now and said she saw Sarah.

At the Old House, Julia is stunned at the rapid reversal. Barnabas outs her true profession by calling her 'doctor,' and tells Carolyn that Hoffman is a blood specialist and psychologist (I thought psychiatrist, but, whatever). Barnabas then gives Julia the bum's rush. He then extracts a promise from captivated Carolyn to tell no one about him or Julia. Oh, and to screw over David; everything he's been saying is just in his imagination. He informs her that Vicki will become Josette and even enslaved Carolyn seems to balk at that for a moment. Blah, blah, must come willingly jazz. Carolyn asks about herself — what is *their* relationship? (that's a tad skeevy, no?). Oh, she's on a higher rung of the enslavement ladder than that sap Willie, so she won't be a servant. If she's extra good, he'll reward her with eternal life (is it a reward or a punishment? He uses it both ways and it's irritating).

Downstairs, Barnabas bids Carolyn adieu. Once she's gone, he tells Julia that Carolyn can be very useful, he should have used her sooner (it's always about him). Julia's ready to hit him with another injection (this treatment is so vague, injections, machinery...). He thinks she's crazy. She correctly counters that it was *his* fault he aged. Bicker and bitch, he cancels the experiment. Julia tries offering a compromise, but arrogant Barney is having none of it. In fact, there's no need for them to be involved in anything anymore. Julia points out that he needs protection during the day and Carolyn can't do it. As Carolyn being there all the time, all of a sudden, would be weird, Barnabas eventually agrees to let her keep an eye on things during the day.

Liz and Roger are still up — at two thirty — waiting for Carolyn. Liz is worried, her brother is calm. Carolyn wanders in and claims she went for a walk for six and a half hours. The vampirically subjugated Carolyn then heads upstairs. Liz comments that her daughter is not herself, something's happened to her. About four hours later, robotic Carolyn comes downstairs and sluttishly stares at the Barnabas portrait while caressing the puncture wounds on her neck.

Episode #352 — Slutty Carolyn foyer redo before she heads into the drawing room. Looking out the window, she thinks of her vow to help Barnabas with Vicki and David, then heads back upstairs.

Carolyn goes to David's room and wakes him. She says she couldn't sleep, as she was thinking about him. She tells him she went to the Old House — but Barnabas could have killed her! — David interjects. No, he showed her the whole house, there's nothing there, nothing to worry about. Doubting David believes she's been tricked somehow. They argue a bit, then she reneges on her Sarah sighting. Cruel Carolyn frightens David with talk of being sent to a nut-house and urges him to say he made everything up.

Julia's down in the drawing room, looking over the crystal. Carolyn sneaks up on her. The doctor inquires how she's feeling and gets a curt 'fine' in response, with the follow-up question of what she's doing there. Julia explains that she's helping Vicki with the chandelier crystals. Carolyn mentions having talked to David and now moves on to Vicki. The claws come out a bit between the two, as each insists they're helping Barnabas. Carolyn then goes upstairs. Vicki strolls into the foyer and Julia calls her into the drawing room to check the crystal again in the lamp light. Julia hypnotizes her and takes her on another field trip. Unfortunately, Carolyn sees them leave.

Julia takes Vicki to Josette's room and tells her that Barnabas plans to transform Vicki into his precious and his bride. She reminds her of the coffin, in use because he's the undead and will force his will on her; she must resist him. They then head back to the main house.

A bit later, Vicki's on the sofa in the drawing room when Carolyn comes in. Vicki was just thinking about ProbablyDeadBurke and is tired of waiting for a phone call about him. Carolyn mentions her walk with Julia. Vicki claims she's been home all day, then heads upstairs to earn her paycheck. Carolyn becomes suspicious; did Vicki lie? Something's amiss. Julia comes home and Carolyn asks her about the walk. Julia tries to brush it off, they just stepped outside for a moment, then heads off through the door under the stairs. Carolyn looks at the Barnabas portrait.

(I didn't mention this last episode, because this one better illustrates my point; why the hell isn't Carolyn laid up in bed, sick as a dog? Remember Maggie and Willie? They could barely move during the day, they just slept, and looked like death warmed over. One would assume Barnabas needed quite a bit of blood to rejuvenate, so why isn't she prostrate in bed? This is a writers' contrivance that breaks with established canon for the sole purpose of serving a particular point in the arc; Barnabas needs a helper now that Willie's gone and things have gone to hell with Julia. Obviously, the show didn't have a bible and was lax in explaining why this situation is different. However, Carolyn's complexion does seem to appear a bit chalky, so there's that.)

Episode #353 — Sluttily enthralled Carolyn voice-overs a monologue to her 'dear' cousin Barnabas (eww). Vicki comes downstairs and asks her to go to the movies. No, how about *you* go to the Old House and talk to Barnabas about the restoration, the blonde minion replies. Vicki's skittish at the suggestion, but doesn't know why. Julia comes home from yet another walk and Vicki conveniently tells her she had a strange dream that the two of them walked to an old house, but she was afraid to enter it. Damage inadvertently done, Vicki goes back upstairs. In the drawing room, Carolyn mentions the walk/dream/Vicki's memory lapse. Julia tries to cover and is made nervous by Carolyn's hostile attitude. Carolyn leaves and Julia realizes she's under scrutiny.

Carolyn's out in the garden, watching the sunset. She starts towards the Old House when Joe comes along (his hair still looks terrible). He's had a change of heart about going to the cemetery. Carolyn tells him there's no need; David lied, Barnabas showed her the house, and *she* lied about having seen Sarah (all these character flip-flops are somewhat maddening). Joe offers to accompany her on her walk, but she suggests he go in to see Vicki instead. She heads off and he looks after her with suspicion.

Carolyn has gone to the Old House and explains she was detained due to Joe's visit. She also informs him that Vicki might not come, she seemed hesitant. Barnabas is perplexed; he must remedy the situation, immediately.

In the drawing room, Joe and Vicki discuss Carolyn and her odd behavior. Maybe she's worried about David. Barnabas shows up. Joe announces he's off to meet Maggie (choke on it, Barney), then tells Vicki to call them sometime, to hang out. Once Joe's gone, Barnabas feigns concern about Burke, then offers to arrange for a private search party. Thanks, but no thanks (Burke is probably a Shuar tsantsa by now). Barnabas reaches to take her hand and she recoils. Oh, he must have startled her, he'll leave. She thanks him for the search party offer.

A little later, Vicki's looking out the drawing room window when Carolyn walks in and wonders where Barnabas is, wasn't he here? Vicki explains that he left and she's so ashamed of the way she behaved when he touched her. She mentions his touch was that of a dead man. Vicki's confused!

At the Old House, Barnabas is pondering to Julia why Vicki recoiled from him. Julia says maybe it's because she's still in love with Burke, dumbass. Or that she knows *he's* interested in her and is trying to avoid the elephant in the room.

This succeeds in aggravating Barnabas. Carolyn rushes in and Barnabas unceremoniously kicks Julia out. The faithful flunky reports her Vicki conversation and the walk that Vicki doesn't remember taking. Barnabas orders her to watch Julia and let him know everything that goes on. He then pronounces that if Hoffman is interfering with his plans for Vicki, she's dead.

Episode #354 — Julia discussion replay/redo. The next day, Julia's reading in the drawing room when Carolyn walks in. Hoffman knows she's being followed around and Carolyn acts a cold bitch. Julia announces she's going to her room and departs. Liz and Roger, both upbeat, come in and tell Carolyn that they're sending David to Boston, though Vicki's not too thrilled to be going along. Roger opines that Burke has to be dead by now. Carolyn says it's a good idea to send her cousin away, what with his wild imaginings. Roger's pleased that she's thinking more rationally and suggests Kitten go to Boston, too; plenty of parties, shopping, young men…Carolyn snaps that she won't go, then strides out to find Vicki. Roger comments that Carolyn's been acting strange lately, which Liz has noticed as well (Roger was in a very good mood in this scene — and he wasn't even drinking!).

Later on, Vicki's in the drawing room, fussing with some flowers, when Julia comes along. The governess explains that they're for Barnabas as a means to apologize for the way she behaved. She then blathers about how super he is. Carolyn interrupts to tell them she's going to town to do some shopping. She leaves the house, but it's a fake-out, she sneaks back in and eavesdrops through the now closed drawing room doors (have I mentioned the ugly, shapeless green dress Carolyn is wearing? It's so unflattering). Julia uses the crystal to hypnotize Vicki yet again. Carolyn hides as they go off on another adventure, then follows.

Julia takes Vicki to the Old House — oh, another previously unseen room of the basement (that wasn't there when Burke and Woodard searched). Carolyn skulks in and eavesdrops. There's a coffin in the room and Julia tells Vicki it's meant for her (is that Maggie's? The one Willie made?). Blah, blah, Barnabas dead, wants her for his bride, resist him! Carolyn hides again as they leave.

Back in the Collinwood drawing room, hypnosis session is over. Julia tests the mesmerism by mentioning the Old House and Barnabas. Vicki comes over a bit anxious, then asks Julia to give him the flowers and say goodbye for her. Liz comes in with the finalized itinerary to Bangor and Vicki says she's glad to be going. Julia's pleased that her Svengali act worked.

Later in the evening, in Vicki's coffin room, Carolyn fills Barnabas in on the day's events. Barnabas bawls that Julia betrayed him. Carolyn tells him that Vicki saw him in his coffin on an earlier trip to the house, then asks what his plan is. Is he going to kill Julia? she cheerily asks. Barnabas responds that he might — or something worse.

Episode # 355 — In the Old House parlor, Barnabas is thinking really hard and says Julia betrayed him. Carolyn doesn't think so and says she's just trying to thwart his plans for Vicki because she's jealous. Ho-hum, Barnabas threatens death, which we know is a non-starter (he's one for six in death threats, Woodard being the only one he followed through on). Carolyn, though under his influence, thinks killing is wrong and tries to talk him out of it. He tells her he wants her help and she responds she can't do it. He claims he'll do the dirty work, he just wants her to get Julia's experiment notes and tells her where the book is stashed. Carolyn still seems iffy and it occurs to me that Barnabas isn't so hot at suppressing victims' free will; they all defy and/or argue with him in some way or other. Blah, blah, notes and don't feel sorry for Julia. Carolyn says she doesn't.

Arriving back at Collinwood, Carolyn runs into Mrs. Johnson, who comments that she doesn't look well. Carolyn says she's fine and asks where Julia is. Working in her room, it turns out. Mrs. J, still looking younger than she did in b&w, heads to the kitchen. Maggie then shows up, looking for Vicki. Too late, the governess has gone to Boston with her charge. Maggie was out of town herself and just heard about Burke. Carolyn's a bit harsh in her pragmatism and Maggie asks her if she's been ill; she doesn't seem like herself and keeps touching her scarf, which seems weirdly familiar. A dog howls and nervous Maggie decides to go home (smart move). Julia runs into Carolyn in the foyer and explains she was distracted from her work by the howling dogs; the canines mean that Barnabas is upset about something. Carolyn lies and tells Julia he wants to see her. Hoffman rushes out, affording the blonde lackey the chance to go to her room (which has a completely different layout again). The notebook is not where Barney said it would be.

Julia arrives at the Old House and from Barnabas' reaction, knows she's been had and that the two cousins are in cahoots. She plays it cool, however, and readies to leave. Slightly panicked, Barnabas calls her Julia again, which she finds curious, and tells her that he wants to begin the experiment again, right away. She says no, she's going home and his vassal won't find what she's looking for. Once again, she warns that if anything happens to her, the contents of the notebook will be discovered.

Carolyn's still in Julia's room, rifling through drawers. She finds the strongbox, breaks it open and finds it empty. Julia walks in and confronts her. Carolyn offers the lame excuse that she was looking for an aspirin. Hoffman knows she's lying and tells her so, then threatens to tell Liz that she was digging through her things. Bitch Carolyn threatens to tell her mother the truth about Julia, then leaves. Julia checks the box and surmises that Barnabas plans to off her.

Episode #356 — At Collinwood, worried Julia, notebook in hand, comes downstairs. With the Barnabas portrait looming over her, she tries to think of a place to hide the book until she can get to the bank the next day and dump it in a safe deposit box. She considers a few places in the drawing room, but no. Walking into the foyer, the clock chimes. Having an ah-ha! moment, Julia stashes the book in a niche in the front of the clock.

Carolyn goes to the Old House and tells Barnabas she couldn't find the book, it wasn't where he said. Also, Julia caught her. Barnabas is worried — she has to go back and find it. She asks him what if Julia tries to kill him and he assures her that won't happen as *she's* going to watch the doctor. Carolyn again inquires that if the notebook is destroyed, does Julia have to die? Well, yes, because — Vicksette!

Thunder rolls and Julia is pacing between the drawing room and foyer. Liz sails down in her deep blue velvet loungewear seeking a sherry. Have one? Sure, why not? Liz then asks about her work and Julia tells her she's almost finished and will be leaving in about a week. Carolyn has come home and walks in, acting bitchy, much to her mother's dismay. Julia heads out to the Old House and Liz starts in on Carolyn, who is a cold, hostile bitch exclaiming that she just doesn't like Hoffman. Liz bitches at her and demands she apologize to their guest. Bitchy Carolyn sits down to wait.

Barnabas is staring out the window. Julia arrives and, damn it, get better, non-drip candles already! Blah, blah, notebook, it's safe with someone in town. If anything happens — exposed. Blah, blah, betrayal! Vicki! Hypnotism! He smugly tells her that Carolyn followed them. Julia tells him to give it the fuck up already; Vicki's in love with someone else and will never come to him willingly. Barney remains obstinate — you betrayed me! Notebook! Die!

Carolyn's pacing the drawing room and complaining. Liz asks her if she's all right and Carolyn wishes everyone would stop asking. Julia comes back and Liz nudges her daughter to apologize. Julia is very gracious, even though she knows Carolyn is full of shit. Liz then goes up to bed and Julia tells Carolyn she knows it's all an act for her mother. Carolyn then says that Julia is jealous and in love with Barnabas. Julia tells her to get away from her, but nothing doing. Carolyn then demands the notebook be turned over and for Julia to leave town. Walking into the foyer, Julia again threatens to tell Liz and the bitchy one dares her to tell her mother everything. Carolyn glances at the clock and notices that it's ticking, but not striking the hour.

Anthony Peterson — Trouble Is His Business

Episode #357 — Carolyn and Julia redo and Carolyn moves to check the clock. Julia stops her by saying someone else knowing about Barnabas can be helpful. They're interrupted by someone pounding on the front door. Carolyn answers to find a brash, trench coated man named Anthony Peterson asking for Roger. Carolyn lets him in and goes up to find Uncle Rog. Julia suggests he wait in the drawing room. Once the coast is clear, she tries retrieving the note-book, but is interrupted by Roger coming down the stairs. He comments that the first Barnabas had the clock made as a wedding gift for Josette (first we've heard of it). Julia gets slightly hysterical and starts laughing for a moment and Roger wonders what the hell? She blames it on nerves and the storm. Peterson interrupts. Roger professes not to know him and Peterson snarks that he must not check his messages (isn't there an accountant at Collinwood Enterprises named Peterson? Yep, episode #242). Turns out, he's a lawyer, representing a cannery worker in a workman's comp case. This Peterson fellow is thorough, saying he's been trying to reach Roger for two weeks. Roger doesn't have any satisfactory answers for the brash lawyer with the withering sarcasm. The men continue arguing, with Peterson snarking about the eighteenth century attitude.

Julia finally gets the book, but when she tries leaving the house, is caught by Carolyn, who's standing on the stairs. Carolyn demands the book and Julia backs away from her. Peterson strides out of the drawing room and heads for the front door. Julia stops him leaving by reminding him about his coat, which he left on the hall table, then asks him for a ride into town. Carolyn offers to drive her and Julia's like, hell, no, then grabs her things and leaves with the good looking Tony. The clock then chimes the quarter hour and Roger steps out into the foyer. Carolyn asks about Peterson and Roger brushes off the am-bulance chaser. He asks her for a game of chess, but she has to run an errand for Barnabas. When Roger wonders aloud what Barney's secret is (for getting people to do things for him) her demeanor changes and Roger asks Kitten if anything's wrong. Oh, no, gotta run, and off she goes. Roger continues to drink.

At Peterson's office, Humphrey Bogart's better looking younger brother sits at his desk, smoking, and eyes the nervously pacing Julia with suspicion. Dogs are howling. Julia finally asks him why he hates the Collinses. He replies that he grew up poor and wants what they have (isn't this cribbing from Burke's sob story?). When he makes a passing comment using the word 'blood,' Julia snaps at him and he observes that she's "not too stable" (hilarious). He tries to figure out what game they're playing and she says there's no game. She notices his floor safe and shows him the notebook, informing him that someone wants it, enough to kill, but won't tell him the contents. Tony thinks she's talking about Roger and Julia becomes a laughing-crying hysterical basket case (and it's a treat). She's so off the rails, he has to shake some sense back into her. She pleads with him to keep the notebook in his safe and promise not to read it. He tells her to lock the book and take the key. She does as instructed and tells him he'll hear all kinds of lies and stories about both her and the book and asks him to take it to the cops if anything happens to her. He offers to drive her home, but she says she'll catch a cab (it's not NYC, you can't just 'catch a cab.' Per Mr. Welles, in episode #1, the town only has one cab).

Once Julia's gone, Tony opens his safe, but before he can deposit the book in it, Carolyn wanders in and introduces herself. He sets the book on his desk and takes a seat. She plants herself *on* the desk, saying she's there to apologize for her Uncle Roger. She traces her fingers over the coveted volume and he says he knows her, but she says that's not possible as they've just met. He goes on to inform the Princess, that he worked as a lifeguard in town and even caddied for her, back in the day (this conversation has a Bogart/Bacall vibe to it). He's suspicious of her, it seems. Talk turns to Julia and kittenish Carolyn says Hoffman is paranoid, then tries fishing for info. Tony says he's her lawyer, not her confessor, then gets up to put the book in the safe. Carolyn then asks him to take her out for a drink. He locks up the book, then manhandles the blonde dame, asking for the real reason she's there.

Episode #358 — At the Old House, Barnabas is browsing through a book when Carolyn comes in, wearing a different dress. She tells him about the book in the foyer clock and Julia going into town with a lawyer. Pissed off Barnabas advances on her — is he going to beat the snot out of her, now that Willie's gone? Turns out, no. Anyway, Carolyn says she followed them and saw the book at Peterson's, but it's in his safe and oh, she told him Julia's crazy. Barney wants to recoup the notebook right away, but Carolyn points out it's nearly dawn. He says she'll have to get it, but she reminds him that she's not a safe-cracker. He then asks if this young lawyer is attractive. Carolyn replies that he's rude, violent…and, yes, he's attractive. Barnabas then pimps her out and blathers about his evil plans for Hoffman; Carolyn sowed the seeds that Julia is mad, so he's running with it. He plans to drive Julia insane and pulls a box containing a hypodermic and empty serum bottle from a drawer. The same items she killed Woodard with (no, she threw the syringe into the fire, complete with breaking glass sound effect).

Later, Carolyn's at the Blue Whale with Tony, in yet another dress. He's still suspicious of her, as she's apparently been trailing him all day, and tells her she needs a full-time job (I already love this guy). She flirts, but he's still guarded. Tony then tries apologizing by offering to buy her dinner, but she refuses. He asks if she's only interested in him because of Julia. She answers by saying she has to meet with a cousin, until eleven, call her then. She admits she is attracted to him, then leaves.

Back at Collinwood, it's six o'clock and Carolyn has changed ensemble again, a little black number this time. Julia comes home and they exchange a few harsh words about Barnabas before Julia goes up to change for dinner. In her room, Julia finds the empty bottle of ~~Windex~~ serum and syringe. Ah, Julia knows it's not the same hypo, because she threw it in the fire (thank you!), then she changes her mind. She thinks it may be Woodard, then tries to think logically — it's a trick, cooked up by Barnabas and Carolyn (well, duh). She puts the items back in the box and leaves the room.

Carolyn's on the phone in the foyer talking to Tony, who's on a payphone as he's out of town. He lets her know that he'll call and see her when *he* wants to, then asks her to have dinner with him the next evening. Julia comes downstairs just as Carolyn is accepting, grabs the phone, and hangs up on him. She confronts the enthralled one with the paraphernalia. Carolyn plays lying bitch as Julia loses her shit.

At the Old House, Barnabas is kicking back in his dressing gown at the desk. Carolyn arrives to report Julia's reaction. He tells her that an Indian he met in Barbados, a warlock, taught him some ritual. The man was arrested for witchcraft, but his cell was empty when they came to hang him. Barnabas then blathers about magic through numbers (huh?). Carolyn scoffs, but Barney insists he was imbued with the power to plant an idea in someone's mind (since fucking when? And where did all this Barbados shit come from? Actually, I know the answer, but won't spoil it for those who don't). Carolyn thinks it's time to leave, but he makes her stay and watch as he — what? Lights some incense in a brass bowl and mutters? There's a whooshing sound and he's disappeared.

Julia's in bed, tossing and turning. She hears the whoosh and, sitting up, sees a shadowy figure in her room, near the window. Woodard, with a slightly distorted voice, speaks, asking her why she killed him, they were friends. Julia flips and passes out. The shadow figure is then gone, but Squeaky Hover Bat is outside the window.

Episode #359 — Morning and Julia's in her room, fiddling with the drapes. Mrs. Johnson comes in to clean and Hoffman asks for her help in taking the window treatments down, as she wants it lighter in the room. Mrs. Johnson thinks that's a bit peculiar, then Julia says she saw someone in her room the night before. Mrs. J logically tells her to let Roger or Liz know. Julia then backtracks, maybe she was half-asleep and stressed. Mrs. Johnson says Julia hasn't been the same since Woodard's funeral. As she goes on about what a nice man he was, Julia snaps at her, then says it was *him* who was in her room, but it was just a dream. Julia then hears Woodard's voice taunting her and loses it, much to Mrs. Johnson's astonishment.

Through a major time jump, it's evening and Tony and Carolyn are on the terrace, after their date. She's acting normal and says she enjoyed the dinner. They chat pleasantly for a minute and she non-verbally let's him know she's interested. They kiss. Unfortunately, howling dogs distract her and she wanders over to the fountain. Tony follows, wondering what the fuck just happened. Carolyn starts acting a bit subjugated bitch again, then asks him to meet her for lunch the next day, to discuss Julia (why not just dump a bucket of cold water on the guy?). He momentarily succeeds in breaking through, but that damn dog gets her attention again. He points out that she's acting weird, just like Julia did the other night. He turns to leave, telling her he's busy, so no lunch.

Nervous Julia goes to her room and voice-over monologues that there's no ghosts (well, at least they changed the drapes, they're sheers now) and she should go back to Windcliffe. She then finds a lab coat with Woodard's name tag on the floor. As she goes to pick it up, a squeaky rat darts out from under it and zips across the floor. She tries to leave the room, but the door won't open. Julia starts pounding on the door and shouting to be let out. She finally gets the door open and finds Mrs. Johnson. She tells Mrs. J about the rat under the coat and Mrs. Johnson says there are no rats in Collinwood and there's no damn coat on the floor. Carolyn comes along and asks what's wrong. Mrs. J hustles off to get some rat poison and Julia tells Carolyn to tell Barnabas to knock this shit off. Carolyn retorts that she's *not* a messenger (no, honey, just a vassal). Julia says she knows Barnabas' vulnerabilities and it's about time she move beyond threatening.

Carolyn has scurried to the Old House — and delivers the message. Barnabas sends her to another room when there's a knock on the door. It's Julia. He tries to act all gracious host, but Julia starts in on him to stop the crap. He acts all worried and says he knows Woodard was in her room, accusing her, because he visited him, too. He then starts with the I'm developing a conscience crap again and oh, it's been a *spiritual* change (this is truly sickening). Carolyn listens to everything from that mystery room with the louvered door off the parlor, near the front window. Barnabas lays the bullshit on thick; Josette is dead, he can't recreate her or summon her ghost. Julia calls bullshit; his Josie is too, too, precious and Woodard never appeared there. The gnome now spreads flattering fertilizer, asking Julia for help, he *needs* her. Julia becomes confused, because she's thinking with both her heart and head. Carolyn looks unhappy. Barnabas asks to see Julia the following night and kisses her hand when she leaves (ick). Carolyn rejoins him and, channeling the best of our man Loomis (gone, but never forgotten), scolds Barnabas for being cruel, as Julia truly loves him (why she does, I'll never fathom). Not liking that nugget of wisdom, he tells her she's tired and summons her closer. Then, I don't know, through a sort of psychic link (?), she dreamily repeats that, yes, she is tired.

Episode #360 — Julia heads to Tony's office. He's on his way out to court. She says she *must* speak with him, it's a matter of life and death! (that old trope?) Someone could die! He asks who, but she won't tell him. Tony decides to risk pissing off the judge and stays. Julia wants to see her notebook; not take it, just see it. He tells her it's locked up, but then opens the safe. When he can't immediately find it, Julia puts on her tinfoil hat and starts squalling conspiracy theory — he's in on it! Did he read the notebook? He finds the article in question under some papers and hands it over. Oh, it's still locked, she observes. Tony says since she doesn't trust him to take the damn thing with her. Blah, blah, argue about keeping it or not. He then advises her to find another lawyer (hey, I bet Frank Garner could use the business! What the hell happened to him, anyway? Did ambitious, uncouth, newcomer Tony Peterson force him out?). Julia says she does trust him and he locks the stupid book in the safe again, saying that he wished he knew what the hell it was all about so he could help her. She says no one can help, then starts crazy talking about finding Sarah, who can.

Joe is at Maggie's for a quiet evening, and teasingly jokes about her homemade cake being store bought (guess Sam is getting tanked at the bar). Julia shows up, asking to borrow Sarah's doll and I am distracted by Maggie's minor wardrobe malfunction (white bra strap, sleeveless brown dress). She relays that the doll disappeared a few weeks earlier (sure, since it served it's plot purpose and is no longer needed). Joe asks why she wanted it and Julia thinks Sarah might appear if she has it. She can't explain why, but she needs to see the girl. Maggie asks Julia if she's upset and if they can help in any way. Hoffman inquires how to contact Sarah. Maggie says she just sort of shows up when needed and that she always saw her in her bedroom. Joe suggests the woods, as that's where David always ran into her. Julia hits on the idea of the crypt. The Magster volunteers Joe to go with Julia, she shouldn't go there alone at night. Julia says no, thanks, it's something she has to do on her own. She admits that Sarah may very well be a ghost. She thanks them for their time and leaves. Maggie tells Joe she feels sorry for Julia, but he reminds her that Woodard didn't trust her.

Julia heads to Eagle Hill and is stopped outside the crypt by Crazy Fake Old Man Caretaker. He warns her the crypt is cursed, but Julia's not afraid. She tells him she's looking for a little girl who sometimes hangs there, seen her? No, stay away, danger, mumbling. Julia hears flute music, which Fake Old Man doesn't. Once the music fades, he says maybe it's a warning, so best she leave. Nothing doing. Danger! Julia's looking at, and drawing away from him, as if he's certifiable (she should know). He finally shuffles off and she heads inside the crypt, calling to Sarah.

Thunder rolls as a storm moves in. Maggie is feeling uneasy since Hoffman's visit. What if the trouble is starting again? Joe says they caught Willie, so that won't happen. What if they didn't get the right person and it does? she muses.

Julia's voice-overing in the crypt. Since it's cold, clammy and Sarah probably is a no-show, she decides to split. However, Sarah is suddenly there. Julia asks her if she can trust Barnabas, that he won't hurt her. Sarah's vague, telling her she'll have to find that out for herself. She then asks the waif wraith if she'll protect her if Barnabas tries to harm her. Sarah replies that she knows who she is and what she did to Dr. Woodard. Julia exclaims that she didn't do anything, Barnabas did. Sarah yells at her that she helped and shouldn't have, then announces she's gotta run. Julia repeatedly asks if Sarah will protect her, but gets no answer, as Sarah's left.

Episode #361 — Accusatory Sarah replay. Once Sarah is gone, Julia tries leaving, but the crypt door slams shut and locks her in. Panicked, she calls out for help. She decides a cigarette will calm her nerves, but before she can light it, she hears a man sobbing. Once it stops, she fires up and hears a hag laughing (the sound effects are on par with what you would hear in a low-rent Jaycees haunted house). Once that's over, Julia leans a hand against the crypt wall, but she pulls away, her hand coated in (watery) blood, which is oozing from behind Sarah's name plaque. Julia gets to sobbing uncontrollably and the crypt door opens on its own. She exits and the door slams shut (who was responsible for all that? Barnabas, Sarah, someone else?).

Arriving back at Collinwood, Julia meets Carolyn in the foyer and finds everyone is from the house and Carolyn is about to go out. Julia would like her to stay and bitchy Carolyn asks if she's afraid, before swanning out. Julia voiceovers that she *is* afraid. She heads into the drawing room and decides to play a game of solitaire, as televisions do not exist in Collinsport. She hears banging, then the room feels cold, just like the crypt, and she believes whatever presence was in the mausoleum is there now. The window blows open and a moment later, the front door (this episode is a Julia voice-over extravaganza). She gives up on her card game and heads to the fire to warm up; the flames flare higher. Julia tries figuring out who's responsible. Barnabas; is he trying to drive her insane? Is it Woodard? The piano starts playing *London Bridge*. Frightened Julia shouts aloud to no one that she's not afraid — then runs from the room, terrified. The reason? A man is standing near the window (Woodard, I presume, but wearing black gloves and hood and I think it's really a woman padded out).

Julia gains the safety of her room and locks herself in. She wonders if Woodard is haunting her. The lights go out. She decides to leave the house, but can't unlock the door. She tries the phone to call for help, but nothing. She then lights a candle, but it goes out. Panic grows. Despite the windows being closed, the drapes are billowing and Ghost Woodard (?) fades in. Julia cries out/squawks in terror. Julia, sobbing, collapses to the floor and begs to be left alone. The phone suddenly rings. It's Woodard with a message; she's going to die, very soon. Grayson Hall gives a tour-de-force performance in histrionics. The doorknob starts to turn, there's a weird sound effect and I guess the wavy distortion of the door is supposed to be the P.O.V. of someone unhinged (but why is the door handle reversed?)

(This episode is not unlike a Grand Guignol play. A limited cast, character isolation, slowly increasing terror and a descent into madness.)

Episode #362 — Phone call from beyond and turning doorknob redo. The door opens and Barnabas pleasantly says hello, acting a polite asshole. Julia pulls herself together and tells him she won't let him frighten her (seems like he did a good job, though). Of course, he denies everything. Desperate Julia offers to do anything — go back to Windcliffe — if he'll stop. He remains inhumane, evil and insufferable. He leaves and meets Carolyn outside the front doors. She tells him he's being cruel. Oh, but *she* was mean to *him* by trying to turn Vicki against him; she needs to be punished! He says she'll end up in an insane asylum until she dies, but first, notebook! Carolyn tells him she got Tony's safe combination through some chicanery during a lunch date (I thought he canceled on her?), so he can break in and steal the book. Oh, no, Pimp Daddy B says, *she'll* get it — by using her feminine charms in order to steal the office keys and she must do it tonight.

Carolyn and Tony walk into Tony's bachelor pad. It's the same damn layout as Burke's tacky motel room, but not tacky, as it's better furnished and looks lived in. Flirt, flirt, fix her a drink? Tony heads to the kitchen, which used to be where Burke's bedroom presumably was, and Carolyn steals the keys from his coat. When he comes back with the potations, she remembers an errand she has to do for Uncle Roger, right away. He doesn't buy it, then offers to tag along. Oh, no, she'll just zip off and be back in an hour, promise! and she leaves.

Pacing in her room, Julia hears someone come in the house and calls out in the hall. It's Roger, who imparts that he barely got home, as some of the roads are flooded (but it's not raining anymore and how did Carolyn and Tony gad about town?). He notices Julia seems a bit unlike her usual self. He answers his own question about where Carolyn is; no doubt with that Peterson fellow. Julia's not pleased to hear that they've already had a couple of dates. Blah, blah, Roger disapproves and mentions something about rebelling (hey, at least Tony's better than Buzz Hackett, he's employed). Julia ends the conversation by saying she has a headache. Roger leaves and she gets on the blower to Peterson. She tells him she *has* to see him. He tries to fend her off, but she hangs up.

Julia arrives at Tony's and blah, blah Carolyn, she's using him to get the notebook. Tony's in full-on Bogie mode as he sips his drink (probably bourbon). She asks about the notebook and he tells her he brought it home with him and he's going to put it in a bank in Bangor. She squawks, but he assures her it's locked up. She demands to see it and he discovers his keys are missing.

Carolyn goes to Tony's office and opens the safe. She starts pawing through the contents and quickly realizes the book isn't there. As she moves to leave, she finds Tony standing there, glaring at her.

Episode #363 — Attempted safe theft redo, but this time, Tony's wearing a fedora to go with his trench coat and turns on the lights when first confronting her. Anyway, he tells her he's moved the book. She makes a break for it, but he grabs her arm (and accidentally slams her against the wall). He's got a few questions for the skirt. He lets her go and she tells him to call the cops, she'd rather that than him knowing anything about the family. Dashiell Hammett type dialogue ensues. Carolyn spins a convoluted lie (culled from fragments of earlier, abandoned storylines). She says that early on in her marriage to Stoddard, Liz was treated badly and turned to a young servant, with whom she became more than friends (the mysterious B. Hanscombe? Shouldn't Frank be in on this?). The man left before Carolyn was born (like her father, originally). Then, along came Julia, to dig info up about Liz, based on the man claiming Carolyn was his daughter. He was going to blackmail the family. The man died, but gave Julia his diary and now *she* is blackmailing them (don't fall for it, Tony). Alas, the blonde plays him for a sap. She says to either take her to the police, or take her home. He opts to take her home (sucker).

The couple arrive back at Collinwood. When Julia steps into the foyer, Carolyn tries to get Tony to leave. He sends her upstairs, then he and Julia start talking. He tells her he knows about the blackmail, so take the notebook back. Julia takes him into the drawing room and is totally perplexed. He shows what a dummy he is for the blonde doll, by repeating Carolyn's blackmail story. Julia says the notebook contents are far more dangerous than some bullshit scandal. She offers to write a letter allowing him to read the book if something happens to her (as her lawyer, couldn't he do that anyway?). He believes her and leaves.

Later, Julia is pacing the drawing room when David comes in, back from his trip (what the hell time/day is it? If the same night, it's late and how did he and Vicki make it to the house if the roads were flooded?). The trip has done David good, he's his old self. He notices that Julia is not herself. She's a bit distracted, then says she's got to go to the Old House, but she's glad he's back. David goes to the foyer, where Sarah appears and welcomes him home. They talk about Boston a little bit and David tells her he would have written her a letter, but — you know (that's actually cute and thoughtful). Sarah becomes distracted and tells him she has to skip to the Old House, someone needs her, then fades away.

Julia is at the Old House (question; does Barnabas do all the cleaning, now that Willie's gone?). Julia and Barney trade some barbs and briefly argue Woodard. Julia lays it on smug Barnabas that she saw and spoke to Sarah. He wants to rush out to the crypt, but she says don't bother, she won't appear to you. Others, sure, *but not you.* Well, that infuriates Barnabas and he starts strangling her. The door suddenly blows open, candles go out and the chandelier starts swinging. Surprised Barnabas drops unconscious Julia to the floor and slowly turns around to find Sarah standing behind him, looking at him with reproach.

Episode #364 — Strangulation interruption redo. Oh, Sarah has come back to him! Barnabas asks why it took so long, while now conscious Julia gets up from the floor and takes a chair, quietly observing. Sarah tells big, bad brother that she's angry with him for hurting people. The asshole lies to her, saying he only did it when he had to. She calls bullshit and says he'll do more bad things (out of the mouths of babes), then reminds him of a rhyme he taught her about evil and good and makes him recite it. She tells him he must be good or be punished. He begs her to stay, but she says she's going and never coming back — *that's* his punishment (man, this ten year old kid doesn't fuck around). She fades out, saying she'll come back when he learns to be good. He calls after her, puling, hands to eyes (I'm not moved by his distress). Julia comforts him, saying that at least she appeared to him. She goes on to say that she's not jealous of Vicki and, oh, by the way, she's home. Julia mentions Sarah again and the sociopathic, black-souled Barnabas issues one of his tiresome, never follow through threats, then bids her goodnight.

In the drawing room, Vicki is talking to Liz, who's wearing lemon yellow loungewear. Preoccupied Liz gives Vicki some bad news; Burke's plane has been found and all the bodies are accounted for. Dumbass Vicki doesn't believe it. Liz says that at least now she knows, but idiot Vicki won't believe until she sees Burke's burnt carcass; stop telling her he's dead! Burke will come back! (Liz, please slap her) She must believe or she'll lose him, she insists, then dashes upstairs. Barnabas stops by and asks to see Vicki. Liz doesn't think that's a good idea, because Burke's dead. Yes, Vicki knows, but refuses to accept it, but she can't go on loving a dead man. Barnabas pipes up that it does happen, but Liz says she won't let it. Oh, yes, Barney agrees, we'll distract her from her grief.

David's in his room and Sarah shows up. She won't tell him what happened at the Old House, but says that those who were there before are angry and have come back, wanting to destroy someone. David worriedly asks if it's him, his father or aunt. She only tells him the dead want to destroy someone and leaves. David yells for her to come back. Liz and Vicki rush in and he relays the cryptic message. Blah, blah, dead. Liz asks if he thought about Sarah while out of town. Julia interrupts, saying she overheard a bit of the conversation. She tells Liz that David is fine; everything he's told them is true.

Episode #365 — A thunderstorm and Liz is pacing the drawing room when Roger comes home, bitching about the inaccuracy of the weather forecast. She tells him about David, then that Julia believes there is a Sarah, but she was afraid to ask for specifics.

Later, Julia, Roger and Liz are talking in the study and the siblings press their houseguest for more info. Julia admits to seeing Sarah and that she's a ghost. She shows them a picture of her in the family album. Roger blusters. Carolyn strolls in and acts a smarmy bitch. Roger says there's no way to prove the ghost claim — Julia suggests a séance. Carolyn snarks, Roger blusters some more and Liz is, surprisingly, on board, reminding him that he scoffed at the last one, then became a believer (not exactly true; the first time with Guthrie, yes, but Liz was catatonic and in the hospital at the time. The second time, Roger was the enthusiastic instigator).

At the Old House, Barnabas voice-over wangsts about Sarah and his lot. The minion shows up and he tries brushing her off, but she quickly tells him about the planned séance.

Barnabas is in the study, telling Liz he's against the séance. Blah, blah, David. Julia and Roger step in; will Barnabas be joining them? What the hell — now Roger is totally on board. The siblings leave to find candles and such to set up. Barnabas asks Julia what if Woodard shows up? She doesn't care, she'll risk it. She walks out and he looks worried.

Carolyn comes downstairs and Barnabas catches her in the foyer. He couldn't stop the séance, but he's got a plan.

In the drawing room, Liz, Vicki, Roger, Carolyn, Barnabas and Julia assemble. Roger is to lead the spirit raising with an assist from Julia. They place the family history on the table, open to a picture of Sarah and begin. Like a hawk, Julia watches as Barnabas and Carolyn exchange glances. Some of the candles gutter out and *London Bridge* flute music is heard. Vicki seems to come over funny. After a cue from Barnabas, Carolyn starts fake channeling Sarah, saying she has no friend named David, she doesn't come there. Vicki watches them, then interrupts, truly channeling Sarah and says that Carolyn is lying and that she's appeared to her. Barnabas shoots daggers at Carolyn (it's not her fault, nitwit). Vicki/Sarah asks where her new nursemaid is, she drew her picture. Roger tries asking questions, but Vicki's on a roll and mentions Barnabas (and oh, he gets pissed). She asks if he'll still love her after he marries Josette and come visit her in the new house? (wasn't Josette always supposed to marry Jeremiah? And didn't Jeremiah build Collinwood? What new fuckery is this?). Anyway, Roger says that she comes there to see David — why? Vicki/Sarah replies the reason is to tell him the story of how it all began, but then says not to take the candle away, not to take the light. The candle on the table suddenly blows out, plunging the room in darkness, and Vicki screams. Barnabas hastily hits the lights. Vicki is gone. A different woman is in her place, seemingly unconscious, and dressed in old fashioned clothing. The woman comes to and says that the carriage overturned. She's alarmed at her surroundings and starts kicking up a fuss, but Roger takes charge. She informs them that her name is Phyllis Wick, from Boston, and that she's been retained by Mrs. Collins as the new governess for Sarah Collins.

Vicki, meanwhile, is outside, in daylight, standing a short distance from the Old House, which looks different. Confused, she wonders aloud where she is.

Lightning Source UK Ltd.
Milton Keynes UK
UKOW02f1230040816

279956UK00001B/214/P